SOUTHERN PATERNALISM AND
THE AMERICAN WELFARE STATE
Economics, Politics, and Institutions in the South
1865–1965

Using the new institutional economics, Professors Alston and Ferrie show how paternalism in Southern agriculture helped shape the growth of the American welfare state in the hundred years following the Civil War. Paternalism was an integral part of agricultural contracts prior to mechanization. It involved the exchange of "good and faithful" labor services for a variety of in-kind services, most notably protection from physical violence. The Southern landed elite valued paternalism because it reduced monitoring costs and turnover. Workers valued paternalism because they lacked civil rights. In order to maintain the value of paternalism to their workers, the agricultural interests needed to prevent meddling from the federal government, which they accomplished through their disproportionate political power. Only the advent of mechanization and complementary technology in the late 1950s and early 1960s finally reduced the desire of Southern agricultural interests to fight the expansion of federal welfare programs.

Lee J. Alston is Professor of Economics at the University of Illinois and Research Associate, National Bureau of Economic Research.

Joseph P. Ferrie is Associate Professor of Economics and Institute for Policy Research Faculty Fellow at Northwestern University and Research Associate, National Bureau of Economic Research.

POLITICAL ECONOMY OF INSTITUTIONS AND DECISIONS

Editors

JAMES E. ALT, *Harvard University*
DOUGLASS C. NORTH, *Washington University of St. Louis*

Other books in the series

ALESINA AND HOWARD ROSENTHAL, *Partisan Politics, Divided Government and the Economy*
LEE J. ALSTON, THRAINN EGGERTSSON AND DOUGLASS C. NORTH, eds., *Empirical Studies in Institutional Change*
JAMES E. ALT AND KENNETH SHEPSLE, eds., *Perspectives on Positive Political Economy*
JEFFREY S. BANKS AND ERIC A. HANUSHEK, eds., *Modern Political Economy: Old Topics, New Directions*
YORAM BARZEL, *Economic Analysis of Property Rights, 2nd edition*
ROBERT BATES, *Beyond the Miracle of the Market: The Political Economy of Agrarian Development in Kenya*
PETER COWHEY AND MATHEW MCCUBBINS, eds., *Structure and Policy in Japan and the United States*
GARY W. COX, *The Efficient Secret: The Cabinet and the Development of Political Parties in Victorian England*
GARY W. COX, *Making Votes Count: Strategic Coordination in the World's Electoral System*
JEAN ENSMINGER, *Making a Market: The Institutional Transformation of an African Society*
KATHRYN FIRMIN-SELLERS, *The Transformation of Property Rights in the Gold Coast: An Empirical Analysis Applying Rational Choice Theory*
ANNA L. HARVEY, *Votes Without Leverage: Women in American Electoral Politics*
MURRAY HORN, *The Political Economy of Public Administration: Institutional Choice in the Public Sector*
JOHN D. HUBER, *Rationalizing Parliament: Legislative Institutions and Party Politics in France*
JACK KNIGHT, *Institutions and Social Conflict*
MICHAEL LAVER AND KENNETH SHEPSLE, eds., *Making and Breaking Governments*
MICHAEL LAVER AND KENNETH SHEPSLE, eds., *Cabinet Ministers and Parliamentary Government*
MARGARET LEVI, *Consent, Dissent, and Patriotism*
BRIAN LEVY AND PABLO T. SPILLER, eds., *Regulations, Institutions, and Commitment*
LEIF LEWIN, *Ideology and Strategy: A Century of Swedish Politics (English Edition)*
GARY LIBECAP, *Contracting for Property Rights*

Continued on page following the Index

SOUTHERN PATERNALISM AND THE AMERICAN WELFARE STATE

ECONOMICS, POLITICS, AND INSTITUTIONS IN THE SOUTH 1865–1965

LEE J. ALSTON   JOSEPH P. FERRIE

CAMBRIDGE
UNIVERSITY PRESS

PUBLISHED BY THE PRESS SYNDICATE OF THE UNIVERSITY OF CAMBRIDGE
The Pitt Building, Trumpington Street, Cambridge CB2 1RP, United Kingdom

CAMBRIDGE UNIVERSITY PRESS
The Edinburgh Building, Cambridge CB2 2RU, UK http: //www.cup.cam.ac.uk
40 West 20th Street, New York, NY 10011-4211, USA http: //www.cup.org
10 Stamford Road, Oakleigh, Melbourne 3166, Australia

First published 1999

Printed in the United States of America

Typeface Sabon 10/12 pt. *System* Penta [RF]

*A catalog record for this book is available from
the British Library.*

Library of Congress Cataloging in Publication Data
Alston, Lee J., 1951–
Southern paternalism and the rise of the American welfare state :
economics, politics, and institutions, 1865–1965 / Lee J. Alston,
Joseph P. Ferrie.
p.   cm. – (Political economy of institutions of decisions.)
Includes index.
ISBN 0–521–62210–7 (hb)
1. Southern States–Economic conditions.   2. Paternalism–Economic
aspects–Southern States–History.   3. Public welfare–Southern
States–History.   4. Public welfare–United States–History.
5. Welfare state–History.   6. Pressure groups–Southern States–
History.   7. Pressure groups–United States–History.   I. Ferrie,
Joseph P.   II. Title.   III. Series.
HC107.A13A765   1999
362.5'8'0975–dc21   97-52779
                                                                        CIP

ISBN 0-520-62210-7 (hardback)

To Mary, Greg, and Eric, and Mari

Contents

Preface

This book is about the interplay of institutions, technology, and contracting. Though it is an example of the "new institutional economics," there was no such well-defined approach when we started this project twenty years ago. In part, this accounts for the book's long gestation. Much of the scholarship on which we rely is the product of research undertaken by others in the new institutional economics over the last two decades. Like those scholars, we had to venture beyond the literatures in economics and history into political science and sociology to answer the questions that we posed. We hope that our work is better for these intellectual excursions.

The genesis for this book was Alston's Ph.D. dissertation. Our collaboration on this topic began in 1980 when Ferrie was an undergraduate in one of Alston's courses. He wrote his undergraduate thesis (which received the Wells Prize in Political Economy) at Williams College on the topic of paternalism and social security in the United States. In the course of our collaboration we had various detours, the most significant being Ferrie's completion of a doctoral dissertation in economics on an unrelated topic. Though the journey to complete this book has been a long one, we believe that the book is better for it – each time we returned to the project, we revised and added new material, often with the benefit of comments from colleagues and the appearance of new findings from scholars working in the field.

The intellectual debts that we owe are numerous. We presented aspects of our work at seminars and conferences around the globe. Many individuals gave us helpful comments and engaged in valuable discussions. Several people deserve special recognition: Robert Higgs patiently listened to Alston for many hours during his dissertation days and throughout this project, and offered his advice and encouragement; Larry Neal came on the scene halfway through this project when Alston moved to Illinois and was the very epitome of a good colleague with his

Preface

comments and encouragement; Douglass North offered his wise counsel throughout and made sure that we never lost track of the "big picture." Though we risk forgetting some people we thank George Akerlof, Mary Alston, James Alt, Terry Anderson, Jeremy Atack, Lee Benham, Ralph Bradburd, Henry Bruton, Leonard Carlson, Ann Carlos, Gary Cox, Paul David, David Farris, Stefano Fenoaltea, Price Fishback, Michael Fortunato, Burleigh Gardner, Victor Goldberg, Claudia Goldin, Avner Greif, Wayne Grove, Tim Hatton, James Heckman, Carl-Ludwig Holtfrerich, Jonathan Hughes, James Kau, Gary Libecap, Peter Lindert, Marvin McInnis, Michael McPherson, Joel Mokyr, David Montgomery, Robert J. Myers, Jeffrey Nugent, Carol Petraitis, Jonathan Pincus, Roger Ransom, Melvin Reder, Joseph Reid, John Roemer, Randy Rucker, Andrew Rutten, Morton Schapiro, Ralph Shlomowitz, Theda Skocpol, Juliet Schor, Ken Shepsle, Pablo Spiller, Richard Sutch, Thomas Ulen, John Wallis, Barry Weingast, Warren Whatley, Steven Wiggins, Gordon Winston, Gavin Wright, and Robert Zevin. For research assistance, we thank Roxanna Barrantes, Wayne Grove, and Bernardo Mueller. We acknowledge financial support from the National Science Foundation (NSF grant SES–8713230). Alston is grateful for support in cash or kind from the Australian National University (Visiting Fellow 1986–1987), the University of California, Davis (Visiting Associate Professor), the University of Colorado, Boulder (Visiting Professor), the University of Washington (Visiting Assistant Professor), the Earhart Foundation, the University of Illinois, Urbana-Champaign, the Liberty Fund, and Williams College. We are also grateful to Alex Holzman of Cambridge University Press for his patience in seeing this project through, and to Herbert Gilbert who edited the manuscript.

Though our professional debts are great, they are clearly exceeded by our personal debts. Without the unwavering love and encouragement of our wives and families, this work would have never begun and surely would have never finished.

Introduction

The rural South has undergone a remarkable transformation in the last half century. The changes in the physical landscape are immediately apparent: the millions of tenants, sharecroppers, and wage laborers who once raised and picked the South's crops and lived in its tumbledown tarpaper shacks are gone, replaced by machines moving methodically across its fields. But the changes in the social landscape that accompanied these physical changes are no less striking: Gone, too, is the complex system of reciprocal duties and obligations that had bound agricultural employers and their workers, the elaborate but often unspoken protocol of paternalism that shaped much of day-to-day life in the rural South. In this book, we will show how paternalism emerged in the postbellum years to reduce the cost of obtaining, motivating, and retaining labor in cotton production following the abolition of slavery. We will also explore the economic and political transformations caused by the decline of paternalism, changes less visible but no less important than the mechanization of cotton production.

The cost of obtaining labor in Southern agriculture included making sure an adequate supply of laborers could be hired and making sure that the laborers who were hired worked hard at their tasks (reducing the cost of monitoring labor) and stayed on through the harvest (reducing turnover in the farm labor force). We will describe the circumstances that caused the emergence of paternalism as part of an implicit contract between employers and workers that helped solve these problems. Paternalism, as part of agricultural contracts in the South, resulted partially from the prevailing institutions in the South and the United States at large. By institutions we mean the informal norms and formal laws of societies that constrain and shape economic decisions. We will explore how Southerners' desire to maintain the system of paternalism helped shape federal social welfare policy in the 1930s, 1940s, and 1950s. We will then explore how the circumstances prompting the use of paternalism

I

changed over time, and how the corresponding demise of paternalism in Southern agricultural contracts influenced federal social welfare policy.

Paternalism emerged in the late nineteenth century as an implicit contract in response to changes in the Southern agricultural labor market caused by the Civil War and emancipation. Planters offered these arrangements when they were unable to satisfy their demand for farm workers after the abolition of slavery. The continued use of paternalism down through the first half of the twentieth century resulted from a technological circumstance: the absence of a mechanical cotton picker, a situation which changed only in the 1950s. The adoption and maintenance of paternalism were also shaped by institutional circumstances. The first was the South's system of social control (the informal norms and practices that dramatically circumscribed the political and economic rights of black and poor white agricultural workers in the South), which was largely shaped by the Southern rural elite after the end of Reconstruction in 1876. Social control in the South made paternalism appealing to agricultural workers, particularly black workers. For paternalism to remain valuable to workers, and for Southern plantation interests to continue to reap the benefits of the system of paternalism, the appearance of substitutes for paternalism (such as government, particularly federal, social welfare programs) had to be prevented. The second institution promoting the adoption of paternalism was the way in which Congress operated for much of the twentieth century, which allowed Southerners to prevent the appearance of these substitutes.

Beginning in the New Deal years, the federal government attempted to interfere with Southern race and labor relations in a variety of ways. If the government's efforts had succeeded, the value of paternalism would have been undermined. In much of what follows, we will describe how political institutions allowed the Southern elite to ward off federal efforts to provide welfare services that threatened paternalism. Beginning in the mid 1950s and continuing through the 1960s, the mechanization of the cotton harvest reduced the economic incentive of Southerners to resist the expansion of federal welfare. At the same time, the nation experienced a revival of interest in the plight of the poor, in part prompted by difficulties absorbing the labor leaving Southern agriculture for Northern cities. The reduced opposition of Southern Congressmen, together with the desire of the Kennedy and Johnson administrations to solidify their urban base of support, resulted in a dramatic enlargement of the scale and scope of the federal government's welfare activities in the 1960s.

In the 1990s, we are well aware of the importance of institutions. The dissolution of the Soviet Union and the resulting difficulties in establishing a market-based economy there have made us acutely aware of the importance of institutions. Yet we are woefully ignorant of how institutions constrain behavior. We are even more ignorant of the factors responsible for institutional change. What follows is a study of the interaction between institutions (the "rules of the game" by which economic actors abide) and contracts (the myriad formal and informal agreements by which parties agree to exchange), the causes of institutional change, and the impact of institutional change on contracts. Throughout the analysis, we take care to specify whose actions are constrained by particular institutions and who has the power to change those institutions. We hope that our methodology will both illuminate the pattern by which the South developed and aid scholars in understanding the importance of institutions elsewhere in the world.

I. A Conceptual Framework for the Analysis of Institutions and Contracts

Our book is a case study of the interaction among institutions, contracts, and economic performance. To illustrate our methodological approach, we will present the conceptual framework that we use to analyze the rise and decline of paternalism and the South's opposition and subsequent resignation to the growth of the federal welfare state. Following Douglass North, we define institutions as the informal norms and formal laws of societies that constrain and shape decision making and that ultimately determine the economic performance of societies (Figure 1).[1] Whereas informal norms do not rely on the coercive power of the state for enforcement, formal laws do in part. Formal laws do not rely entirely on the coercive power of the state because some of their force is derived from the beliefs of its citizens. For example, if more people believe that littering is wrong, the costs incur to police littering are lower.

As Figure 1 shows, the norms and laws of society determine the rights that individuals possess. The norms and laws of a society were very important historically in determining technology and remain a determinant today. Nevertheless, in order to concentrate on the link between institutions and transaction costs, we will treat technology as conceptually exogenous. When appropriate, we will relax this assumption.[2] Rights often carry with them obligations; for example, citizenship carries the obligation to defend one's country. The list of rights is almost endless, so the following are illustrative rather than exhaustive: the right to political participation, the right to own, sell, and use property or one's labor, and the right to education. We will concentrate on the property

[1] North, *Institutions* and *Structure and Change*.
[2] See Mokyr, *Lever of Riches*, for a discussion of the importance of the determinants of technology and their importance for economic performance.

3

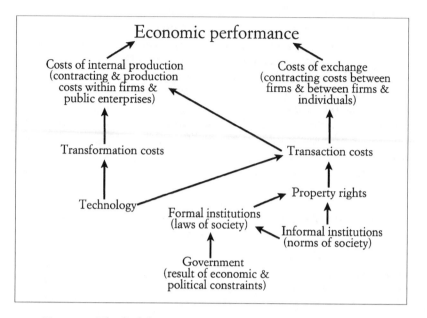

Figure 1. The link between institutions (formal and informal) and economic performance

rights that citizens possess – their right to control resources – though our definition of resources is broad enough to include all of the rights enumerated above. For rights to be valuable, they must be enforced either by governments or by private parties. Though self-interest is often the incentive for people to engage in productive activities, the property rights of society determine the form those productive activities can take.

Property rights, along with technology, determine the transaction costs and transformation costs associated with exchange and production.[3] Transformation costs are the physical costs (in an engineering sense) of combining inputs to produce output. The transformation costs of production depend on the technology in society. The transaction costs of production are the invisible costs of production. They include: (1) monitoring labor effort; (2) coordinating the physical factors of production; and (3) monitoring the use of the physical and financial capital employed in the production process.

Both technology and institutions may affect the transaction costs of production in a variety of ways. For example, technology can both reduce the direct costs of monitoring through better surveillance and re-

[3] Robertson and Alston, "Technological Change," present a schematic framework for analyzing the impact of technology on the transaction costs of production.

duce the need to monitor. For example, in agriculture, when workers chop weeds by hand, monitoring costs are higher than when workers weed with a John Deere cultivator. Whether on the farm or in the factory, machines by their very nature reduce the discretion of labor. They standardize the production process and thereby reduce the variation in the marginal product of labor. In addition, technology influences the transaction costs of coordinating production; no doubt the computer is largely responsible for the observed horizontal integration in commercial banking in the United States in the past decade.

Institutions can also affect the transaction costs of production. For example, in some cultures if people believe in working hard (perhaps because of past incentives), providing "an honest day's work for an honest day's pay," then the monitoring costs borne by the residual claimant are lower. Or, if the law makes it difficult to fire workers for shirking, then monitoring costs increase. Overall, the transaction costs of production are the result of the institutions in a society and technology.

The transaction costs of exchange include the costs associated with negotiating and enforcing contracts. For some transactions, costs of exchange are low because informal norms suffice to uphold bargains. Most local communities have well-established customs that limit opportunistic behavior. Similarly, repeat transactions often give a sufficient incentive to deal fairly. Though local or repeat exchanges may have low transaction costs, the gains from such trade are limited because the extent of the market with whom individuals can deal locally or repeatedly is limited. Formal institutions are necessary if the full gains from specialization in an extended market are to be captured.[4] For example, the extension of the market may require that more trades occur among anonymous parties or that more trades occur where payment and delivery are not simultaneous. Institutions can reduce the potential for unscrupulous behavior inherent in such arrangements.

The presence of "honest" courts and a body of law that upholds contracts and safeguards exchanges is a formal institution that determines the property rights of individuals which in turn affect the transaction costs of exchange. This does not imply that the courts are used frequently, only that they form a backdrop for exchange. The availability of recourse to law and the courts provides the assurance necessary for anonymous or nonsimultaneous exchange to take place. In the absence

---

[4]We use the term "full gains" because some trade can be accomplished through self-generated reputation and the prospect of repeat business without relying on outside formal government institutions. This is particularly evident in the case of international transactions in which the participants do not share a common body of law.

of honest courts, contracts will be written in ways that will safeguard the exchange should one party desire to act opportunistically.[5]

At times there may be insufficient safeguards such that the result is no exchange. For example, large investments are generally required to reap economies of scale. A part of that investment may not be readily transferable to other uses (i.e., the investments are asset-specific). Before the investment is made, if there is a fear that some of the value of the investment will be expropriated, firms will not invest as much as they would in the absence of such fears. Expropriation could occur either through actions taken by the state (such as regulation or nationalization) or through actions taken by one of the parties (such as refusing to execute the exchange without a renegotiation of terms).

Given the set of institutions in a society, residual claimants will construct contracts with the suppliers of inputs to minimize the sum of transformation and transaction costs. The result is a variety of contracts with differing transaction cost and production cost components, and different total costs of production which in turn influence economic performance.

The conceptual framework presented in Figure 1 and discussed thus far is basically static; it illustrates the ultimate importance of institutions for economic performance but it does not address the determinants of institutions and institutional change.[6] To understand the process of institutional change, it is useful to think about economic performance or economic growth as a process of creative destruction in which there are both winners and losers.[7] The losers have an incentive to lobby government for institutional change to protect them from the ravages of the market, while the winners have an incentive to lobby for the status quo. Consumers have an interest in the outcome, but given the existence of rational ignorance and free rider problems consumers tend not to be as effective as special interests in the political marketplace.[8]

We can think of those who lobby for changes in institutions or for the status quo as the demand side of legislation. But special interest groups

---

[5] Williamson, *Economic Institutions of Capitalism*, describes how contractors shield themselves from the potential opportunistic behavior of others. For an example of the importance of institutions in safeguarding investments in telecommunications, see Levy and Spiller, "Institutional Foundations."

[6] The following draws on Alston, "Empirical Work."

[7] This term was coined by Schumpeter, *Capitalism, Socialism, and Democracy*, Ch. 7.

[8] By rational ignorance we mean that it does not pay for the consumer to be as informed about legislation as special interest groups are. The free rider problem arises because of the large numbers of consumers and difficulties in organizing collectively. Both these problems may be attenuated by political entrepreneurs; see Denzau and Munger, "Legislators and Interest Groups."

do not enact legislation. Their demands are filtered through a political process shaped by government institutions – what we call the supply side of legislation.[9] Historically, in the United States, political parties and the committee structure in legislatures have played major roles in shaping political outcomes.[10] In this work, we specify both the demand-side and supply-side forces in a particular historical setting. This allows us to say a great deal about the determinants of institutions and the dynamics of institutional change.

II. The Conceptual Framework Applied to Paternalism

In our framework, paternalism is an arrangement that emerged as the proximate result of high transaction costs associated with premechanized agriculture and the insecure property rights of agricultural labor in the South. Paternalism shaped the lives of rural people in the labor-intensive agricultural regions of the Southern United States. What we describe as paternalism – what has in other contexts been described as a patron–client relationship – was the behavior exhibited by landowners toward their agricultural workers and the reciprocal behavior displayed by workers.

Paternalism developed within the South's system of social control and evolved along with that institution. Social control embodied both formal laws and informal norms or practices that dramatically circumscribed the property rights of black and poor white agricultural workers in the South. The result was the dependency of agricultural workers on the white rural elite. Manifestations of social control included laws (or in our framework institutions) that resulted in: low levels of expenditure on education, old-age security, and welfare; the exclusion of blacks and many poor whites from the electoral process; a pronounced lack of civil rights; and the tolerance of violence. Both economic self-interest and beliefs (or social norms) motivated the "demand" for social control. On the "supply" side, the same forces that pushed for social control also controlled the levers of political power. Our work is an examination of the economic role of paternalism in the South's system of social control

---

[9] By using the terms demand and supply we do not mean that there is necessarily a unique outcome; the term bargaining may be more appropriate. For the most part economists have paid too little attention to the supply side of government. See Alston, Eggertsson, and North, *Empirical Studies*.

[10] On the importance of parties, see Cox and McCubbins, *Legislative Leviathan*. For the instrumental role of committees, see Shepsle, *Giant Jigsaw Puzzle*, Shepsle and Weingast, "Institutional Foundations of Committee Power," and Shepsle and Weingast, "Legislative Politics." We will have considerably more to say about committees in the following chapters.

and how that role changed over time in response to changes in technology.

How did paternalism operate? Given the existence of social control, agricultural workers – especially blacks – had an economic incentive to entrust themselves to a patron who could provide the security and services workers could not obtain for themselves. In exchange, patrons received "good and faithful" labor.[11] The exchange was not simultaneous. Only workers who demonstrated their loyalty over time received protection. In Chapter 1, we describe the emergence and development of paternalism in agricultural contracts following the Civil War and also examine the economic functions of paternalism in the twentieth century.

As long as the South remained "an armed camp for intimidating black folk" – the phrase coined by W. E. B. DuBois to describe the region in the late nineteenth century – protection was a valuable service planters could deliver to their black workers.[12] In our framework presented in the previous section, the demand for protection was prompted by insecure property rights. A powerful patron can be viewed as a substitute for the state. Although blacks needed protection more than whites, the capriciousness of local and state law enforcement and judicial systems meant that white workers might also benefit from a patron. For protection to remain valuable to workers, planters had to prevent substitutes from emerging for their services. Local and state governments, by providing civil rights and greater welfare benefits, could have reduced the value of planter protection. However, planters either controlled the judicial, legislative, and enforcement branches of local and state governments outright or allied themselves with these forces. The federal government posed more of a threat. The federal government shared the costs of a variety of welfare programs, and the prevalence of these arrangements increased with the New Deal. With cost sharing came attempts by the federal government to set national standards. Furthermore, many New Deal programs directly threatened the system of social control in the South.

Southern planters were not defenseless against those in Congress who wanted to change the South. Far from it. To understand the South's ability to prevent federal programs from affecting paternalism and the system of social control, we need to examine the politics of the South and the institutional workings of Congress, the supply side of the federal government. We do this in Chapter 2.

The plantation elite, allied with the "county courthouse gang," domi-

---

[11] The term "good and faithful" labor in this sense comes from Ronald Davis, *Good and Faithful Labor*.
[12] DuBois, *Souls of Black Folks*.

nated Southern politics by the turn of the twentieth century. The result was a one-party system that effectively disfranchised blacks and many poor whites. To be elected and stay in office, politicians had to serve the interests of the rural elite. And serve them they did. At the national level, Southern Congressmen were expected not only to bring home the pork but also to prevent federal intervention in Southern labor and race relations – the hallmarks of social control. Disproportionate Southern political power resulted from the one-party system of the South, the importance of Southerners within the Democratic party, and the committee structure of Congress. Though Southerners as a bloc never had sufficient votes to determine legislative outcomes, they occupied nodes of power and could use their power, in concert with other Congressmen seeking the same outcomes. The one-party system gave Southern Congressmen more seniority than their colleagues in the rest of the country, and because of the way committees worked, greater seniority enabled Southerners to exercise considerable legislative agenda control.

Southerners exerted their political power in efforts to assure the maintenance of social control well into the twentieth century. In assessing the motivation of three typical Southern Senators in the mid twentieth century, George Mowry maintains that "[i]f their Congressional votes meant anything, they were not wedded either to the Democratic party, to national conservatism, or to states' rights but rather used both the party and the concepts as instruments to secure and maintain the existing socioeconomic society at home in the South, and of course to secure their own personal careers."[13] Southern power on the supply side of government enabled a coalition of Southerners and other social conservatives to check the demands for the expansion of many welfare services in ways that did not interfere with Southern agricultural labor or race relations.

Evidence of the tenacity with which Southerners defended social control during the New Deal years is found in a variety of welfare and labor legislation. For example, Southerners promoted the exclusion of farm workers from the Fair Labor Standards Act (FLSA) and both the Old-Age and Unemployment provisions of the Social Security Act. In addition, Southern Congressmen acted to keep local control over those welfare programs – Aid to Dependent Children and Old-Age Assistance – that did not explicitly exclude agriculture. Further evidence comes from the life and death of the Farm Security Administration (FSA). At first, Southern landlords welcomed – or at least did not resist – the FSA or its predecessor, the Resettlement Administration, because the FSA's programs did not initially interfere in labor or race relations. Once reform

[13] Mowry, *Another Look*, p. 70.

9

was on the agenda of the FSA, Southerners used their influence to gain local control over some threatening programs, limit current appropriations, and, in 1946, stop future appropriations for the FSA. In Chapters 3 and 4, we describe the political maneuvering of Southern Congressmen during the 1930s to prevent the Social Security Act and the FSA from directly weakening the Southern system of social control.[14]

As rural labor markets tightened during World War II, landlords sought ways to retain a cheap and dependent labor supply. In our framework this tightening of labor markets can be viewed as an increase in the costs of internal production, which would prompt Southern landlords to lobby for protection from market forces. Their political agents came to the rescue. The Tydings amendment in 1942 to the Selective Service Act of 1940 provided deferments to agricultural workers. The Pace amendments to the Farm Labor Act of 1943 prevented the expenditure of federal funds for the transportation of agricultural workers out of a county without the permission of the county farm agent. At the behest of Southerners, an international agreement with Mexico was reached in 1942 for the importation of temporary agricultural labor. Mexican labor greatly augmented the Southwestern supply of labor and thereby discouraged outmigration from the Deep South to the expanding West. Limiting migration from the South prevented wages from rising more than they otherwise would have. Of course all farm owners benefitted from reducing labor costs but, because Southern agriculture was not yet mechanized, labor costs were a considerably greater percentage of costs than in mechanized agricultural regions (e.g., the corn and wheat regions).

Although designed as a temporary war measure, Congress gave repeated legislative approval for the legal importation of Mexican labor until 1964. Over the postwar years, Southern legislators disproportionately supported importation of Mexican labor, yet only Texas and Arkansas landowners employed many Mexicans. However, importation of Mexican labor elsewhere enabled paternalism to linger on in the rest of the South. In Chapter 5, we discuss the beneficial legislation and programs initiated in World War II to maintain a cheap and dependent supply of labor for agricultural interests – in particular Southern landlords.

The complete mechanization of Southern agriculture, along with the introduction of complementary technology, lowered the transaction and transformation costs of cotton production. The reduced transaction costs eroded the economic foundations of Southern paternalism. Labor can

---

[14] For an examination of the South's role in shaping the FLSA, see Seltzer, "Political Economy."

Introduction

never be too cheap, but it can be too dependent. Dependency made economic sense in the presence of the high supervision and turnover costs that accompanied premechanized agriculture. Mechanization reduced supervision costs in two ways: (1) it reduced the variation in the marginal productivity of labor; and (2) it greatly reduced the demand for labor. With mechanization, monitoring labor became easier because workers had less scope for shirking and workers were likely to shirk less for fear of losing their jobs in an environment of high unemployment. With lower supervision costs, the maintenance of paternalism would have entailed costs for landlords without any reciprocal benefits. Furthermore, with the dramatic decline in the demand for labor resulting from mechanization, turnover was no longer a matter of concern to planters. As a result, paternalism withered away. In Chapter 6, we present circumstantial evidence consistent with the hypothesis that mechanization was responsible for the decline of paternalism.

Along with a reduced incentive to supply paternalism as part of the compensation of agricultural workers, mechanization reduced the incentive of landlords to fight substitutes for planter paternalism (i.e., federal welfare programs) through their political agents. However, this does not mean that those who held political power in the South welcomed the welfare state with open arms. Far from it. Ideologically, most of the Southern elite still found the welfare state repugnant and social control worth maintaining. Nevertheless, once mechanization decoupled the economic and ideological motivations for resistance to the welfare state, resistance became less virulent. The South now fought to dampen the impact from civil rights on social control and attempted to structure welfare programs to preserve social control. In Chapter 6, we describe the role of Southerners in shaping the Economic Opportunity Act to encourage rural outmigration, a role that would have been paradoxical if paternalism still had been important to the Southern elite.

From 1940 to 1965, the Southern farm population fell from approximately sixteen million to five million. Such demographic change had the potential to diminish the political power of the rural South and the South in general. If this occurred, the welfare state may have expanded because the South was overwhelmed politically. Yet, for the most part, Southerners retained their political dominance. Despite outmigration, the Southern delegations to Congress changed little over the course of mechanization. Most importantly, the more senior Congressmen continued to get elected. Hence, Southerners maintained their disproportionate share of committee chairs and their control of the legislative agenda. For example, the Food Stamp Act, which replaced some aspects of planter paternalism, first had to pass through House and Senate Agriculture committees that were chaired and dominated by Southerners. In Chapter 6, we

11

show that much of Southern gatekeeping power over legislation remained intact throughout the 1960s.

The passage of welfare and civil rights legislation in the New Frontier and Great Society years dramatically changed the lives of millions of poor black and white people in the North and South. The rural elite in the South was by no means the only player in this process. Generally, scholars attribute the success of this legislation to the liberal Northern faction in Congress. No doubt, the impetus for change came from the North, while other interests outside the South also opposed change.

But change within the South was probably crucial (in the language of political science, decisive) for the success of welfare state legislation. Though the distance moved by the South from implacable opposition to the welfare state in the 1940s and 1950s to grudging acceptance of it in the 1960s and 1970s may not seem great, this was a great enough change to allow a flood of welfare legislation through Congress and onto the desks of three presidents. In the following chapters, we will examine the changes within the South, to understand both how the region's economic and political systems were transformed as paternalism passed from the stage, and how that transformation resonated at the national level in the culmination of a process of government growth that had begun more than thirty years before, in the depths of the Great Depression.

I

The Economics of Paternalism

I. Introduction

For much of the century between the end of the Civil War and the 1960s, paternalism was an important aspect of the rural way of life in the American South. In fact, the clearest difference between labor markets in the South and those in the rest of the United States was the elaborate system of paternalism that shaped most of the South's agricultural labor arrangements. We imply no value judgments by our use of the term "paternalism." By paternalism – or the term "patron–client relationship" which we use synonymously – we simply mean the exchange of goods such as protection for dependable labor services.[1] Paternalism is a relationship involving employer provision of a wide range of goods and services in exchange for loyal service – a long-term commitment to an employer that transcends the textbook impersonal exchange of labor services for cash – and a measure of deference.

The benefits planters provided to their loyal tenants varied and depended on the specific relationship between landlord and tenant. They included old-age assistance, unemployment insurance of a sort (carrying the tenant through a poor season), medical care, intercession with legal authorities, recreational amenities, housing, garden plots, fuel, hunting privileges, general advice, credit, donations to schools and churches, and aid in times of emergencies, among others.[2]

These patron–client relationships have existed over time in various cultures. Similar benefits have been provided by large planters in the regions of South America dominated by plantation agriculture: in both

---

[1] Though at times this relationship may entail ties of affection, we do not argue that this was or should have been the norm. That such bonds of affection did or did not exist has no bearing on the following analysis.

[2] For documentation, see Alston and Ferrie, "Resisting the Welfare State," and the sources cited therein.

the Brazilian Sertaõ, a cotton-producing region, and the sugar-producing regions of northeastern Brazil, for example. They have been observed in a variety of village economies in Asia: in the coastal region of the Philippines and in the Subang region of Java. In the Transvaal of South Africa paternalism played a role in agriculture well into the latter part of the twentieth century. In fact, such arrangements are found in virtually all countries where large-scale agriculture and traditional social systems prevail.[3] Similar arrangements have existed in nearly all countries at one time or another. Such relationships also existed in feudal Europe.[4]

Throughout history and across cultures, landlords have provided paternalistic benefits. How are we to explain the presence and persistence of these benefits? In this chapter, we explore the historical origins of paternalism in the South, describe in detail some of its essential elements, and offer an economic explanation for its origins and existence. We suggest that these arrangements helped to reduce labor costs in an economy where directly monitoring labor was costly and where workers were unable to purchase some goods, such as protection from violence and insurance against various economic hardships, directly in the marketplace. In subsequent chapters, we demonstrate how the existence of this system of paternalism motivated much of the South's resistance to the growth of the U.S. welfare state and how the disappearance of paternalism reduced that resistance.

II. Some Historical Background on the Appearance of Paternalism in the South

The system of paternalism in place by the turn of the twentieth century was not a simple extension of the antebellum master-slave relationship into the postbellum Southern economy.[5] It was instead the product of the dislocation occasioned by the Civil War and the actions of planters trying to secure an adequate labor supply in these circumstances.

The initial response of planters to the difficulties of keeping laborers

---

[3] For references to these relationships in South America, see Allen W. Johnson, *Sharecroppers*; Hutchinson, *Village and Plantation Life*; and Barraclough and Domike, "Agrarian Structure." For references in Asia, see Hayami and Kikuchi, *Asian Village Economy*. For a discussion of aspects of paternalism in the Transvaal of South Africa, see Van Onselen, *The Seed is Mine*. For references in England, see Newby, *Deferential Worker*. For an elaboration of the issues in this section, see Alston and Ferrie, "Social Control."

[4] See Bloch, *Feudal Society* and *Slavery and Serfdom*.

[5] We are grateful to Robert Higgs for providing much of the primary source material on which this section is based.

Welcome

Visit and share in His love.

2
3
4
5

*
15

16

in the immediate postwar period was to offer former slaves a variety of nonmonetary inducements to remain at least through the harvest of the present crop. The rise of virulent racism in the post-Reconstruction period presented planters an opportunity to offer their workers protection from racist violence and the capricious judgments of a racist legal system, in exchange for continued dependable service in the planters' fields.

Their role as protector of the physical safety of their workers evolved in the twentieth century into a more general role as protector of workers in commercial and legal transactions and in many dealings with the world outside the plantation. The faithful labor services they received in exchange for that role ensured the opposition of planters to federal interference in Southern labor and race relations in the first half of the twentieth century.

After the Civil War, Southern agriculture faced enormous difficulties. The abolition of slavery, the coercive system that had organized labor relations before the war, was clearly the greatest problem. Though the South suffered tremendous physical destruction, including the loss of livestock, fences, and barns, and though many of its fields had been neglected throughout the war, what most concerned planters was the lack of a system to assure an adequate supply of labor.[6]

Fields could be rehabilitated and new workstock and animals purchased after a season or two of hardship – farmers had often been forced to do so in the past after natural disasters – but replacing slavery with a new system was a more daunting task. Most of those hiring large numbers of hands after the war were the same planters who had controlled the largest plantations before the war. There was little turnover in the "plantation elite" as a result of the war.[7] After Reconstruction, it was the planter elite rather than the petty merchants who retained the greatest political and economic power in the rural South. For example, crop lien laws gave planters rather than merchants first claim on the output of sharecroppers indebted to both.[8] Laws relegated sharecroppers to the legal status of wage workers, enhancing the power of landlords.[9] Some former masters, those "who had dealt honorably and humanely towards their slaves," were able to retain many of their former fieldhands.[10] Most planters, though, particularly those who were not so

---

[6] Cloud, "Cotton Culture"; U.S. Department of Agriculture, *Report of the Commissioner.*

[7] Mandle, "Re-establishment of the Plantation Economy"; Wiener, *Social Origins of the New South*; and Wayne, *Reshaping of Plantation Society.*

[8] Woodman, "Southern Agriculture and the Law," p. 328.

[9] Ibid., pp. 324–6.

[10] See U.S. Congress, *Joint Committee on Reconstruction*, p. 125.

highly regarded by their former slaves, had greater difficulty in satisfying their demand for labor.[11]

The Freedmen's Bureau stepped into this chaos as an intermediary, at least for a short time. The bureau, an agency of the federal government, initially enjoyed the trust of the freedmen. As a repository of their trust, it could "disabuse them of any extravagant notions and expectations . . . (and) administer them good advice and be voluntarily obeyed."[12] The bureau had the power to compel the observance of labor contracts and for this earned the early respect of planters.

The Freedmen's Bureau, however, did nothing to change the fact that the abolition of slavery had raised the cost of labor. Ransom and Sutch argue that emancipation decreased the labor supply of former slaves who in effect bought greater leisure. Fogel suggests that planters increased their demand for labor after emancipation, because more workers were needed to do the work that had previously been done under the onerous gang system.[13] Both effects would have increased the price of labor. During the period of excess demand for labor that existed until the adjustment to this new, higher equilibrium wage, some planters raided their competitors for labor and bitterly complained as their own workforces were raided.

By 1869, the bureau had ceased to function as a go-between and guarantor. Both planters and freedmen seem to have seen less need for the offices of the agency after only three years experience with it, perhaps because of a desire for greater flexibility than the bureau-approved contracts allowed.[14] The bureau had attempted to stabilize the agricultural labor market in the first confused years after emancipation. The bureau's legacy was its intermediation – the first by any federal agency and the last for a long time – in the South's evolving system of labor relations. Though such intervention was attempted again by the Resettlement Administration and the Farm Security Administration in the 1930s, the context had changed considerably by then and the results were altogether different.[15]

The demise of the Freedmen's Bureau left planters and freedmen to contract among themselves directly. Writing in 1872, one observer noted conditions much like those in the immediate aftermath of the war: Workers were being hired away by competing employers, leaving plant-

---

[11] See Freedmen's Bureau, *Report*, p. 95. See Litwack, *Been in the Storm*; and Jaynes, *Branches Without Roots*, pp. 207–23, for a discussion of the disorder in agricultural labor markets immediately following the Civil War.
[12] Schurz, *Report*, p. 40.
[13] Ransom and Sutch, *One Kind of Freedom*; Fogel, *Without Consent or Contract*.
[14] Shlomowitz, "Freedmen's Bureau," p. 35.
[15] See Alston and Ferrie, "Resisting the Welfare State"; and Chapter 4.

ers with insufficient labor to bring in the crop, and employers were failing to fulfill the terms of their contracts with their workers.[16] Securing adequate labor was described as "a matter of grave uncertainty and deep anxiety" for every planter.[17]

In these circumstances, some planters chose a new course – turning to honesty, fair dealing, and a host of nonwage aspects of their relationship with their workers as additional margins for competition.[18] The amenities that employers offered their workers included improved housing, garden plots, firewood, and plantation schools and churches.[19] These perquisites were seldom explicitly stipulated – planters continued to prefer verbal rather than written leases.[20] Jaynes describes the introduction of such arrangements between planters and their wage workers in the immediate antebellum period, even before the demise of the Freedmen's Bureau.[21] He does not explore the persistence of these relationships into the post-Reconstruction period or into the twentieth century as we have elsewhere.[22]

Jaynes views "market paternalism" – his term for these arrangements – and tenancy and sharecrop contracts as substitutes used by planters for reducing monitoring costs. Such paternalistic arrangements were, however, actually more likely to be given to tenants and croppers than to wage workers. A long-term relationship like that between planters and their tenants and croppers made such arrangements more effective as monitoring devices. Such arrangements were also increasingly important as wage workers in gangs were replaced by geographically dispersed tenants and croppers. The assignment of tenants and croppers to specific plots created an incentive for planters to reduce turnover and prevent the departure of tenants and croppers in possession of location-specific farming knowledge. The literature on paternalism in the late nineteenth and early twentieth centuries supports the view that these arrangements continued with the transition away from an exclusive reliance on wage labor, and that these arrangements were in fact of even greater value to

---

[16] Stearns, *Black Man of the South*, pp. 107–8.

[17] Southerner, "Agricultural Labor," p. 329.

[18] See Paul Taylor, "Tenancy and Labor," p. 329; and Bruce, *Plantation Negro*, pp. 180–1.

[19] Godwin, "Testimony," p. 476; H. C. Taylor, *Agricultural Economics*, p. 337; DuBois, "Negro Farmer," p. 514; U.S. Industrial Commission, *Report*, p. 778; Tebeau, "Planter–Freedman Relations," p. 138; and Stone, "Negro in the Yazoo-Mississippi Delta," p. 250.

[20] E. V. Wilcox, "Lease Contracts," pp. 2–4; Hoffsommer, *Significance of Land Tenure*, p. 389; and U.S. Industrial Commission, *Report*, pp. 437–8.

[21] Jaynes, *Branches Without Roots*, pp. 78–9, 104–6, 121.

[22] Alston and Ferrie, "Social Control."

planters when they employed tenants and croppers than they had been when only wage workers were employed.[23]

By the end of the nineteenth century, another role, in addition to that of provider of these amenities, had been assumed by large planters – that of protector of their workers. As early as the 1880s, landlords were willing to offer their advice to their workers and to protect them from exploitation at the hands of the local merchant.[24] By the turn of the century, the role of protector expanded to include protection from violence.

White hostility toward freed blacks had been evident since the end of the war, but had to some extent been kept in check by the Reconstruction governments.[25] The end of Reconstruction saw such hostilities emerge into the open.[26] For example, "white-capping," driving blacks from their homes and forcing them off the lands owned by the largest landowners and merchants, was reported in several Mississippi counties in the early 1890s.[27] With disfranchisement, the entire machinery of the state became an instrument with which to coerce blacks. For example, the South's judicial system displayed a clear bias, meting out sentences to blacks in the South far more severe than those given for corresponding crimes in the North.[28]

The disfranchisement of blacks and poor whites that helped create the South's regime of social control could not have occurred without the cooperation of the white rural elite. Indeed, Kousser argues convincingly that the new political structure in the South was shaped by black belt socioeconomic elites.[29] This is the sense in which we view the institution of social control in the South as "endogenous": It was the product of decisions made by the white rural elite.

Wright argues that disfranchisement "was a by-product of the agrarian movement," a movement which he describes as a result of weak world cotton demand in the 1890s.[30] Kousser provides a similar explanation for the disfranchisement of both blacks and poor whites,

---

[23] This literature is cited in ibid.

[24] U.S. Congress, Senate, Committee on Education and Labor, *Labor and Capital*, p. 164.

[25] Truman, *Report*, p. 10; Schurz, *Report*, pp. 47–105; Stearns, *Black Man of the South*, p. 103.

[26] Tebeau, "Planter–Freedman Relations," p. 139. For a more general view of the experience of blacks in the postemancipation Southern economy, see Higgs, *Competition and Coercion*.

[27] Otken, *Ills of the South*, pp. 86–8; Holmes, "Whitecapping," pp. 166–9.

[28] Woofter, *Negro Migration*, p. 143.

[29] Kousser, *Shaping of Southern Politics*, p. 238.

[30] Wright, *Old South, New South*, p. 122.

though one that does not rely on the impact of world cotton demand.[31] Blacks were excluded from the electoral process by the black belt elites because "The end of Negro voting would solidify their control over their tenants and free them from having to deal with elected or appointed black officials, a type of contact almost all Southern whites found distasteful."[32] The elites excluded poor, up-country whites to prevent conflict over issues such as taxes and, more generally, to achieve political hegemony in state politics.

The rise of the institution of social control led in turn to the increased use of protection in paternalistic contracts. Planters increasingly offered protection to their faithful black workers as the social and legal environment became more hostile toward blacks – a hostility that, over several decades, the white rural elite was instrumental in creating. Thus, to limit the departure of their own workers from the South, many planters came to serve as the protectors for their workers as well as the providers of many of their material needs. Planters had posted bond for their workers and accompanied them to court before, but with the pronounced change in the political, legal, and social climate at the turn of the century, such practices took on added importance.[33]

In the following years, the scope of planters' paternalism expanded. The result was a system of thorough paternalism in which planters looked after most aspects of their workers' lives, and workers responded by offering their loyalty to their patron. Planters had to some degree solved the labor supply problem they had faced at emancipation: Provision of paternalism allowed them to tie black workers to the land in a world of free contracting, though not as firmly as the law had bound black workers under slavery, because coercion was no longer as viable and exit was an option. They were able to reduce the cost of monitoring labor by providing workers with valuable services, which they would forfeit if they were caught shirking. They offered both black and white workers a wide array of nonwage benefits, as well as assistance in commercial and legal transactions, and in addition provided their black

---

[31] Kousser, *Shaping of Southern Politics*, pp. 6–8.

[32] Ibid., p. 7.

[33] See examples from the 1870s in the papers of the Pitts family, North Carolina cotton planters whose records are preserved in the Southern Historical Collection at the University of North Carolina, Chapel Hill. Woodward, *Origins of the New South*, also notes the use of paternalism as a protective device for blacks. "Another considerable Negro element saw nothing better than to take refuge under the paternalism of the old masters, who offered some protection against the extreme race doctrines of the upland whites . . . . [the publication] *The Nation* . . . rejoiced that 'Thousands of them' had discovered 'that their interests are bound up with the interests of their old masters.' " Ibid., p. 218.

workers with protection from the power of the state and the racial hostility of many whites.

The ability of planters to keep labor both cheap and dependable required not only that they continue to supply the full range of paternalistic benefits to their workers, but also that the external threat posed by a racist state continue. Furthermore, planters needed to ensure that no other party stepped forward to act as the workers' protector in commercial and legal dealings. In short, planters had an interest in maintaining a racist state and preventing federal interference in race and labor issues.[34]

III. Some Aspects of Paternalism in Agriculture in the U.S. South

By the early twentieth century, planters had come to act as intermediaries between their workers and much of the outside world. Planters exercised control over the credit extended to their workers, but they were also willing to "stand good" for their workers' debts with local merchants. Half of all Southern landlords surveyed in 1938 said they would routinely "stand good" for their tenants' debts, whereas only three percent of Northern landlords said they would do so. The study's author described this finding as "evidence of the paternalistic side of the landlord-tenant relationship in the South, an aspect which is insignificant in the North. . . ."[35] Planters reported significant outlays for the payment of doctors' bills, the establishment and maintenance of schools and churches, and various unspecified forms of entertainment.[36] And planters commonly paid legal fines incurred by workers and served as parole sponsors for their workers.[37] Woofter described some of the specific social and economic aspects of paternalism in the American South in the 1930s:

[T]he landlord is also often called upon for services of a social nature, for the large plantation is a social as well as an economic organism and the matrix of a number of plantations often constitutes or dominates the larger unit of civil government in the locality.

Among efficient landlords, tenant health is one of the major considerations and doctors' bills are paid by the landlord and charged against the tenant crop. Those tenants who have a landlord who will "stand for" their bills are far more likely to get physicians' services than are the general run of tenants.

[34] The political power of the rural elite is discussed in Chapter 2.
[35] Schuler, "Social Status and Farm Tenure," p. 172.
[36] Woofter, "Plantation Economy," table 14-A.
[37] Ibid., table 14-B.

The Economics of Paternalism

Landlords are also expected to "stand for" their tenants in minor difficulties such as may grow out of gambling games, altercations and traffic infractions. This function is, of course, not exercised indiscriminately. A good worker will, in all probability, be 'gotten off' and a drone left in the hands of the law. . . . [T]he landlord assumes responsibility for such tenants who are arrested for minor offenses, especially during the busy season.[38]

Some planters felt it was their duty to look out for their tenants, and some tenants felt it was their right to be looked after. These dependency relationships carried mutual obligations that were stronger the longer the relationship had been intact. Some relationships between tenant and planter in the 1930s reached back over several generations into slavery, though, as we saw in Section II, the paternalistic relationship that existed after emancipation was not a direct descendant of the master–slave relationship.[39] One study noted: "[U]sually where the tenant is a favored worker, 'a good nigger,' or a member of a family which has worked for several generations for the planter's family, the solidarity between landlord and tenant is very strong, and the obligations and benefits of each party are increased."[40]

In the American South, perhaps the most important aspect of paternalism was the protection planters offered from violence perpetrated by the larger community. Planters considered it their role "to look after their people." One planter remarked, "If my people do something wrong, I will punish them, but no mob of townspeople can touch them."[41] Protection was important for all agricultural workers, but particularly for black workers, because they lacked civil rights and society condoned violence. As one scholar has suggested

The South's paternalism by no means precluded the use of violence. Although a relatively inefficient instrument by which to achieve social cohesion, the use of force was omnipresent as a backup means to ensure social viability. And, indeed, the use of terror was part of the postbellum southern way of life. . . . Violence was . . . employed in reaction to a violation of approved behavioral norms, particularly attempts to escape deferential patterns by southern blacks. Furthermore the use of violence was aimed not only at the individual transgressor, but also possessed symbolic importance for the other members of the black community. The ability to inflict violence on one individual acted as a deterrent against attempts to introduce more egalitarian behavioral patterns.[42]

[38] Ibid., pp. 31–2.
[39] Davis et al., *Deep South*, p. 239; Powdermaker, *After Freedom*, p. 325.
[40] Davis et al., *Deep South*, p. 234.
[41] Private correspondence from Burleigh B. Gardner, author of *Deep South* (August 30, 1984).
[42] Mandle, *Not Slave, Not Free*, p. 64.

Though the planter elite initially fostered a hostile racist environment in order to wrest political control from the upland whites, once their political power was entrenched, they feared that a threatening racial atmosphere would encourage outmigration. This became increasingly important following World War I because many blacks now had contacts in the urban North, and Ku Klux Klan activities began to spread into plantation areas. LeRoy Percy of Greenville, Mississippi, one of the most influential members of the planter elite in the Delta and indeed in the entire South worked to pass resolutions in his home county condemning the Klan.[43] Following a speech by a Klan organizer in February 1922, Percy spoke for an hour encouraging his fellow whites to reject the Klan. His fear was the exodus of labor:

But I know the terror this organization embodies for our negro population and I am here to plead against it. . . . The shifting of the population from the South to the North – you cannot stop that trend. It is going on as the result of industrial call to better opportunity. You cannot stop it but you can expedite it. Instead of making it a matter of 35 or 50 years, during which the South can readjust itself, you can make it an exodus within a year. . . . You can make three parades in the county of Washington of your Ku Klux Klan and never say another word and you can start the grass growing in the streets of Greenville.

Percy concluded: "Friends, let this Klan go somewhere else where it will not do the harm that it will in this community. Let them sow dissension in some community less united than is ours. Let this order go somewhere else if there is any place it can do any good. It can do no good here." After Percy's speech a resolution was put forward condemning the Klan. The crowd resoundingly voiced its approval. The Klan did not disappear, but Percy along with others in the Delta continued their fight against its inroads in their region. In February 1923 Percy told a friend: "I am intensely worried about the labor, uneasy for fear the negroes will not stay with us even to make this crop. . . . I regard the menace from the weevil, great as it once seemed, slight compared to the migration of the negroes from the South."

Paternalism was more than sheltering workers from physical threats; it could also involve interceding in commercial transactions, obtaining medical care, providing influence or money to bail a son out of jail, or settling familial disputes.[44] For example:

[I]n time of trouble . . . a tenant turns to his landlord as his natural protector. In case of illness, the planter sends a doctor. If the tenant is in jail, the planter pays

---

[43] The local, regional, and national influence of Percy are chronicled in depth in Barry, *Rising Tide*. The following quotes are found in Barry, pp. 145–9.
[44] These examples are illustrative rather than exhaustive.

his fines or hires a lawyer, and uses his influence to have the tenant released. One prosecuting attorney told of instances in which planters have made agreements by which the tenants would receive light sentences in return for a plea of guilty.[45]

The benefits and services provided by landlords were often more mundane, showing the important role that landlords played in even the most common experiences of workers' lives: "Mr. Sampson [a plantation owner] is never too busy to visit a pregnant colored woman, to 'judge' a dispute between tenant neighbors, or to encourage a tenant boy to enter a calf in the county Agricultural Extension Service contest."[46] As several of the previous quotations make explicit, black workers were more likely to be the recipients of paternalism than white workers. In addition, plantation owners, more so than landlords employing few workers, tended to provide paternalism. We will discuss the rationale for these tendencies in the next section.

This elaborate system of benefits prompts two questions: (1) why were such paternalistic goods and services provided in the first instance; and (2) how can we account for the observation that some workers were more likely to receive paternalistic benefits and some employers were more likely to provide them? Is there an economic logic to the system of paternalism that allows us to explain both its existence and its particular characteristics? We now offer an economic rationale for the system of paternalism that answers these questions and also helps explain the staunch resistance of Southern landowners to the expansion of many federal government welfare functions that we document in subsequent chapters.

IV. The Economics of Paternalism

Paternalism is most prevalent in premechanized and nonscience-based agriculture. Before the advent of scientific advances that stabilized yields, workers possessed farm-specific knowledge, which gave landlords an incentive to curb the migration of tenants with such knowledge. Before mechanization, monitoring labor effort was costly because workers were spread over a considerable physical distance, and linkage of reward with effort was difficult because there could be considerable variation in output, the cause of which was difficult to determine. Examples

---

[45] Davis et al., *Deep South*, p. 234. For additional examples of paternalism in the American South, see Alston, "Race Etiquette"; Alston and Ferrie, "Social Control"; and Woofter, "Plantation Economy."

[46] Rubin, *Plantation County*, p. 27.

abound: Did the mule go lame naturally or did the worker mistreat the mule? Was the shortfall in output due to too little rain or too little work effort? Paternalism reduced these monitoring costs by reducing workers' tendency to shirk, by raising the costs of shirking, and by increasing the length of the time horizon over which workers made decisions.[47]

Paternalism may reduce workers' taste for shirking if it is viewed by workers not as a market transaction but rather as benevolence from the patron. Under such conditions workers respond with goodwill gestures (more work intensity) of their own.[48] Paternalistic benefits may reduce the worker's "marginal propensity to shirk" for every given level of cost of detection if the worker views them as goodwill gestures from the landlord. In this case, provision of benefits helps the landlord cast himself as a benevolent patron, thereby legitimating at the same time his role in the social and economic hierarchy. Workers respond with a measure of loyalty where they are assured by the landlord's gestures of the legitimacy and fairness of the exchange of their labor for paternalism. As Hayami and Kikuchi have noted in Asian village economies: "to behave like a benevolent patron was the efficient way for a landlord to establish his status as a legitimate member of the elite and the least costly way to enforce his contracts with tenants in the local community."[49] This also appears to have been the case in the American South.[50]

More importantly, paternalism may act as an "efficiency wage:" Because some of the services acquired under paternalism are not available in markets, workers, who value such services, are not indifferent between the present paternalistic work relationship and the casual labor market. The lack of indifference encourages greater work intensity because workers are afraid of losing their paternalistic benefits if caught shirking. For example, in discussing the variety of services provided by a patron, Hayami and Kikuchi remark that "the discovery of shirking in one operation . . . would endanger the whole set of transactions."[51]

Presumably landlords could induce loyalty by simply paying higher wages than those that exist in the casual labor market. The rationale for using paternalism is that there is a cost advantage over cash. If landlords have access to the machinery of the state and can foster a discriminatory environment – unequal educational benefits or unequal treatment under

---

[47] The mechanisms through which paternalism could reduce monitoring costs are discussed in greater detail in Alston and Ferrie, "Social Control."

[48] A similar model is described in Akerlof, "Labor Contracts."

[49] Hayami and Kikuchi, *Asian Village Economy*, p. 72.

[50] Davis et al., *Deep South*; Powdermaker, *After Freedom*; Raper, *Preface to Peasantry*; Rubin, *Plantation County*.

[51] Hayami and Kikuchi, *Asian Village Economy*, p. 218.

the law, for example – they are able to increase the value of the paternalistic goods they supply. Over some range, the provision of paternalism costs the landlord less than the cash value of paternalism for some workers.

Once the value of planter paternalism has been created, competition among landlords and their inability to price discriminate perfectly among workers (because workers' labor supply functions are unobservable) imply that some workers will receive greater rents than others, thereby fostering greater work intensity. For example, some workers may value protection more than others or some may have different attitudes with respect to displaying deference. This means that there will be inframarginal workers who earn rents, and the potential loss of those rents motivates their unstinting work effort.

Finally, provision of paternalism may help to increase the length of the time horizon over which workers make decisions, even in the absence of a fear of being caught shirking and forfeiting paternalistic benefits that have not yet been paid. Because paternalism is a long-term contract of sorts, it may induce in workers a sense that they, as well as the landlord, gain from investments that show a payoff only in the distant future, such as improvements to soil fertility. This is especially true for fixed-rent tenants who are residual claimants of any given year's output. If landlords' promises of the payment of paternalistic goods and services in the future convince workers that their situation is more than just temporary, they may be more willing to make long-term investments that raise total output (and hence the returns to both landowner and worker) above what it would be if they had to negotiate a new contract each year and forgo such investments.

One perhaps puzzling aspect of these paternalistic transactions is that workers were expected not only to work hard in the fields but to display deference toward their landlords. By deference we mean the subservient behavior displayed by employees toward their employers. Higgs and Alston have described this deferential behavior:

In addition to performing faithfully his duties as servant, laborer, or tenant, a dependent in his dealings with the patron would: never contradict the patron; never use the patron's front door, no matter what the occasion; always address the patron courteously as mister or sir; keep his head bowed slightly; never sit down unless invited to; always remove his hat; be humble at all times; appear extremely grateful for any favors, even if they were due; never interrupt the patron's conversation; and always appear happy.[52]

No doubt some of the deference landlords received was due in part to their being members of the white upper class in a racially divided and

---

[52] Higgs and Alston, "An Economist's Perspective."

class-conscious society. However, it appears that both black and white landlords acted as protectors and were accorded similarly deferential respect by their tenants, both black and white.[53]

Why would landlords want deference, when without it labor costs would be lower? It may be that repeated deferential behavior increases work effort. By distancing themselves from workers, landlords may instill fear and thereby generate more intensity. In addition, establishing a hierarchical relationship may legitimate the existing distribution of wealth and thereby maintain it.[54] Deference may also be a consumption good in the utility function of landlords.

The distribution of paternalistic benefits across agricultural classes is not expected to be uniform. Instead, the frequency with which benefits are provided will vary across classes of workers (tenants, croppers, or wage workers), along with the frequency with which they are provided to workers within classes. To some extent, direct supervision, contract mix, and paternalism are substitutes. Yet the direct costs of supervision vary across workers. It depends on what assets a worker brings to the production process.[55]

For example, in the short-run, workers vary in their stocks of human and physical capital (farming know-how and mules or tractors). If the landlord supplies all the factors of production except labor, his costs of directly supervising work effort are less than if he supplies only land. When supplying advice and physical capital, the landlord has an incentive to visit the farm regularly to monitor the treatment of his capital and to give direction. Given his presence for these reasons, the marginal cost of supervising labor work effort is relatively low. But the marginal cost of supervising labor work effort of an experienced farmer who owns capital is relatively greater. To reduce the cost of supervising workers who own more assets, landlords adjust contract form – wage to share or fixed rent – and give paternalism to induce self-supervision. Because wage workers are closely supervised, paternalism may not reduce shirking sufficiently to warrant its cost.

Fostering greater work intensity is not the primary motivation for supplying paternalistic goods to all workers, though. Fixed-rent tenants already have an incentive not to stint on their labor because they are residual claimants to output. Nevertheless we see fixed-rent tenants receiving paternalistic goods. To the extent that paternalistic goods are

[53] Davis et al., *Deep South*, pp. 233–4, 270–3.
[54] See Fenoaltea, "Authority, Efficiency, and Agricultural Organization," pp. 693–718, for a discussion of this effect in Medieval agriculture in England.
[55] This analysis extends that found in Alston and Higgs, "Contractual Mix," pp. 327–53.

landlord-specific and usually require a long-standing relationship, supplying paternalism will discourage the job mobility of tenants by raising the cost of leaving a specific patron-client relationship.

Landlords want to tie certain tenants to their plantations if all workers do not know how to farm all plots of land equally well. For some plots, experienced tenants may know the optimal combinations of factor inputs to maximize output better than the landlords. In these instances, landlords have an incentive to supply paternalism to their better tenants to discourage mobility. Provided there are sufficient numbers of tenants on each plantation with plantation-specific skills, competition among tenants on each plantation will ensure that landlords will capture some of the rents from the knowledge of tenants.

The time horizons over which to maximize the returns to land also differ between owners and tenants. Because of their weaker ties to the land, tenants have less of an incentive than owners to engage in activities that bring returns in the future. To encourage tenants to value future returns more highly, owners may be willing to offer a long-term paternalistic relationship.

The incentives to workers from paternalism and different contract forms are not identical. Contract form induces self-supervised work effort on this year's crop, whereas paternalistic benefits raise the costs of losing a job and thereby both increase work intensity and reduce the benefits of changing employers. Because landlords have more incentive to monitor the work effort of croppers than of fixed-rent tenants, paternalistic goods may be provided to croppers to substitute for some direct supervision. As was the case with tenants, to the extent that croppers possess farm-specific human capital, they may receive some paternalistic goods to reduce mobility. Our explanation provides a theoretical rationale for the observed provision of paternalistic goods primarily to croppers and tenants.

Even within a particular class of workers, however, we would not expect the distribution of paternalistic benefits to be uniform. That distribution depends not just on employers' willingness to supply benefits but also on workers' demand for them. For example, white workers were not as likely as black workers to be the beneficiaries of paternalistic arrangements, both because they had a lower demand for protection from violence, and because they were not as likely as blacks to be employed on plantations.[56]

Of course, because paternalistic goods are highly personal in nature (for example, legal assistance), we would expect that close contact be-

---

[56] Some white farm workers did enter into paternalistic relationships, however; Genovese, *Roll, Jordan, Roll*, p. 661.

Southern Paternalism and the American Welfare State

tween workers and landlords would increase the likelihood of their provision. Plantation owners tended to reside in close proximity to their workers, which in part explains why plantations and paternalism so often coincided. Plantation owners were more likely than other employers to supply paternalism because in these areas the ties between the landlord and the tenant and his family often extended over several years or generations.[57] Plantation owners were also more likely to supply paternalism because of economies of scale in the provision of some aspects of paternalism, such as housing or medical care. Finally, because plantation owners also had more political power than small landowners, they had more ability to offer protection from the law. The cost of providing this sort of paternalism varied inversely with political influence, which in turn was a function of farm size. This is perhaps the most important reason why paternalism in the American South was associated with plantations.

For much of the late nineteenth and early twentieth centuries, individual Southern plantation owners had the local political influence to ensure the delivery of protection and, by the turn of the century, the collective political influence at the state level to create a discriminatory sociolegal environment from which they then offered dispensation.[58] Furthermore, from the end of Reconstruction through the 1960s, plantation owners collectively had the political power at the national level to prevent, or at least limit, federal interference in Southern race and labor relations.[59]

V. Evidence on the Extent of Paternalism in the South

We can begin to get an idea of the greater use of in-kind benefits in the South by comparing estimates of the value of farm perquisites such as housing, fuel, foodstuffs, livestock use, and garden privileges as a percentage of total wages (cash plus perquisites) in various geographic regions across the country in 1925. As Table 1.1 shows, the South tended to use relatively more in-kind benefits than other regions. In the three Southern regions, the ratio of in-kind wages to total wages exceeded 40 percent. Only in the East North Central region, where tenancy was important, did in-kind benefits come close to their relative magnitude in the South.[60]

[57] We present evidence in the next section on the lower mobility of tenants and sharecroppers in the plantation regions of the South.

[58] Kousser, *Shaping of Southern Politics*.

[59] Cox and McCubbins, *Legislative Leviathan*; Havard, *Changing Politics of the South*; Key, *Southern Politics*; and Mowry, *Another Look*.

[60] We can reject at the 95 percent confidence level the null hypothesis that the mean percentage of in-kind benefits to cash wages was equal between the South and the rest of the nation. The relevant *t*-statistic is 3.38.

Table 1.1. *Cash wages and the value of perquisites of farm laborers by geographic region (1925)*

Region	(1) Average monthly cash wages[a]	(2) Average monthly perquisites[b]	(3) Col. (2) / [Col. (1) + Col. (2)]
New England	$63.21	$25.08	28.4%
Middle Atlantic	54.07	31.84	37.1
East North Central	46.44	32.37	41.1
West North Central	47.41	31.15	39.7
South Atlantic	32.78	26.97	45.1
East South Central	31.53	24.71	43.9
West South Central	36.05	27.63	43.4
Mountain	56.49	35.13	38.3
Pacific	73.79	33.00	30.9
Total U.S.	46.31	30.34	39.6

Notes:
[a] Monthly money payments to noncasual hired farm laborers
[b] Monthly farm value of perquisites of noncasual hired farm laborers. Perquisites include board (table board in the employer's home or paid for by him elsewhere, lodging in the employer's home or buildings or paid for by him elsewhere, laundry work done in the farm house or elsewhere at the employer's expense); shelter (the rental value of the dwelling occupied by the farm laborer's family provided or paid for by the employer, wood, coal, gas, electricity); dairy and poultry (milk, butter, eggs, chickens for meat); meat (pork, ham, bacon, lard, beef, and other meats); flour and meal (wheat flour, corn meal); vegetables and fruit (potatoes, other vegetables, apples, other fruits); miscellaneous foods; privilege of keeping livestock (chickens, pigs, cows, horses, or mules); feed for livestock; pasture or range for livestock; garden space; use of employer's horses or mules; use of employer's farm tools and vehicles; garage space; and miscellaneous perquisites.
Sources: Cash wages and perquisites from Folsom, "Perquisites and Wages," table 17, pp. 23–4.

For several reasons, these figures underrepresent the extent to which Southern plantation owners relied more on in-kind benefits than did small Southern landholders and Northern farmers: (1) given their perceived role in Southern society, plantation owners may have placed a greater value on the deference they received from providing in-kind benefits; (2) to the extent that the provision of these benefits was subject to economies of scale, plantation owners would supply more; (3) because of their political influence, plantation owners could provide benefits such as legal aid, whereas small landowners lacked the necessary influence over local judges and officials that would have allowed them to do the same; (4) because supervision costs become more important with farm size (because of the strain placed upon the limited supervisory capacity of the owner by the greater number of workers to supervise and the increased spatial separation of workers), the role played by in-kind benefits in reducing supervisory costs also becomes more important; and (5) studies of Southern agricultural life consistently emphasize the connection between plantations and paternalism.[61]

Evidence from an earlier period of the association between in-kind benefits and plantations is contained in a special investigation of Georgia plantations conducted by the United States Census Bureau in 1911. This survey was unique because it surveyed large farm owners in the South, rather than the group usually enumerated by the Census Bureau, farm operators, which included tenants and croppers (who were not owners), thereby obscuring data on large ownership units. This census asked whether landlords gave laborers gifts, livestock privileges, prizes, rent-free patches of land, holidays, funerals, meetings, circuses, excursions, picnics, and land or financial support for churches and schools. Unfortunately, it is not possible to tally systematically the percentages of landlords who gave benefits or the value of the benefits, because the schedules are not complete. Nonetheless, it appears that the use of in-kind benefits of this sort was nearly universal. The fact that the Census Bureau included such a question on its schedules suggests a belief that plantations tended to use these in-kind benefits as an integral part of the compensation package.

Alston and Kauffman provide indirect evidence on the existence of paternalism.[62] They found that, particularly in plantation areas, black cash tenants paid higher cash rents per acre than did white cash tenants in the same area. They argue that black cash tenants paid "paternalism premiums" for protection from potential abuses. The estimated magnitude of the premium is eight percent above that of a white cash tenant and represents about 6.5 percent of the average income for cash tenants in the South. In a competitive market, blacks would not pay such a premium unless they received corresponding benefits. The fact that turnover for black tenants was less than turnover for white tenants indicates that black tenants still captured some value from paternalistic benefits over and above the premium that they paid.

There is also evidence in a study from the New Deal period that agricultural labor arrangements in the South differed significantly from those

---

[61] Davis et al., *Deep South*; Charles S. Johnson, *Shadow of the Plantation*; Myrdal, *American Dilemma*; Percy, *Lanterns on the Levee*; Powdermaker, *After Freedom*; Raper, *Preface to Peasantry*; Rubin, *Plantation County*.
[62] See Alston and Kauffman, "Social Norms of Racial Discrimination."

in the North.[63] This study found that paternalism was far more prevalent in the South than in the North.[64] In the South, supervision was more frequent and more detailed, and landlords exercised greater control over their tenants' credit and stood good for their debts more often than in the North. In addition, such control was more frequently exercised over black workers, who worked in disproportionate numbers on plantations rather than small farms, which emphasizes again the link between plantations and paternalism.[65]

The evidence on the existence and provision of paternalistic goods is extensive.[66] All the studies of labor relations in Southern agriculture indicate that tenants and croppers received more paternalistic goods than wage workers. This is consistent with our view that paternalistic goods substituted for direct monitoring. In addition, wage hands tended to cultivate plots of land closest to the house of the landlord, suggesting more frequent supervision and thus less of a reason to provide paternalism to wage workers.[67]

Tenants and sharecroppers in the plantation regions of the South tended to move far less frequently than those outside the plantation regions. As Table 1.2 shows, Southern tenants on plantations had on average been living on their present farm roughly twice as long as tenants not on plantations in the 1930s. This reduced mobility in the plantation regions enabled landlords to offer benefits that required long-term personal relationships. At the same time, this evidence suggests the success of landlords in using paternalism to tie tenants to their farms. The striking difference between black and white mobility in every tenure class is consistent with the greater demand by blacks for protection.

Our explanation for low mobility in plantation areas and for black workers differs from Wright, who maintains that Southern agricultural labor markets consisted of two interlinked markets: a local market of tenants and sharecroppers and a larger geographic market of wage hands.[68] Wright argues that the need to secure credit limited the mobility of tenants and sharecroppers. His explanation, however, is unable to

---

[63] Schuler, "Social Status and Farm Tenure."

[64] These survey results are discussed in greater detail in Chapter 4.

[65] This is also consistent with black workers having a greater demand for paternalistic benefits because of the sociolegal discrimination they faced; Higgs and Alston, "An Economist's Perspective."

[66] For examples, see Davis et al., *Deep South*; Powdermaker, *After Freedom*; Raper, *Preface to Peasantry*; Rubin, *Plantation County*; and Woofter, "Plantation Economy."

[67] Wright, *Old South, New South*, p. 92, drawing on the study by Woofter in 1936, gives evidence consistent with this view, though he does not draw this implication.

[68] Wright, *Old South, New South*.

Table 1.2. *Occupancy on present farm by race
of operator, region, plantation and
nonplantation, and agriculture class (1934 and
1940)*

	Years on present farm[a]	
	White	Black
All farms[b]		
Tenants		
New England	7	8
Middle Atlantic	7	6
East North Central	6	7
West North Central	6	6
South Atlantic	5	8
East South Central	5	8
West South Central	4	7
Mountain	5	6
Pacific	5	7
Sharecroppers		
South Atlantic	4	5
East South Central	3	5
West South Central	4	5
Farms on plantations[c]		
Tenants	9	14
Sharecroppers	5	7

Notes:
[a]"Present" is 1940 for "All farms" and 1934 for "Farms on plantations"
[b]Based on enumeration of all farms in U.S.
[c]Based on sample of 646 plantations in 6 Southern states: Alabama, Arkansas, Georgia, Louisiana, Mississippi, and North Carolina
Sources:
[b]U.S. Census Bureau, *Sixteenth Census,* Vol. I, table 14, pp. 392–9
[c]Woofter, "Plantation Economy," table 41, p. 98

account for differences in mobility across regions (plantation versus non-plantation) or race (black versus white).

Though labor was dependent, was it cheap? In 1925, the unweighted Southern regional average of cash wages plus perquisites paid to farm workers was approximately $60, more than 25 percent lower than the $87 average for the rest of the country (Table 1.1). During World War

II, wages in most Southern states increased less than the national average.[69] By the end of the war, Southern farm wages were still considerably below the national average.[70]

To maintain their cheap, dependent labor force, planters had to prevent the out-migration of labor and the in-migration of capital. Wright argues that although labor did migrate to the North, the Southern labor market was not integrated into the national market until after World War II.[71] His argument hinges on path dependence – the extent to which circumstances at a point in time are the result of circumstances at previous points in time. Migration flows in the nineteenth century tended along latitudinal lines, in part because migrants brought with them climate specific knowledge about crops.[72] Slavery and the turbulence of the postbellum period further insulated the South and helped produce a distinct Southern culture. Once the South was perceived as different by Southerners and others, cultural differences acted as a further check on migration. The lack of large numbers of expatriate Southerners outside the South also stemmed out-migration: The network externalities that induce people to move where they have many personal contacts were absent for most Southerners.

The low levels of education in the South may have also increased the costs of migration. Literacy and numeracy increase both the likelihood of employment in a new location and the flexibility with which one adapts to a new situation. Southerners spent considerably less on education than did Northerners. The desire of a politically potent coalition of Southern planters and mill owners to keep the costs of migration high can explain much of the Southern aversion toward spending on education.

[69] Walter W. Wilcox, *Farmer in the Second World War*, p. 76.
[70] Lebergott, *Manpower*, p. 540.
[71] Wright, *Old South, New South* and "Economic Revolution."
[72] Steckel, "Economic Foundations."

2

The Politics of Maintaining Paternalism

The value of paternalism to the Southern rural elite depended on the availability of substitutes for paternalism. The appearance of substitutes provided by the government – programs providing old-age security, unemployment insurance, medical care, or greater security in commercial and legal dealings – would have raised the cost of monitoring labor and reduced the elite's ability to keep labor dependable and cheap. Substitutes for paternalism provided by the private sector – the provision of farming supplies and household goods on favorable terms from local merchants, the opportunity for Southern workers to migrate to jobs outside the South, or the appearance of new employment opportunities within the South created by inflows of capital from outside the South – would have raised reservation wages. The Southern planter elite worked to prevent any of these developments in order to limit the threat to their form of labor relations.

Southern landowners did not operate directly in politics but instead used Congressmen as their political agents. The Democratic party in the South dominated politics after Reconstruction and was controlled by landowners and merchants in the counties dominated by plantation agriculture – the black belt elites. In the early 1870s the commitment to Reconstruction by the North began to wane due to allegations of corruption and the economic recession of the 1870s.[1] In the South the fall in agricultural prices hurt all farmers, and poor white farmers reacted more favorably to the racist rhetoric of the Redeemer (Democratic) governments than if times had been good. The varied factions supporting the Southern Redeemers "shared however a commitment to dismantling the Reconstruction state, reducing the political power of blacks, and reshaping the South's legal system in the interests of labor control and racial

[1] Foner, *History of Reconstruction.*

34

subordination."[2] The retreat from Reconstruction was consummated in the "Bargain of 1877," which resulted from the contested presidential election of 1876 between Tilden and Hayes. The "bargain" entailed the exchange of the electoral votes of Louisiana and South Carolina in favor of Hayes for a commitment from the Republicans to allow "home rule" in those states.[3] This bargain sounds fragile but it sealed what had been a slow Northern retreat from Reconstruction.

The failure of Reconstruction to bring about lasting political and economic emancipation for the Freedmen despite the North's victory in the Civil War, a failure that laid the groundwork for the South's system of paternalistic labor relations, was in some ways inevitable. It followed from the inability to build a Southern Republican party that would represent the Freedmen where the Southern Democrats did not. The problems faced in building such a party in the South were the result of a combination of circumstances: the difficulty of balancing the demands of its two likely constituencies on fiscal issues (Freedmen wanted more funding for education, and upcountry yeomen wanted a lower tax burden), even though both were ready to stand in opposition to the plantation oligarchy; the awkward position of Southern Republicans as newcomers in a national Republican party that was more concerned with the national debt and the gold standard than with the promotion of railroads and industry that would have won Southern Republicans' support; and the consequent reliance of Republicans in the South on poorly financed state-level improvement projects that went under in the Recession of 1873, prompting Northern complaints of mismanagement and venality.[4]

These "party-building" difficulties were compounded by the continued threat of physical violence against supporters of such a new party in the absence of complete federal control of law and order and frequent Klan activity. Despite the North's military victory in the war, federal coercive power in the South was weakened by troop reductions in the three years after 1865, by the need to shift resources to the Western frontier as conflict with Native Americans intensified, and by Democratic gains in the House of Representatives in the 1874 election.[5]

In some areas the impact of the plantation elite was felt immediately after the war: New vagrancy and antienticement laws were passed early in Reconstruction. Other changes took longer for the planter elite to achieve. These changes included: The clarification of lien laws (through

[2] Ibid., p. 248.
[3] Ibid., p. 244.
[4] Valelly, "Party, Coercion, and Inclusion," pp. 45–51.
[5] Ibid., pp. 48–9.

the state legislatures) to ensure that the landlord's claim to the crop superseded the rights of country merchants or wage laborers; the resolution of the legal status of sharecroppers (through the courts) to that of wage workers rather than tenants; and the virtual disfranchisement of blacks and many poor whites (through the legislatures and courts). The crucial role of the South's rural plantation elite in this gradual process is stressed by Kousser who argues that it took about twenty years for the planters to achieve domination and shape the South's political and legal structure to their liking:

> The new political structure was not the product of accident or other impersonal forces, nor of decisions demanded by the masses, nor even the white masses. The system which insured the absolute control of predominantly black counties by upper-class whites, the elimination in most areas of parties as a means of organized competition between politicians, and, in general, the nonrepresentation of lower class interests in political decision-making was shaped by those who stood to benefit most from it – Democrats, usually from the black belt and always socioeconomically privileged.[6]

The new political structure gave the plantation elite and their allies a firm grip on politics in the South. The black belt elite no longer had to stuff ballot boxes or engage in intimidation. Disfranchisement now ensured the political hegemony at the state level of this socioeconomic upper class. After suffrage restrictions were enacted in the South, the fall in mean white turnout ranged from 3 percent in Georgia to 66 percent in Louisiana. Throughout the South, mean black turnout fell 62 percent. The decline in turnout was accompanied by a 45 percent fall in the number of adult males voting for opposition parties.[7]

The history of the South's crop lien laws and the evolution of the legal status of sharecroppers clearly illustrate the gradual evolution of the political environment that made paternalism viable.[8] But these developments also highlight the extent of conflict within the South's rural elite. Though the Democratic party dominated Southern politics in the decades following the end of Reconstruction, for much of that time it was not a monolithic Democratic party. The interests of merchants and large plantation owners frequently collided down through the last quarter of the nineteenth century and the first decade of the twentieth. Only in the early twentieth century was the plantation elite able to consolidate its hold over the Southern Democratic party. The South's striking ability to wield power at the national level in defense of paternalism (which we describe in the following chapters) may blind us to the continuing cleav-

[6] Kousser, *Shaping of Southern Politics*, p. 238.
[7] Ibid., pp. 240–2.
[8] The development of the South's crop lien laws and changing status of sharecroppers are described in Woodman, *New South – New Law*.

ages within the Southern Democratic party throughout the first half of the twentieth century. A brief look at the history of the South's crop lien laws and the changing legal status of sharecroppers will reveal the interests within the party in the South that had to be harmonized before the South could defend paternalism in the national political arena when the threat of outside interference emerged in the New Deal.

The crop lien laws were the most important source of friction between plantation owners and local merchants in the first forty or so years after emancipation. These laws were passed by Southern state legislatures in the immediate aftermath of the Civil War to assure creditors that their loans would be repaid when they advanced supplies to cash-strapped Southern farmers.[9] The operation of these laws was straightforward when a farm's owner was also its operator. As freed blacks became tenants, agreeing to pay the rent on their land after the crop was brought in and borrowing from local merchants to finance the purchase of supplies and cover living expenses, things got more complicated. Both the landowner and the merchant would often have liens against the same crop. When the crop provided too little revenue to satisfy all these claims against it, conflict arose over whose claim should be satisfied first.

For planters, this was about more than merely whether they would receive at the end of the growing season the rent agreed upon at the start – it was also about control over their workforce. When planters were the sole source to which tenants could turn for credit, planters could exercise significant control over virtually every aspect of their tenants' lives; with nowhere else to turn, tenants had no choice but to accept the paternalism offered by planters. The crop lien laws complicated these arrangements. As Woodman notes,

Ironically, then, the lien law, designed to help the planters get credit and maintain control over their workforce, became a means for workers to escape dependency upon their employers by providing them with an alternative source of credit. When the freedmen seized their new opportunity, they created new and unforeseen conflicts, which freedmen, planters, and merchants all attempted to resolve in a manner that afforded each the greatest benefit.[10]

Court decisions throughout the South in the late 1860s provided little comfort to landowners, as the decisions usually turned on the specific circumstances of each case and established no universal principles of lien superiority.[11]

[9] Ibid., pp. 6–7.
[10] Ibid., p. 24.
[11] See ibid., pp. 32–56, for examples of the ambiguities created by the postbellum lien laws and subsequent court cases in Georgia, Mississippi, North Carolina, South Carolina, and Louisiana.

Though problems with the postbellum lien laws were apparent in most states as early as 1867, nothing was done to clarify the ranking of liens while the political power of the black belt plantation elites was weak. The declining fortunes of radical Republicans and the appearance of Redeemer Democrats in many Southern legislators, however, prompted a review of lien law in the early 1870s. For example, Georgia (in 1873) and Mississippi (in 1875) established the priority of a landlord's lien when credit was extended to a tenant to cover rent. This did not entirely settle the issue – court cases challenging landlords' liens for rent continued through the early 1930s – but it did provide a greater degree of certainty than had existed immediately after the war. The lien laws of the 1870s also did not end conflict between planters and merchants, but simply foreclosed one avenue of competition between them: the struggle over control of tenants' credit. By the early 1880s, it was clear that landlords rather than merchants would exercise that control, making it easier for landlords to exercise control over other areas of their tenants' lives, thereby laying one of the important foundations of the system of paternalism.

The second area in which the planters struggled for control with merchants in the first decade after the war was the legal status of sharecroppers. Because they possessed few resources and did not realize any income until the crop was harvested and sold, croppers had an acute need for credit, credit local merchants were quite willing to supply when the first postbellum crop lien laws gave them a good chance of repayment. As Woodman notes, "Landowner-employers quickly realized that their ability to control these advances, which directly affected the well-being of the croppers and their families, could be a powerful weapon to insure their croppers' obedience – unless, of course, the cropper could get advances from other sources."[12]

Southern courts over the late 1860s resolved some of this conflict by defining croppers to be nothing more than wage laborers compensated with a share of the crop, rather than cash. This left control over the crop in the hands of the landlord and gave the cropper nothing against which to borrow from local merchants. The question of lien superiority causing such problems with tenants was rendered moot by stripping the cropper of the principal collateral on which a merchant could take a lien.

This opened up a new area of contention, however. Radical Republicans had strengthened the laws allowing laborers to take liens against their employers for the payment of wages, and in some states required that wages be paid only in U.S. currency. Now, croppers' liens could

[12] Ibid., p. 87.

conflict with those of merchants who had advanced supplies to the croppers' employers. By the late 1870s, Redeemer legislatures had addressed these concerns by subordinating laborers' liens to those of merchants.[13]

Once the conflicts between planters and merchants over crop liens and the status of croppers were resolved in the planters' favor, the Southern rural elite could turn to using their political power at the local and state levels to prevent interference from the federal government in Southern labor and race relations when Washington turned its attention to the South in the early 1930s. Because of their control of the Democratic party within their states, the black belt elites controlled their states' delegations to Congress from the late nineteenth century until the second half of the twentieth century. As V. O. Key noted in 1949, "the black belts manage to control almost the entire Southern delegation in opposition to proposals of external interference."[14]

Key argued that the basis for Southern unity was race. Though much of the power of race as a unifying issue in Southern politics resulted from the pervasive racism of Southern whites in general, we believe that race was important for another reason as well: it enabled politicians to cater to the economic interests of the white upper class while maintaining the support of whites in general. Though some poor whites prospered as a result of the South's system of social control, many did not because some of the mechanisms for social control, such as poll taxes, were based on class rather than race. Through their promotion of a racist ideology, Southern politicians were able to maintain the support of poor Southern whites who were hurt by these mechanisms. Race as an issue also solidified the support for Southern politicians from the white elite: To the extent that plantation owners believed the racist rhetoric of Southern politicians, plantation owners could enrich themselves while satisfying their racial prejudices.

One area in which Southerners strenuously resisted interference from outside the South was labor relations in agriculture. Federal interference would have included the promotion of welfare programs, old-age assistance, and civil rights. As we saw in Chapter 1, a lack of civil rights for blacks reduced labor costs in plantation agriculture by making blacks in agriculture more dependent on the white elite for protection from arbitrary violence. In Chapter 3, we describe how the Southern Congressional delegation prevented agricultural labor from being covered under

[13] Ibid., p. 79. These changes occurred in Mississippi (1875), Arkansas (1875), Alabama (1874), South Carolina (1877), Georgia (1873), Tennessee (1879), and Texas (1874).
[14] Key, *Southern Politics*, p. 668.

the Social Security Act. We discuss in Chapter 4 how Southern politicians opposed the Farm Security Administration in the late 1930s once that agency's agenda turned from promoting recovery from the Depression to advocating fundamental reform in Southern agriculture. In Chapter 5, we show how Southerners advocated farm labor legislation during and after World War II in order to prevent the migration of Southern agricultural workers out of the South.

The successes of Southerners in these efforts prompt a question: Given that the Southern delegation did not represent a majority in either chamber of Congress, how were Southern legislators able to satisfy the desires of their constituents in these ways? First, after Reconstruction and until the advent of the New Deal, there was an absence of pressure to intervene in the South. The New Deal represented a departure from noninterference when it switched its agenda toward reform. Reform was thwarted in part as a result of remarkable Southern unity on voting, particularly on issues dealing with race and to a lesser degree on issues dealing with federal interference in other matters.[15]

A larger part of the reason for the disproportionate power of Southern Congressmen is how Congress functions as an institution. Though Southern Democrats were never an absolute majority in Congress, they represented a substantial and influential faction in the Democratic party. Though there is presently a lively debate over whether parties have had much influence over decision making in Congress in the twentieth century, it is difficult to deny that parties ultimately shape decisions if only because appointments to committees are made by the party leadership.[16] The influence of Southerners within the Democratic party thus afforded them some power through the party's control of committee assignments.

An even more important reason for disproportionate Southern influence, however, is that Congress has historically ceded short-run authority over legislation to committees. This is important because legislative outcomes can differ from the outcomes desired by the median party member when a committee's composition differs from the composition of the party. Thus, a Southern minority within the Democratic party could thwart the desires of the majority of the party in the short-run if they dominated certain "control" committees.[17] Committees at times may thus be an even more important source of power than parties. For this reason, a look at representation on committees, particularly the

---

[15] Ibid., pp. 345–55 and 667. Key's formal analysis of Southern unity only covered the years 1933, 1937, 1941, and 1945.

[16] For a synthesis of the issues surrounding the debate, see Cox and McCubbins, *Legislative Leviathan*.

[17] Cox and McCubbins, *Legislative Leviathan*, label the House Ways and Means, Rules, and Appropriations Committees the control committees.

composition of control committees, will illuminate the sources of the South's political power.

Decision making in Congress is not completely democratic. Although every Congressman has one vote, considerable authority is delegated to committees that decide if and when legislation comes up for a vote. Ceding control over legislation to committees prevents sudden reversals in legislation. This is because committee members in part self-select themselves onto committees, which implies that committee members will have preferences different from the preferences of the median member of the House or Senate. For example, Congressmen from agricultural states tend to care more about agriculture than Congressmen from nonagricultural states and request assignment to the Agriculture Committee. This makes it less likely that legislation will be reversed suddenly, because senior committee members must change their preferences or be replaced by members with different preferences for laws to change. It is not sufficient merely for members to form a new coalition or for Congress as a whole to change its preferences.[18]

This arrangement does not imply that committee authority is absolute. One way to view committee members is as agents of their respective parties.[19] The authority committees are allowed to exercise depends in part on the cohesiveness of the majority party and the extent to which committee members are representative of their parties. Shepsle has argued convincingly that committee members – at least for special interest committees like agriculture – have preferences that are different from the preferences of the median member of their party.[20] However, this does not necessarily imply that committees have complete autonomy to exercise their preferences. Much depends on the cohesion of the parties. When parties are composed of factions, as the Democratic party was from the New Deal to 1970 when the Voting Rights Act changed constituencies in the South, coalitions need to be formed and enforced in order for a party to be effective in policy-making.

By allowing strong committees to exercise agenda control, the Democratic party held together an alliance based on Southern support for the party platform and federal noninterference in Southern labor and race relations. Committee power, though, was still not absolute. Senior com-

---

[18] Weingast and Marshall, "Industrial Organization of Congress"; Shepsle and Weingast, "Institutional Foundations"; Shepsle and Weingast, "Legislative Politics."

[19] For an elaboration of this view, see Kiewat and McCubbins, *Logic of Delegation*; and Cox and McCubbins, *Legislative Leviathan*.

[20] Shepsle, *Giant Jigsaw Puzzle*. Cox and McCubbins, *Legislative Leviathan*, dispute this claim of Shepsle, but the evidence of Cox and McCubbins is based on measures of ideology rather than narrow economic interest. Measures of economic interest are what one would ideally want to use in testing the Shepsle hypothesis.

mittee members had to satisfy some faction within the Democratic party, whether Southern conservatives or Northern liberals. Nevertheless, in the postwar period, it is clear that committees and their senior members were the repositories of legislative power.

Committees shape legislation in several ways. In the House, if and when any piece of legislation reaches the floor are determined by the House Rules Committee. In both the House and Senate, committees have agenda control within their policy jurisdictions. Legislation originates in and is shaped by committees with jurisdiction over particular policy areas. For example, only the House and Senate committees on Agriculture have the authority to submit to the floor legislation that deals with agriculture. Out of the infinite number of bills that could pass through Congress, committees can choose the bills that best suit the interests of committee members while still commanding a majority of votes in Congress. Alternatively, if the committee is not interested in an issue, even though the majority of Congress is, it can simply fail to report a bill to the floor.

Even after legislation passes in the House or Senate, committees still exercise disproportionate power. Differences in proposed legislation between the House and Senate are settled in conference committees comprised of representatives of each chamber who are members of the relevant committees from which the proposed legislation emanated.[21] In addition, after legislation becomes law, committees watch over its implementation.

As in Congress as a whole, decision making within committees is not democratic. In describing committees in the post-World War II period, Smith argues that "widely recognized norms of apprenticeship and committee deference served to limit effective participation to a few senior committee members. Moreover, the distribution of resources and parliamentary prerogatives advantaged senior, majority party, committee chairmen in both chambers."[22]

Whether it was norms of behavior or constraints on the party that gave senior members disproportionate power is a subject of debate. We favor the view that it was the constraints of the party because it appears less ad hoc. For example, to say that the same norms of behavior existed in the pre-World War II period but were not as strong requires that we explain why Congress allowed committees to become so strong. Chairmen of committees set committee meeting times, made appointments to subcommittees, hired the professional staff, led the floor debate on the legislation reported out of their committees, and served on conference committees to reconcile differences between the two chambers.

---

[21] In the House, the Speaker picks the conference delegation.
[22] Steven S. Smith, *Call to Order*, p. 13.

The Politics of Maintaining Paternalism

Seniority also matters outside committees. Seniority increases a Congressman's influence by increasing the ease of logrolling votes. Because votes on many issues must be traded over time, the increased certainty of continued service that seniority signifies increases the ease with which trades can be made.[23] More senior members may also have more benefits to trade, perhaps because of more senior committee status. Greater seniority also affords a Congressman greater scope for acting on personal ideological preferences that may be different from those of their constituents. If constituents decide to "vote the rascal out," they will have an agent who is less senior and hence less powerful than his predecessor. We argue in Chapter 6 that senior Southern politicians in the sixties had considerable scope for voting their ideological preferences.

The importance of party coalitions and seniority in the institutional workings of Congress makes apparent why the South could succeed in blocking federal interference: Southern Congressmen at times constituted about half the membership of the Democratic party in Congress. Though their representation declined in the 1950s, they still had far greater seniority than Congressmen from outside the South because of the one-party system in the South and the South's obsession with race.

Relative Southern seniority manifests itself in Southern dominance of committees. In Tables 2.1 and 2.2 we show the seniority of Southern Congressmen for two periods: 1930 to 1946 and 1947 to 1960. For now, we are focusing only on the pre-1960 era when we believe the maintenance of paternalism was still important to Southerners. We broke the data into two periods to allow us to concentrate on political power in two eras: (1) during the New Deal and World War II years; and (2) during the postwar years. In the second period, described as the era of the "classic committee system" by Bensel in his analysis of committee power and Congressional voting patterns, the power of committee chairmen was at its zenith. Congress reorganized committees in 1946, resulting in fewer standing committees: nineteen in the House and fifteen in the Senate. Congressmen became more specialized, with House members assigned to only one standing committee and Senators assigned to two.[24]

Committee chairs, especially in the House where there was more specialization, became more powerful with reorganization because of expanded jurisdiction and increased control over staff appointments. During the heyday of committee chairmen, they could withhold legislation

---

[23] Crain, Leavens, and Tollison, "Final Voting," found evidence consistent with this view: Bills sponsored by more senior members both passed more frequently and passed more rapidly than those sponsored by junior members. They may or not subscribe to the arguments that follow.
[24] Bensel, *Sectionalism*, p. 319. Steven S. Smith, *Call to Order*.

from the floor singlehandedly.[25] Knowing the power of the committee chairmen, other committee members shaped legislation so it would meet with the approval of chairmen. In the House, committee chairmen catered to the chairman of the Rules Committee in order to get legislation to the floor.[26]

The relative seniority of Southern Congressmen and a sense of their disproportionate power can be seen in Tables 2.1 and 2.2. In the House, from 1930 through the reorganization of committees in 1946, Southerners dominated the Ways and Means, Agriculture, and Judiciary committees: A Southerner chaired these committees in fourteen of the seventeen years and Southerners usually had over half of the first five seats. Southerners also had disproportionate influence in the 1930s on the Rules and Appropriations committees. In short, Southerners in the House had considerable agenda control on both the "control" committees – Rules, Ways and Means, and Appropriations – and on the Agriculture and Judiciary committees.

In the early Roosevelt years, Southern political power was enhanced by a tacit deal between Roosevelt and the Southern contingent: Support for the New Deal was exchanged for a relatively free hand in writing and rewriting legislation to fit the peculiarities of the South. The accommodation of Southern positions on race and labor relations provided the Democratic party with more than simply support for New Deal domestic policies; it purchased support for "a vast increase in world affairs and the protection of U.S. foreign investment and trade ties."[27] Rexford Tugwell, among the most radical of Roosevelt's advisors, described the Southern Democrats in Congress as "the only dependable body of men who can be counted on to stick by their bargains and pass legislation."[28]

This accommodation was born of both political expediency and the president's political instincts. As Brinkley notes,

His inclination, rather, was to conciliate, to broaden his base, to win the loyalties of existing leaders. In the South, that meant not only remaining solicitous of political elites in the distribution of patronage and the administration of programs. It meant avoiding issues altogether when those issues seemed likely to create antagonisms. Hence, the New Deal's reluctance to challenge segregation in the South, its willingness to tolerate racial discrimination in the administration of its own relief programs, its acceptance of racial wage differentials, its refusal

---

[25] Steven S. Smith, *Call to Order*, pp. 8–9. Deering and Smith, *Committees in Congress*.
[26] Dierenfield, *Keeper of the Rules*, p. 231.
[27] Bensel, *Sectionalism*, p. 372.
[28] Schlesinger, *Coming of the New Deal*, p. 415. As we note in Chapter 6, Kennedy and Johnson also relied on Southern support to pass legislation.

The Politics of Maintaining Paternalism

Table 2.1. *Seniority of Southern Democrats on House committees,*
1930–60

Committee	Years chaired by Southern Democrat		Average number of first five Democratic seats held by Southern Democrat	
	1931–46	1947–60	1931–46	1947–60
Rules	3	6	2.9	3.0
Appropriations	6	0	2.6	2.3
Ways and Means	15	10	2.8	3.4
Agriculture	15	10	4.3	4.7
Education	4	—	1.6	—
Labor	0	—	1.4	—
Education/Labor	—	8		2.0
Judiciary	15	0	3.4	1.3

Notes: Democrats held a majority in the House from 1931 to 1960 in each
Congress except 1947 to 1948 and 1953 to 1954. We employed the *Congressional Quarterly* definition of the South: the former Confederate states plus Kentucky and Oklahoma.
Source: Congressional Directory, various years

to endorse antilynching legislation, its notable lack of enthusiasm for supporting
union-organizing in the South.[29]

The president's unwillingness to support the antilynching bill introduced in 1935 by Senators Wagner (NY) and Costigan (CO) and vehemently opposed by Southern senators reveals Roosevelt's need for Southern support and the lengths he would go to retain it: "The Southerners
by reason of seniority in Congress are chairmen or occupy strategic
places on most of the Senate and House committees. If I come out for
the antilynching bill now, they will block every bill I ask Congress to
pass to keep America from collapsing. I just can't take that risk."[30] The
purge of "radicals" in the Agricultural Adjustment Administration
(AAA) in 1935 is evidence of the same sensitivity to the wishes of Southern planters and their agents in Washington. When Southern representatives expressed their outrage over a directive from the AAA requiring
that planters retain not just the same number of tenants but the same
individuals as tenants after signing contracts with the AAA, Roosevelt
eliminated the office that had drafted the directive and fired the staff.[31]

[29] Brinkley, "New Deal and Southern Politics," pp. 101–2.
[30] Schlesinger, *Coming of the New Deal,* p. 438.
[31] Leuchtenburg, *Roosevelt and the New Deal,* p. 139.

Table 2.2. *Seniority of Southern Democrats on Senate committees,*
1930–60

Committee	Years chaired by Southern Democrat		Average number of first five Democratic seats held by Southern Democrat	
	1931–46	1947–60	1931–46	1947–60
Rules	5	0	3.2	1.0
Appropriations	13	4	3.4	2.7
Finance	13	10	3.4	3.5
Agriculture	13	10	3.2	4.0
Education/Labor	1	—	1.5	—
Labor	—	6	—	1.4
Judiciary	0	4	3.4	2.3

Notes: Democrats held a majority in the Senate from 1931 to 1960 in each
Congress except 1947 to 1948 (Republican majority), 1953 to 1954 (Republican
majority), 1931 to 1932 (tie), and 1955 to 1956 (tie). We employed the *Con-*
gressional Quarterly definition of the South: the former Confederate states plus
Kentucky and Oklahoma.
Source: Congressional Directory, various years

After reorganization in 1946, the power of Southerners did not wane.
Indeed, it increased, because their relative seniority did not change and
reorganization enhanced the power of committee chairmen. In the postwar period, Southerners dominated the Ways and Means and Agriculture committees, chairing the committees ten of the fourteen years. A
Southerner also chaired the now combined Education and Labor Committee eight years and the Rules Committee six years. Only in the chairs
of the Judiciary and Appropriations committees did Southern presence
decline, though on Appropriations a Southerner held the second-ranking
seat from 1949 to 1960.

For the Senate, the evidence is similar. From 1931 to the reorganization in 1946, Southerners dominated the Appropriations, Finance, and
Agriculture committees: A Southerner chaired the committees in thirteen
of the seventeen years. Southerners also had considerable power on the
Rules Committee, chairing it from 1941 to 1946 and averaging three of
the top five seats throughout the period.[32]

In the postwar period, the strength of Southerners on balance re-

[32] The Senate Rules Committee is not nearly as powerful as the House Rules Committee.

mained constant. They continued their dominance on the Agriculture and Finance committees, increased their strength on the Labor committee, and lost some seniority on the Rules and Appropriations committees, though Democratic Senator Russell (GA) was the second-ranking member on the Appropriations committee from 1953 until he took over the chair in 1969 and had been a member of the Appropriations Committee since 1933.

Although Southerners in either the House or Senate may have been weak on particular committees, it is important to keep in mind that bills have to be reconciled between the two chambers. As long as Southerners were well represented in either chamber they would have influence at the conference meetings.

Southern power was also enhanced through the formation of the "conservative coalition" – a bloc of Southern Democrats and Northern Republicans aligned on a variety of issues. The coalition solidified during Roosevelt's second term when Southern Congressmen believed that Roosevelt had breached the implicit contract in which Southern Congressmen supported Democratic legislation in exchange for freedom from federal meddling in the South's labor and race relations. Evidence on voting behavior indicates that this coalition strengthened over the postwar period. Indeed, the power of the "conservative coalition" to block "liberal" Democratic legislation led to the formation of the Democratic Study Group in the late 1950s and the eventual reorganization of the committee system in the early 1970s.[33]

In an examination of sectional voting patterns in Congress from 1880 to 1980, Bensel presents a number of empirical measures of committee power, all of which support the view that the period from 1947 through the early 1960s was one in which committees and their chairmen exercised an unprecedented degree of latitude.[34] One source of committee power is deference to committee decisions on the floor. Such deference is easier when fewer recorded roll call votes are taken. In this period, the number of roll call votes fell to an all time low (an average of only 0.4 per day, as opposed to 1.8 per day by the 1980s). Further evidence of deference to committee decisions can be seen in the relatively low number of defeats of special orders reported by the Rules Committee in the House: During 1929–68, an average of 2.2 were defeated in each Congress, whereas in the six Congresses since 1968, the average had risen to nearly six.[35]

---

[33] In Chapter 6, we discuss in more depth the motivation for the reorganization of committees.
[34] Bensel, *Sectionalism*, pp. 362–6.
[35] Ibid., p. 364.

Southern Paternalism and the American Welfare State

The political power of Southerners was not latent. In the next several chapters we discuss the actions taken by Southern legislators in the 1930s, 1940s, and 1950s to maintain the value of paternalism. In particular we will document the success of Southern legislators in: (1) defeating or altering the coverage of farm workers under the initial Social Security Act; (2) limiting appropriations for the Farm Security Administration once its agenda became the reform of Southern agriculture; and (3) originating and continuing a program for the importation of Mexican farm labor.

3

Southern Opposition to the Social Security Act

I. Introduction

The system of labor relations in the South that we described in Chapter 1 was a dominant force in the region's economy, but it was fragile in at least one important sense. The relationship between planters and their dependent laborers would have been undermined by government or private sector provision of goods and services that workers viewed as substitutes for paternalistic benefits. With the onset of the Depression, there was little danger of new private sector investment in the South that would have provided workers with an alternative source of jobs and benefits. With the entire U.S. economy flat on its back, there was also little that the individual state governments could do. The only credible threat came from the federal government, particularly the system of social insurance that resulted from the Social Security Act of 1935. The threat posed by the Social Security system and the Southern rural elite's response to it reveal a great deal about the South's system of paternalism and the political strength of the forces arrayed in defense of it.

Before the Social Security system was conceived, the federal government had more immediate needs to address. High levels of unemployment across the nation since 1930 had strained the system of providing poor relief. Before long-term structural change could occur, the government had to find ways of making sure the unemployed would simply survive to see that new system. New systems of relief provision had to be established. The Great Depression presented the Southern rural elite with a particularly vexing challenge in this respect: How could it accept the government assistance that so many plantation owners desperately needed to sustain their labor force until prosperity's return without allowing the government to replace them as the benefactors of their workers?

Relief and social insurance would have weakened the South's system of paternalistic labor relations in more subtle ways. By providing federal benefits to Southerners unable to provide for themselves because of unemployment, sickness, or the infirmities of old age, a Social Security system would have made workers less likely to turn to their landlords. Though their landlords would carry them through a poor season, pay for a visit from the local doctor, or provide a small pension or plot of garden space to elderly fieldhands, the price Southern farm workers paid for these benefits was their loyal work in the field and deference to their patron. Social insurance would substitute for the paternalism of planters by providing benefits in return for the payroll contributions of workers to the Social Security system.

In this chapter, we describe the role played by Southerners in shaping the New Deal poor relief and Social Security Act to minimize the federal government's interference in the relationship between Southern landlords and their workers. We first briefly describe the background to the federal government's entry into the provision of poor relief in the 1930s. The battles over who would control the distribution of emergency relief in the years before the Social Security Act determined much of the form the act eventually assumed. We then explore several alternative explanations for why Southern states were opposed to welfare spending in general and the Social Security Act in particular. We then turn to what the architects of the Social Security Act thought should be done about agriculture, and what Southern representatives led Congress to do instead. The inclusion of agricultural workers under the Social Security system was both desirable and feasible, according to the system's proponents. The exclusion of agricultural workers until the 1950s was done largely at the behest of Southern Congressmen and was done in ways consistent with their desire to prevent the spread of government-supplied benefits that would be seen as substitutes for the paternalism they offered to their faithful, dependent laborers. Though the federal government, as part of the emergency relief process, also set out to attack rural poverty specifically – both the short-term difficulties many farmers experienced because of the Depression and the chronic, long-term poverty that was seen by many as particularly acute in the South – these programs were initially only a minor part of the story. We will explore these rural initiatives (and the South's opposition to them) in the next chapter. Here we focus on relief and social insurance for the general population and the South's response to it.

II. Early Relief and FERA

The first attack on the South's system of social control and on the viability of paternalism came not from the system of cradle-to-grave social insurance to which Americans have become so accustomed over the last half century, but from the federal government's attempts to provide relief on an emergency basis early in the Depression. This battle had to be fought and won before the larger struggle over Social Security could occur. In fact, the outcome of the battle over the terms on which emergency relief would be provided shaped the Social Security system in several important ways. The battle over emergency relief is also crucial to the story of the South's opposition to the growth of the welfare state because it reveals the support from outside the South for limiting that growth. Southern plantation elites were not the only interests concerned by the expansion of federal welfare activities – they were merely the most powerful. They were able to hold off much of that expansion as part of a larger coalition, and were crucial in that coalition's demise in the 1960s when their desire to protect social control and paternalism was reduced.

The provision of poor relief had historically been a local function in the United States, largely a legacy of the English poor laws that the colonial governments adopted at their inception.[1] This patchwork system, based upon municipalities rather than parishes as in England, was little changed in the original thirteen states from the time of initial settlement until the early twentieth century and was adopted with little change by new states as they entered the union. Though the English updated their poor laws in 1834, the U.S. system remained modeled after the Tudor design. As a result, even as late as the 1920s, the U.S. system was set up to cope with the poverty of people who because of infirmity or the loss of the household's wage-earner were unable to fend for themselves – the chronic poverty of the non-able-bodied. The system was not equipped to deal with the intermittent poverty of households in which the principal breadwinner had been thrown out of work by an industrial depression. Local systems of poor relief were further hampered by a lack of resources: Their funds were often drawn only from local tax revenues, which were reduced by the same forces that caused need to grow.

Some changes were made in the first two decades of the twentieth century. The most important were an awakening of interest in the problem of poverty and attempts by state governments to distinguish among different types of poor people. The relative prosperity of the period from 1900 through the end of World War I and the prominence of Progressives in many city governments led to heightened interest in urban poverty. This new interest led to the growth of a professional class of social

---

[1] See Hughes, *Governmental Habit*, pp. 46–8, for a description of the extent to which the "safety net" adopted by the colonies reflected their English pedigree.

workers and the expansion of private charitable institutions, though these developments were felt less in the South because of its ruralness and dependence on agriculture.[2] At the same time, several state governments erected special programs for the blind, the aged, and mothers with dependent children, but these programs remained in local hands and inadequately funded.[3]

The inability of these local systems of relief to deal with the Depression was soon apparent. State governments provided additional funding after 1930, but they faced the same problem as the localities: Their ability to fund relief out of tax revenues was reduced by the business downturn just as the need for relief was increased. The federal government entered the picture in 1932 with the passage of the Emergency Relief and Construction Act, which authorized the Reconstruction Finance Corporation (RFC) to loan up to $300 million to states and municipalities at a 3 percent rate of interest for emergency relief expenditures, and provided $200 million for state construction projects and $322 million for federal public works. The RFC exercised no control over the agencies that ultimately dispensed the money to relief recipients, and in fact "conceived itself to be a banking and not a social agency."[4]

The federal government did not become intimately involved in the provision of relief until the beginning of the first Roosevelt administration. As part of its "First Hundred Days" of frenzied legislation, Congress passed the Federal Emergency Relief Act, which authorized $500 million in grants (rather than loans as under the RFC) to states for the provision of relief. The act also recognized that the plight of the rural poor (who might be able to provide for most of their own needs with only slight help from the government) was fundamentally different from that of the urban poor (who possessed no resources other than their own labor). As a result, it provided funds to fight rural poverty through "rehabilitation" of farm families saddled with burdensome debts, inadequate capital, or submarginal land. We will return to these issues in the next chapter.

Like the RFC, the Federal Emergency Relief Administration (FERA) was a funding agency rather than a social welfare agency. The combination of the tradition of local control of relief spending, the need to act quickly, and the belief that FERA's existence would be short-lived prevented the development of a federal agency that would do much

---

[2] For a description of these developments, see Patterson, *Struggle Against Poverty*, pp. 20–34.
[3] See Williams, *Federal Aid for Relief*, pp. 11–12.
[4] Ibid., p. 56.

more than send quarterly checks to the states. Opposition to even this limited federal role was immediate in some quarters. Professional social workers, for example, resented the intrusion of the federal government into the business of providing relief.[5] The control FERA exercised through the strategy for distributing relief dollars among the states used by FERA's administrator, Harry Hopkins, aroused staunch opposition from the states. This struggle over distribution shows the strength of the opposition across the nation to federal control over welfare spending.

FERA's initial authorization in 1932 stipulated that half of its funds would be distributed on a matching basis to the states (one federal dollar for every three state dollars), and half would be distributed as discretionary grants determined by Hopkins. This was the result of political compromise in writing the act between those who wanted to limit federal discretion in directing welfare spending at the very outset (favoring matching grants, through which states could control federal involvement by adjusting their own expenditures) and those who feared that the situation was so desperate in the poorest states that even the combination of their own meager resources and matching federal dollars would do little good.[6] Hopkins and FERA preferred the discretionary grants, because they allowed FERA to reach the maximum number of recipients with its limited resources. These grants were offered on an essentially all-or-nothing basis by Hopkins, who required that states use them solely for relief. Wallis points out that a simple model of intergovernmental transfers demonstrates the superiority (from FERA's perspective) of discretionary grants. By specifying the total number of cases that a state had to serve and the total amount of resources it had to spend on them, FERA reached more recipients at lower cost per case than if it simply reduced the "price" that each state had to pay to serve each case, as a matching grant would do.[7] The sizes of the grants made to states were determined each quarter on the basis of FERA's evaluation of their need. By the end of 1933, new authorizations for FERA dropped the matching grants and left all of FERA's funding as discretionary grants by Hopkins.[8]

FERA's activities were a source of concern to Southern interests who feared that federal interference would weaken social control and pater-

---

[5] This opposition is discussed in Patterson, *Struggle Against Poverty*, pp. 57–8.

[6] See Williams, *Federal Aid for Relief*, pp. 182–3, for a discussion of this compromise.

[7] Wallis, "Fiscal Federalism," pp. 515–18.

[8] Williams, *Federal Aid for Relief*, p. 185.

nalism. The Southern states were particularly distressed by FERA's requirement that recipients of work relief receive a minimum wage of thirty cents per hour. Williams notes: "The requirement . . . was productive of considerable criticism, particularly in the South."[9] The Civil Works Administration (CWA), in contrast, set different minimum wage rates in different regions of the country. For example, it paid unskilled laborers forty cents an hour in the South, forty-five cents in the Midwest, and fifty cents in the Northeast.[10] The CWA was a wholly federal program, however, so it is possible that the greater cognizance it took of regional labor market norms was the price it paid for acceptance by the states. As we suggest in the next chapter, the difference in the South's attitudes toward the Farm Security Administration (FSA) and the Agricultural Adjustment Administration (AAA) may reflect a similar difference in the relative flexibility of these agencies in adapting to conditions in the South: The AAA was far more willing to accede to the wishes of large landowners, and enjoyed greater support than the FSA throughout the South.

Southerners also balked at FERA guidelines forbidding discrimination on the basis of race in providing relief to individuals. Southern states often used a stricter enforcement of eligibility rules for blacks than for whites, discrimination that FERA was "powerless" to prevent.[11] Dissatisfaction with FERA was not limited to the South, however. Many states were unhappy with the arrangement by which FERA made its discretionary grants, since a matching grant that allowed them to serve the same number of cases would have also allowed them to increase spending on nonrelief items. FERA's attempts to interfere in personnel matters was similarly opposed in a number of states.[12] In many cases, opposition to FERA represented little more than the familiar struggle between states and the federal government for the power to act and the ability to reap the political benefits of action.

The breadth of opposition to FERA's policies can be seen in the states that were formally sanctioned for repeatedly violating FERA's guidelines. Two forms of sanction were employed: "federalization" of a state's relief program (in which FERA appointed a new administrator and brought relief distribution under direct federal control) and withholding a state's relief funds until compliance was achieved. Relief programs were federalized in six states: Oklahoma (1934), North Dakota (1934), Massachusetts (1934), Ohio (1935), Louisiana (1935), and Georgia

[9] Ibid., p. 105.
[10] Ibid., p. 120.
[11] Ibid., p. 172.
[12] Ibid., pp. 154–9.

(1935). Funds were temporarily withheld from Colorado (1933), Missouri (1935), Alabama (1933), and Illinois (1934).[13] Of these ten states, half are in the northeast or Midwest.

Though opposition to FERA was widespread, political leaders in the South had additional reasons for opposing FERA and FERA-style direct relief. This can be seen in the results of FERA's spending policies: In the Northeast states, federal relief dollars accounted for less than 60 percent of all (federal, state, and local) relief expenditures between 1933 and 1935, while in the South federal dollars accounted for more than 90 percent. Though part of this disparity no doubt reflects the South's limited resources for paying relief even if it desired to do so, it also reflects the South's attitude toward paying relief. Williams suggests: "The proportion of federal assistance was high in these southern states because state ability was extremely low and because the imponderable elements, such as debt limitations, the extent of popular willingness to support relief, etc., often tended to keep state and local contributions at a low level."[14]

Over the course of its short life, FERA saw increasing opposition from a variety of states: As the sense of desperation passed with the first year of relief dollars from Washington, friction between FERA and the states became more pronounced. Again, though, the objections were particularly strong from the South.[15]

In 1935, the federal government sought to erect a permanent relief system to replace the emergency system in operation since 1933. It planned to retain responsibility for employable individuals and provide work for them through the Works Progress Administration (WPA), but hoped to return responsibility for unemployables (the aged, the blind, and mothers with dependent children) to the states, and offer grants to help finance their care. The vehicle through which this transformation would occur was the Social Security Act of 1935.

III. Alternative Explanations for the Southern Aversion to Welfare Spending

A number of hypotheses have been advanced to explain the low benefit levels and narrow coverage of social welfare programs in the South in the 1930s. The limited scope and scale of the South's welfare apparatus have been attributed to the area's conservative bias and inherent opposition to federal meddling in its affairs, to its low levels of per capita

[13] Ibid., pp. 177–8 and 203–4.
[14] Ibid., p. 225.
[15] Ibid., p. 236.

income and consequent inability to offer more substantial benefits, and to its latent racism and consequent unwillingness to extend welfare services to its predominantly black rural poor. No doubt all these factors played a role. Our criticisms of these explanations should not be interpreted as implying that poverty, racism, and ideology have no explanatory power; rather, they are offered to show our reluctance to embrace any mono-causal explanation.

The picture of a "Solid South" united in its opposition to the interference of social reformers and federal bureaucrats bears little resemblance to the view of the South during the New Deal more familiar to students of the period. Southerners were in fact among Roosevelt's staunchest allies throughout the first part of the New Deal: They welcomed the Agricultural Adjustment Administration, were among the earliest to join the clamor for federal relief funds as the Depression drained their state reserves, and had a hand in drafting most of the administration's recovery legislation.

Only when the emphasis shifted from recovery to reform, after the 1936 election, did a solid opposition begin to coalesce, and even then the disaffection was not generalized but limited to the "county-seat elites" who had the most to lose from high levels of welfare spending and strict federal oversight of programs. Those same rural interests, however, had earlier been among the supporters of the administration's recovery measures that entailed a substantial amount of federal relief spending and oversight. The opposition of Southerners to relief and federal interference *per se* is thus less apparent than the opposition of particular privileged interest groups to long-term welfare measures and the guiding hand of federal administrators. The Solid South was not particularly solid in its opposition to all federal interference, at least through 1940.[16]

The Agricultural Adjustment Administration (AAA) provides a striking example of strong Southern support. Left largely in the hands of local agricultural interests and loathe to interfere in landlord-tenant relations, the AAA was warmly received in the South. Not surprisingly, the largest Southern planters gained the most from the AAA's programs. Mordecai Ezekiel, one of Roosevelt's agricultural advisors, wrote:

There can be no question that the farm owners, constituting less than half of those engaged in agriculture, have been the dominant element in the preparation and administration of AAA programs heretofore. In certain commodities, notably cotton, this has resulted in their receiving the lion's share of the benefits resulting from the programs.[17]

[16] See, for example, Tindall, *Emergence*, p. 618.
[17] Quoted in Nourse et al., *Three Years*.

This stands in marked contrast to the Southern reception of programs such as the Economic Security Act as initially proposed which threatened to interfere in landlord-tenant relations and give Southern elites little control. The same was true of the Farm Security Administration and its reception by Southerners.[18]

The lower per capita income in the South may at first seem a more plausible explanation of its inability to provide welfare, particularly welfare financed by the states themselves (the early state Old-Age Pension and Mothers' Aid programs, for example). That poverty, however, does not explain why the South was likewise unusually chary in dispensing federally funded welfare. In fact, the South should have been a strong proponent of a new federal pension system, because the federal pension system in existence at the start of the twentieth century – which provided pensions to veterans and their widows and dependents – actually redistributed money from the South to the North.

Because pensions had historically been funded out of revenue generated by tariffs on imported manufactures, the South helped finance the system. But because the South's share of the veteran population was smaller than its share of the total population, the region received less money in pensions than it paid into the system in tariffs. Early in the nineteenth century, the South contained a disproportionately small share of veterans because so much of its population was comprised of slaves who did not serve in the military. After the Civil War, Confederate soldiers were ineligible for federal pensions. Federal veterans' pensions were legislated as early as 1790, and were being paid out of revenues generated by the tariff as early as 1816. Southern opposition to the resulting redistribution of income was first voiced in 1818. Per capita Civil War pensions were $3.36 in Ohio, $1.49 in New York, and $3.90 in Indiana, whereas Southern states such as Georgia, Alabama, Mississippi, North Carolina, South Carolina, and Louisiana received less than 50 cents per person.[19]

Under these circumstances, Southern states had ample reasons to support the erection of a federal system that would pay pensions regardless of previous military service and finance those payments out of a general income tax. For example, because Old-Age Insurance benefits were to be paid out of a federal trust fund with monies collected from all states, the scheme would have transferred income from richer states to the South. Instead of supporting the scheme, however, Southerners altered it so that

[18] See Chapter 4, and Alston and Ferrie, "Resisting the Welfare State."
[19] See Quadagno, *Transformation of Old Age Security*, pp. 31–47, for a discussion of the historical link between veterans' pensions and tariffs. The figures quoted are from p. 46.

farmers and farm workers, who comprised the bulk of the region's primarily rural population, were excluded, and the transfer was prevented. When considering the South's opposition to federal Old-Age Assistance, Old-Age Insurance, and Aid to Dependent Children (ADC), the claim that the South was unable or unwilling to pay because of its small tax base and its low-wage economy seems less believable than the hypothesis we advance – that the payment of these benefits in Southern states threatened paternalism by landlords.

The issue of racism is more complex. It is clear that in many cases of relief giving, outright discrimination prevented many blacks from receiving benefits equal to those received by whites. Lieberman has advanced the view that racial discrimination motivated the exclusionary aspects of the Social Security legislation.[20] For the South, it is difficult to distinguish issues of race from issues of class. In many instances the two motives are not separable with the available evidence.

Two points must be borne in mind, though. First, discrimination against blacks in areas where they comprised the bulk of the low-wage agricultural labor force (in the black belt counties, for example) does not necessarily point to racism on the part of relief-giving agencies. Discrimination may have been based more on class than on race in the South: Opposition to welfare spending may have resulted from a desire to maintain a pool of cheap laborers, while blacks were a disproportionate share of the low wage labor force. The desire to maintain low agricultural wages, rather than simple white supremacy, is plausible if in predominately white areas, low wages were also paid. A resolution of this issue requires an analysis of data on state benefits disaggregated by counties. The existing evidence is sufficiently ambiguous that we are unable to accept racism as the sole explanation.

Second, in considering the wholesale exclusion of agricultural workers from the Old-Age Insurance and Unemployment Insurance provisions of the Social Security Act, the issue of racism seems largely irrelevant. White tenants and croppers were excluded along with blacks, even though whites outnumbered blacks in absolute terms in nearly every Southern state through the 1950s. If white elites were intent upon preventing blacks from receiving federal Old-Age and Unemployment Insurance compensation, they did so at the expense of an even greater number of whites. Further, no grandfather clauses or literacy tests were invoked to allow the payment of benefits to whites as had been used to allow them to circumvent the disfranchisement laws at the turn of the century. It appears that Southerners were interested in excluding a particular class, rather than a particular race.

[20] Lieberman, "Race and the Development of the American Welfare State."

Southern Opposition to the Social Security Act

Another explanation that has been offered for Southern opposition to spending on welfare is that such expenditures would directly increase labor costs. Programs that supplemented workers' incomes regardless of their employment status, such as Mothers' Aid and its successors, Aid to Dependent Children (ADC) and Aid to Families with Dependent Children (AFDC), would have had the direct effect of increasing wages because the reservation wage of those eligible in marginal occupations (seasonal workers) would increase. In addition these programs would increase supervision costs because the cost to employed workers of losing their jobs would fall and the relative gain expected from shirking would increase.[21] Resistance to welfare programs, therefore, was partly due to a desire for cheap labor: Welfare programs such as ADC would have fundamentally altered the terms of trade between employers and both present and prospective employees, increasing the wage and supervision costs of Southern planters. The actions of Southerners in shaping and manipulating the ADC program to ensure a steady supply of seasonal labor provide ample evidence on this point.[22]

But many of the welfare programs contemplated during the New Deal (Old-Age Insurance and Unemployment Insurance, for example), which would have affected the South, were already present in one form or another. They were usually supplied by planters to loyal workers as in-kind benefits. As we have seen, this elaborate system of paternalistic in-kind benefits which evolved from the South's peculiar history was used to reduce direct wages and turnover and supervision costs. The Southern rural elite was thus not opposed to workers' receiving such benefits. What the elite feared instead was that workers would receive them from another party – the federal government.

Finally, none of these explanations, either singly or in conjunction with any other, seems to explain the sudden increases in social welfare spending in the South and elsewhere in the 1950s and early 1960s: Agricultural labor was at last brought under the Social Security Act in 1950, 1954, and 1956. Aid to Families with Dependent Children rolls grew astronomically, and much of the promise of the New Deal welfare state was realized in the Great Society – all within the space of fifteen years. No significant changes in the South's ideology, poverty, or racial composition are apparent to explain these quickly accomplished changes.

---

[21] See Weisskopf, Bowles, and Gordon, "Hearts and Minds," pp. 381–450, for an analysis of how this mechanism operates in the contemporary United States.
[22] See the discussion in Section IV.

IV. Some Political Considerations

In Chapter 2, we described how Southerners were able to shape the debate in Congress over many programs such as welfare that would have interfered in Southern labor relations. Three features of the political and institutional climate of the late 1930s, conditioned by the need for rapid and concerted action on the part of the New Dealers, lowered still further the cost to Southerners of exercising their influence and increased their probability of success. First, Roosevelt was unable to count on the support of many Midwestern progressives. He appears to have struck a tacit deal with Southerners in Congress: Support for the New Deal was exchanged for a relatively free hand in writing and rewriting legislation to fit the peculiarities of the South.[23] The results of this deal are evident in the reworking of the administration's Economic Security Act to exclude the South's low-wage labor force, which assured minimum federal meddling.

Second, because the administration wanted rapid action on the New Deal's legislative package, most of the work on its formulation took place in House and Senate committees which avoided months of open debate, compromise, and negotiation on the floor of Congress. Passage of the Economic Security Act was rushed through Congress so that state legislatures could pass the necessary enabling legislation before the summer recess.[24] The South's one-party system and the seniority it afforded Southern Congressmen meant, as we discussed in Chapter 2, that they dominated and often chaired the committees which were responsible for the New Deal legislation. Thus, both the House Ways and Means Committee and Senate Finance Committee which produced the Social Security Act were chaired by Southerners.[25]

Finally, the need for speed in drafting and implementing the legislation virtually assured that existing institutions rather than new agencies would administer the program locally. The Old-Age Assistance and Aid to Dependent Children provisions of the Social Security Act were therefore left to the administration of the state Old-Age Pension and Mothers Aid programs which, as we shall see, offered significantly lower benefits in the South than elsewhere. Southern landholders exploited their power to maintain tenant dependency by channeling funds through these locally controlled agencies. In general, the New Deal has been criticized for doing just the opposite – creating an agency and an administrative order for each new problem.

[23] See Chapter 2 for a description of this arrangement.
[24] See Witte, *Development of the Social Security Act*, p. 75.
[25] U.S. Congress, *Congressional Directory* (1933), p. 192.

V. The South and the Social Security Act

Two problems emerge in trying to link the continuance of the low-wage, labor-intensive economy in the cotton South and the opposition of Southern landholders (and the legislators they controlled) to the enactment of significant social welfare legislation. First, we would not expect Southerners to admit they were blocking legislation to preserve the viability of cotton cultivation and to secure their positions. We could expect a more subtle course similar to the South's later camouflaging the race issue with arguments about states' rights and big government. Second, as we note below, quantitative evidence is limited because the votes for changes to the Economic Security Act were not recorded.[26]

To overcome the first difficulty, we have cast a jaundiced eye on much of the rhetoric clouding the debate over Social Security. Therefore, rather than study the fiery orations of Southerners, we compared what Southerners actually did to what they could have done to bring agriculture under the Social Security Act. To overcome the second difficulty, we will demonstrate qualitatively that there was a pattern of Southern indifference (if not outright hostility) to the provision of welfare to the rural poor that is consistent with the hypothesis we have advanced. First, we survey the work of the Committee on Economic Security (CES) that wrote the original Economic Security Act and studied the viability of including farmers and agricultural laborers under the various provisions of the act. This establishes the background against which Congress acted in 1935. Then, the role of Southerners in the debates preceding crucial decisions and their role in executive session votes, for which we have information, is considered. Finally, we document the actual levels of benefits paid under the provisions of the act that included agricultural laborers and the continued struggle to include agricultural workers in those that did not.

Observations consistent with the view that Southerners opposed the growth of a federal welfare state in order to protect their paternalistic relations with their workers include: (1) Low levels of state relief were provided in the South before the New Deal; (2) Arguments regarding the administrative difficulty of including agriculture were considered weak by the CES staff, who recommended their inclusion; (3) Agriculture was included in most European social insurance schemes, and increasingly so through the 1930s; (4) After 1935, when Old-Age Assistance and ADC

---

[26] The problem of data availability is important for the issue of coverage under the Old-Age Insurance and Unemployment Insurance provisions of the act, because no votes were recorded and because all agricultural workers (from all states) were excluded.

were subsidized by the federal government, Southern states continued to provide relatively lower levels of welfare assistance than other states even after controlling for income and race; and (5) Southerners successfully resisted congressional pressure to include agricultural workers in the Old-Age Insurance and Unemployment Insurance programs.

Early Relief and the Committee on Economic Security

Expenditures for relief were notoriously low in the South during the early years of the Depression. Of the thirty-one states with old-age pension laws on their books in 1934, only Maryland and Delaware could have been considered remotely Southern. By comparison, industrial states such as New York, New Jersey, and Massachusetts spent substantial amounts on pensions. A comparison of spending in the South with other agricultural regions points to something unique about the South: Numerous Midwestern states, as well as California which had a significant agricultural sector, were paying out pensions by 1934. Similarly, the states that did not provide Mothers Aid or that paid very low per capita benefit levels were predominantly Southern, while industrial and Midwestern farming states were among the states providing benefits.[27] This was the situation when the Social Security system was first contemplated in 1934 to 1935.

The CES was set up in 1934 and was charged with formulating a program of social insurance that was national in scope and provided a system of cradle-to-grave protection for all Americans. In the course of its work, the committee produced numerous studies on all aspects of the Social Security question including the viability of a system that would embrace the agricultural population. Six staff reports, dealing specifically with the problem of providing economic security for agricultural workers, emanated from the committee.[28] Though these reports were never followed up in any detail, their impact is visible in the act that emerged from the committee and that included agricultural workers.

According to the executive director of the committee, Edwin Witte, the committee never recommended that agricultural workers should be

---

[27] Mean per-recipient Mothers Aid for the Southern states paying pensions in 1934 was $19.68. For non-Southern states paying Mothers Aid, the mean was $25.82. Committee on Economic Security, *Social Security in America*, p. 247.

[28] The staff reports of the Committee on Economic Security relating to agriculture can be found in CES, *Reports*. Apparently, only two complete sets of these reports have survived, both in typescript – one in the archives of the Department of Health and Human Services and one in the archives of the Social Security Administration. These reports were confidential until very recently (apparently because the staff's recommendations were so at variance with the act as it emerged from Congress in 1935) and may still be read only at the respective archives and not photocopied.

explicitly excluded from Old-Age and Unemployment Insurance. The committee did recommend the exclusion of tenants and croppers because neither group worked under an explicit contract and were thus considered self-employed. The committee did, however, recognize how incorrect this classification was. Most croppers and many tenants were more akin to wage workers than to owners in the extent to which they could make independent decisions regarding how to run the land they farmed. As a result, the committee recommended that at the very least croppers be reclassified as agricultural laborers. At the same time, the committee recommended that a special Old-Age Insurance program be set up to cover tenants, croppers, and other self-employed persons.[29] The committee further recommended in hearings in Congress that the problem of providing security in agriculture "was one of the aspects of economic security requiring further study."[30]

The first staff report on agriculture, "The Economic Security Program in Relation to Farm Operators and Employees," recommended that agricultural workers (as well as croppers who were more often classified as operators than workers) be included in the Unemployment Insurance, Old-Age Assistance, and Old-Age Insurance schemes. Old-Age Assistance was to be noncontributory and unearned (more like relief for the aged than social insurance). Old-Age Insurance, on the other hand, was to require contributions from the recipient and some link between payments by the recipient and eventual payments to the recipient. The distinction is important. If Southerners wanted to prevent Old-Age Insurance from interfering with paternalism, they would have had to make sure that all agricultural workers were excluded from the program. To prevent interference from Old-Age Assistance, they merely had to manipulate the benefits paid in their states.

The report proposed that agricultural employees be included in the general Unemployment Insurance program on the same basis as industrial employees, and that the inclusion of agricultural employees in firms with six or fewer employees (the lower limit on coverage under the industrial scheme) be seriously considered.[31]

The second report, "Economic Security of Farmers and Agricultural Workers," similarly recommended the inclusion of farm laborers in Unemployment Insurance, and urged that croppers be included.[32] The same report recognized that the inclusion of croppers might "present

[29] Witte, *Development of the Social Security Act*, p. 152.
[30] See U.S. Congress, House, Committee on Ways and Means, *Hearings on the Economic Security Act*, p. 58.
[31] Bean, "Farm Operators and Employees," pp. 802–10.
[32] Folsom, "Farmers and Agricultural Workers," p. 827.

peculiar difficulties" because they "receive payments for their work as a share of the proceeds of the crops on which they work, at the end of the crop season."[33] The report suggested, however, that the cropper and landlord could pay their insurance premiums at the time settlements were made. The problem of the seasonality of the work, with several long periods of idleness between the busy planting and picking seasons, could have been overcome by making payment of benefits conditional "upon failure of the cropper to secure a contract for the succeeding year by the time when such contracts are customarily made."[34] Croppers were recommended for inclusion throughout the report because of their low standard of living and the similarity of their status with that of hired labor.[35] Coverage of the broader class of tenants was likewise recommended in a program to insure against "unemployment through inability to rent land or secure other work."[36]

The recommendations of the second report addressed the problems arising from covering agricultural workers. Perhaps more important than the supposed administrative difficulties, then, were the political considerations outlined in a third report. "The Bearing of the Program of the Committee on Economic Security Upon Farmers and Farm Laborers" suggested that "inclusion of farm laborers in the [Unemployment Insurance] scheme would lead to the defeat of any legislation that might be proposed."[37]

Thus, some difficulties were anticipated in the inclusion of farmers and farm workers in an Unemployment Insurance program. But, the problems were not insuperable – farm owners would have been excluded because they were not employed under a contract; croppers and tenants, by virtue of the contractual nature of their employment, were more akin to wage labor and therefore deserved to be covered along with agricultural laborers. The principal problems expected from including these groups were political. Despite what Witte reported, it appears that in the staff reports, the exclusion of agricultural workers, tenants, and croppers was never seriously advocated. On the contrary, inclusion was urged in all three studies, but the problems posed by political considerations were recognized.

In an early summary memorandum, "Major Issues in Unemployment Compensation," dated December 3, 1934, Witte himself reported, "The coverage recommended is a compulsory coverage of all employers with

---

[33] Ibid.
[34] Ibid.
[35] Ibid., p. 819.
[36] Ibid.
[37] Ham, "Farmers and Farm Laborers," p. 872.

six or more employees, including those engaged in agriculture. . . ."[38] Just two months later, however, in an updated version of the same report, he stated, "inclusion of these groups of [agricultural] workers is difficult administratively and for short-time and intermittent workers is of relatively little value. . . ."[39] What came between the two versions of the Witte report was the "Staff Report on Unemployment Insurance" that urged a minimum firm size restriction but no explicit exclusion of agricultural labor.[40]

The final report from the CES appears to have been influenced by committee members largely unfamiliar with the problems of agriculture and likely to succumb to arguments of administrative difficulty. These members appeared more willing to bow to political pressure to get the bulk of the bill passed and seem to have used the minimum size exclusion urged in the staff report as a pretext for excluding agriculture entirely from this provision of the act, in the manner evinced by the shift in Witte's tone from December to February.[41]

The program for old-age security outlined in the staff reports similarly embraced agricultural labor, and urged adoption of a program to cover croppers, tenants, and owners with even more enthusiasm than had been displayed for covering these groups under Unemployment Insurance. The crucial difference here was the recognition that although farm owners and operators (croppers and tenants) might not suffer from unemployment in the same way as industrial workers, they would still have to provide for their retirement years. The proposed program thus included a scheme to cover "the large number of scattered, low-paid migratory workers, the farm croppers, tenants, and even small proprietors" excluded from receiving Unemployment Insurance.[42]

Support for the inclusion of agriculture in the Old-Age Insurance scheme was not limited to members of the staff charged with studying the problems of agriculture and economic security. In a report on the broader topic of "Provision for Old-Age Security," prepared by the CES general staff, for example, it was conceded that:

---

[38] Witte, "Major Issues" (1934), p. 3.

[39] Witte, "Major Issues" (1935), pp. 17–18.

[40] "Staff Report," pp. 1–2.

[41] Warren Samuels, a student of Witte's and later his assistant at the University of Wisconsin, agrees that the document that eventually emerged from the CES was highly political in nature. He suggests that Witte was fully aware of this (despite the equivocations in this book). Witte was interested, however, in forging a coalition of sufficient strength to get the bulk of the act passed and was willing to bend to political pressure (from Southerners in this case) to achieve that end. Private conversation with Samuels, May 1983.

[42] Bean, "Farm Operators and Employees," pp. 802–3.

There are no special difficulties in the way of old-age insurance for agricultural workers, such as are encountered in plans for unemployment insurance. The agricultural employee, moreover, is an extremely low-paid worker and has un-questionable need of old-age protection. Except for the advantage of having a common coverage for old-age insurance and unemployment insurance, there would be no excuse for omitting the agricultural group from old-age insurance requirements.[43]

Though this report stopped short of urging a reclassification of tenants and croppers as agricultural laborers and thus did not go quite so far as the staff reports outlined above, it showed that the supposed administrative difficulties were not great, and the need to include them was acute.

Further support for the inclusion of agriculture was provided by two studies of foreign social insurance programs conducted by the CES staff. Both studies noted the tendency of foreign programs to increase coverage through the early 1930s. Three factors were emphasized because they promoted these changes: (1) the severity of the agricultural depression which in many places dated back to the early 1920s; (2) the increasing interrelatedness of agricultural and industrial depressions which elimi-nated cities as outlets for the rural unemployed; and (3) rapid mechani-zation in agriculture. Except for a lag in mechanization in the South, these conditions prevailed in the United States.[44]

The recommendations of those most closely associated with agricul-ture on the CES staff were modified when incorporated into the commit-tee's final report. For Unemployment Insurance, modifications were rec-ommended to overcome the anticipated administrative difficulties. Likewise, croppers and tenants were reclassified as agricultural workers to avoid problems. The final CES staff report, however, excluded work-ers in firms of six or fewer employees without explicitly excluding agri-culture even though the exclusion would "deprive the majority of agri-cultural laborers of the benefits given others," and avoided entirely the issue of reclassification.[45] The recommendations on old-age security, on the other hand, were largely followed in the final CES report. A special scheme to cover "farm owners and tenants, self-employed persons, and other people of small incomes . . ." was included in the bill sent to Con-gress.[46] Existing state old-age pension systems were to receive a subsidy from federal funds as well.

[43] Armstrong, "Provision for Old-Age Security," p. 4.

[44] Kiehel, "Agricultural Workers"; and Jaros, "Foreign Unemployment Schemes." Final versions of both studies can be found in Committee on Economic Security, *Reports*.

[45] Folsom, "Farmers and Agricultural Workers," p. 819.

[46] See U.S. Congress, House, Committee on Ways and Means, *Hearings on the Economic Security Act*, p. 58.

Southern Opposition to the Social Security Act

Action in Congress – 1935

The Social Security Act that emerged from Congress in 1935 was considerably different from the bill proposed by the CES, particularly in its treatment of the farm population. Farmers and farm laborers were excluded from both the Old-Age and Unemployment Insurance provisions of the act, despite CES staff recommendations to the contrary. No special schemes were included to cover these workers, and the administration of the programs which did not explicitly exclude agriculture, Old-Age Assistance and Aid to Dependent Children, was left largely in the hands of the states.

These changes might be explained as the product of weak support for the inclusion of agriculture (owing to administrative difficulties), with their ultimate exclusion coming as the result of the ostensibly disinterested recommendation of Secretary of the Treasury Henry Morgenthau, Jr., rather than from the machinations of any particular interest group.[47]

The issue was not clear-cut, though. As we have shown, there was substantial support within the CES staff for including agricultural laborers, tenants, croppers, and owners. As we shall see, the "recommendation" of Morgenthau was but one of the options he found acceptable, but it was the one seized upon by Southerners on the House Ways and Means Committee and the Senate Finance Committee. Southerners displayed a strikingly defeatist attitude toward the inclusion of agriculture when they were not urging its outright exclusion and were the staunchest advocates of state control of programs that did not exclude agriculture.

At the very outset, the opposition of Southerners to the provisions of the act covering agricultural labor was evident. Among the members of the House Ways and Means Committee described as unsympathetic were Robert Doughton (North Carolina), Fred Vinson (Kentucky), and Jere Cooper (Tennessee).[48] The Senate Finance Committee was seen as a more formidable obstacle to agriculture's inclusion, because "a very large percentage of the members of this committee were from south of the Mason and Dixon line, and several . . . were among the most conservative of all senators."[49]

Southern opposition was quickly manifested: The House Ways and

---

[47] Morgenthau outlined some of the problems the inclusion of agriculture might create. See "Statement of the Secretary of the Treasury on the Economic Security Bill," pp. 9–10.

[48] Though Vinson was from Kentucky, which is not a Southern state geographically, we have grouped him here and throughout this chapter with representatives from the South. In doing so, we are following a well-established practice of including Kentucky in the "political" South. This is the grouping used by, among others, *Congressional Quarterly* in its analyses of voting behavior.

[49] Witte, *Development of the Social Security Act*, p. 100.

Means Committee, which contained those "unsympathetic" Southerners, excluded agricultural laborers from the Unemployment Insurance program "as a matter of course."[50] The special Old-Age Insurance program for tenants, croppers, and farm owners was similarly deleted without much ceremony by the committees. Attention then turned to the more general old-age security provisions of the act which could have covered tenants and croppers as well as agricultural laborers.

The first mention of the exclusion of farmers and farm workers from the Old-Age Insurance program was made by Representative Vinson in his questioning of CES Director Witte. Vinson suggested that administration of the program might be easier if these groups were excluded entirely from the insurance program, even if this resulted in an increase in the cost of the state-run pension systems (which would have still covered these groups).[51] Only a moment earlier, however, Witte had addressed the administrative difficulty issue by suggesting that different collection mechanisms might be employed for different groups. In the case of farm workers and domestic workers, who would have had little contact with the internal revenue system being suggested as the basis of the nation-wide network for collection of premiums, a stampbook method might have eliminated many of the anticipated difficulties.[52] The British chose this method in 1936 when they began to bring agricultural labor under their social insurance system.[53]

Nonetheless, in pressing for agriculture's exclusion, Vinson evinced a peculiarly negative attitude toward Social Security for farmers and farm workers, an attitude that was increasingly characteristic of the Southern members of these committees as the hearings progressed. In most if not all cases where a choice had to be made between including agriculture by trying to overcome some difficulties and excluding them almost "as a matter of course," Southerners favored the latter approach. This attitude is best displayed in the questioning of Secretary of the Treasury Morgenthau.

Morgenthau had been persuaded by junior Treasury officials "that the bill must be amended to exclude these groups of workers [agricultural workers and domestics] to make it administratively feasible," and made a statement to that effect in his testimony.[54] Witte has suggested that it was this recommendation rather than the workings of partisan or interest group politics which excluded agricultural workers. The fact of the

[50]Ibid., p. 132.
[51]U.S. Congress, House, Committee on Ways and Means, *Hearings on the Economic Security Act*, p. 112.
[52]Ibid.
[53]See Kiehel, "Agricultural Workers."
[54]Witte, *Development of the Social Security Act*, p. 153.

68

matter is, however, that Morgenthau found several other options equally satisfying, including bringing agricultural workers under the bill immediately and dealing later with the peculiar problems their inclusion might pose. Morgenthau even went so far as to describe this alternative as "ideal."[55]

Though Morgenthau found such alternatives wholly unobjectionable, Representative Vinson seized upon his initial position as his last word on the subject. Vinson and other Southerners followed this approach as the hearings progressed. In its later executive sessions, according to Witte, "the committee was influenced far less by difficulties of administration than by the fact that it was felt that farmers would object to being taxed for old-age protection for their employees."[56] The attitude of defeatism displayed by Vinson and the other Southerners in the public hearings suggests that the opposition in the executive sessions came less from the fear of objection from farmers in general than from that of Southern farmers and landlords specifically.

Southerners apparently pressed for the exclusion of "agricultural laborers" (in addition to croppers and tenants) for three reasons: (1) to protect such paternalistic relations as existed between planters and wage workers; (2) to prevent the payment of benefits to croppers and tenants should they be reclassified as laborers; and (3) to ensure that tenants and croppers downgraded to laborer status through the incentives of the AAA would continue to be denied benefits.

Though tenants, croppers, and wage workers in agriculture had been eliminated from both the special and general Old-Age Insurance programs, there was some recognition on the part of Southerners that these groups would still be eligible for the state-administered Old-Age Assistance programs subsidized under Title I of the act.[57] Attention turned to adjustment of the pension section to assure maximum local discretion in providing benefits to the groups excluded from the federal program.

At the very beginning, the Old-Age Assistance provision of the act was very bitterly attacked by Senator Harry Byrd of Virginia because it dictated to states the size and recipients of pensions. He was joined in this position by "nearly all of the members of both committees [who likewise feared] federal interference."[58] The changes made in the

---

[55] See U.S. Congress, House, Committee on Ways and Means, *Hearings on the Economic Security Act*, p. 911. Morgenthau apparently recognized that delaying inclusion would only make eventual coverage more difficult.

[56] Witte, *Development of the Social Security Act*, p. 153.

[57] U.S. Congress, House, Committee on Ways and Means, *Hearings on the Economic Security Act*, p. 911.

[58] Witte, *Development of the Social Security Act*, pp. 153–4.

House and Senate were directed toward diminishing such federal interference.

Under the original bill, states were enjoined from imposing any conditions for the receipt of Old-Age Assistance. As the provision emerged from the House Ways and Means Committee, it was stated negatively, so states could impose any conditions they saw fit, as long as they were no more stringent than those in the original bill.[59] The original bill required that state pensions, when added to the recipient's income, furnish "a reasonable subsistence compatible with decency and health."[60] This provision was eliminated entirely, leaving states "free to pay pensions of any amount, however small."[61] The revised bill also made it more difficult for the federal government to withdraw approval of any state plan and eliminated the need for federal approval of "selection, tenure of office, and compensation of personnel."[62] Finally, the revised act transferred federal administration from the Federal Emergency Relief Administration to the independent Social Security Board, to avoid the equation of Old-Age Assistance with relief, "which the committee was very anxious to avoid."[63]

Each change strengthened the hold of states over their own pension programs. In the language of our model, it became easier for Southerners to control the substitutes for planter paternalism. Therefore, they set state-provided benefit levels to minimize the effect on the demand for planter paternalism. The result was the successful protection of the landlord-tenant relationship.

In addition to eliminating agriculture from the act's Unemployment and Old-Age Insurance programs, and restricting federal control over state pension plans, both committees under pressure from Southerners, and other Congressmen aligned with them, similarly limited benefit levels and federal oversight under Title IV, the Aid to Dependent Children program (ADC). Because this program, the forerunner of Aid to Families with Dependent Children (AFDC), provided relief irrespective of employment status, it did not involve the administrative difficulties of premium collection and monitoring encountered with Old-Age and Unemployment Insurance. Justification for the exclusion of agriculture would have been less apparent, so the attention of Southerners again turned toward reducing federal control and enabling states to set benefit levels and restrictions. Once these programs were in the hands of the states,

[59] Ibid., pp. 144–5.
[60] Ibid.
[61] Ibid.
[62] Ibid.
[63] Ibid., p. 134.

many in the South did not attempt to disguise their desire to manipulate the program to maintain a cheap, dependent labor force.

Under the original act, states were required to pay ADC benefits that would "provide a reasonable subsistence compatible with decency and health," as under the original Old-Age Assistance program. This requirement was again eliminated entirely here, apparently because of "objection to Federal determination of adequacy on the part of Southern members who feared Northern standards would be forced on the South in providing for Negro and White tenant families."[64] Determination was instead left in the hands of state and local administrators.[65]

The members of the House Ways and Means Committee went even further. They inserted a provision into the act that set an upper limit on the amount of federal assistance provided to the states under Title IV. When Secretary of Labor Frances Perkins objected to the restriction, Committee Chairman Pat Harrison of Georgia "expressed the view that it was probably alright to start this aid at a very low figure, as subsequent Congresses could easily expand it," displaying the same cavalier attitude toward the expansion of relief that had characterized Southerners on both committees throughout.

As our hypothesis suggests, then, the coverage of agriculture in Old-Age Insurance was an area of much contention in the House and Senate. The system that emerged from Congress bore scant resemblance to that proposed by the CES. The only provision of the act that survived in its entirety was the federal subsidy of state old-age pension programs. The pensions were to be distributed through the various existing state pension systems with states and localities left free to determine benefit levels, expenditures, and restrictions. The arrangement was apparently appealing as a compromise between those desiring to see a modicum of security provided for all groups and those desiring to exclude selected groups or to provide them with significantly lower benefit levels. In fact, the wide latitude given to states in setting eligibility criteria allowed Southern states to pay a "supplement" to Confederate veterans, over and above their regular state old age pension. Because these veterans were white, this distinction created a great disparity between pensions paid to blacks and whites in the South.[66]

Throughout the struggle over Social Security in Congress, the South was joined by a variety of interests. States outside the South that resented

---

[64] Abbott, *Child and the State*, p. 240. That both black and white tenant families were specified by Southerners as the problem tends to diminish the plausibility of the simple racial explanation of the South's aversion to welfare discussed previously.

[65] Witte, *Development of the Social Security Act*, p. 163.

[66] See Quadagno, *Transformation of Old Age Security*, p. 136.

the oversight of their relief programs by FERA joined with Southern representatives in supporting restrictions on the Social Security Board's ability to shape the personnel policies of state agencies administering Old-Age Assistance, Unemployment Insurance, and Aid to Dependent Children. States that desired greater flexibility in setting relief spending priorities than they had enjoyed under FERA's system of discretionary grants joined the South in pushing for a system of matching grants to fund the categorical assistance programs established by the Social Security Act. Finally, many Americans – including Roosevelt himself to some extent – favored decentralization, out of a belief that a centralized system would not survive a court challenge, a belief in states as the best "laboratory" through which experimentation and learning could occur, or a belief in states' rights.[67] The South did not invent opposition to the welfare state – it merely capitalized on it, to shape federal programs in ways that minimized the harm they would do to the region's system of social control and paternalism.

Action After 1935

The passage of the Social Security Act in 1935 did not signal an end to the fight to save paternalism. Southern landed interests had succeeded in barring the payment of Old-Age and Unemployment Insurance to the agricultural population, but Old-Age Assistance and Aid to Dependent Children administered through the states were not directly restricted in this manner. In the absence of mechanization, which we have suggested would have sounded the death knell of paternalism, the battle against federal paternalism would have continued to rage on two fronts: (1) in the states, where the manipulation of benefit levels and restrictions achieved the same effect as outright exclusion, and (2) in Congress, where the issue of agriculture's inclusion under Social Security would continue to be pressed.

As altered at the insistence of Southern representatives in Congress, the Old-Age Assistance and ADC provisions of the Social Security Act gave the states a great deal more latitude in setting benefit levels and determining the ease with which benefits could be obtained than did the original Economic Security Act. The original act was stringent because the CES staff recognized a return to state responsibility generally resulted in a reduction of benefits. Various devices were used by states to make relief more "economical" when responsibility for short-term direct relief reverted to them in 1935.[68]

---

[67] Patterson, *Struggle Against Poverty*, p. 71.
[68] "Returning Relief to the States."

Two methods appear to have figured most prominently in the South. In the first years under the Social Security Act, Southern states manipulated both benefit levels and eligibility rules. Southern states continued to pay relatively lower benefits than other states even after the passage of the Social Security Act and the start of federal subsidy of state programs. At the same time, throughout the 1930s and 1940s, Southern states devised elaborate restrictions to assure that those most needed in cotton cultivation were kept off the welfare rolls.[69] Both mechanisms were clearly aimed at maintaining dependency.

In Congress, as well, Southerners' fight against the encroachment of federal paternalism continued. There was considerable support from organized labor, the National Association for the Advancement of Colored People (NAACP), the National Urban League, and the Social Security Board for broadening the Social Security Act to cover agricultural labor, and for reclassifying Southern tenants and croppers as agricultural laborers rather than farm operators (to allow these groups to come under the purview of a broadened plan).[70] Despite their support, the category of excluded workers was in fact broadened when the act was revised in 1939, leaving the inclusion of agriculture but a distant prospect through the first two decades of the act's operation and leaving the South's curious system of paternalistic labor relations intact.

Pressure to expand the Social Security Act's coverage and include agricultural workers and farm operators continued into the 1940s. In 1948, though the Social Security Board recommended that agricultural workers be included in the Old-Age Insurance program, they were not included in the bill that Democrat Robert Doughton's (NC) Ways and Means Committee reported to the House. Despite the broad support for inclusion of agriculture, "southern democrats countered that no farmers came to their hearings to argue for coverage."[71] Though the Senate Finance Committee reported a bill that did include agricultural workers,

---

[69] See, for example, Piven and Cloward, *Regulating the Poor*, p. 134. Louisiana and Georgia were among the first states to adopt employable mother rules under which "AFDC families with children seven years old and older [would] be refused assistance as long as the mother was presumed to be employable in the fields."

[70] See "National Urban League Asks Inclusion of Domestic and Agricultural Workers"; "AFL Report Including Agricultural Workers"; "CIO Urges Inclusion of Agricultural Workers"; Bureau of Research and Statistics, Division of Old-Age Benefits Research, "Expansion of Coverage"; "Statement of Arthur J. Altmeyer, Chairman of the Social Security Board, Before the Senate Finance Committee on Amendments to the Social Security Act"; Paul Taylor, "Relation of Tenancy and Labor in Agriculture"; "Old-Age Insurance for Agricultural Workers"; John J. Corson to O. M. Powell, "Conference with Farm Labor Committee of the Department of Agriculture"; "Alternative Plans for the Coverage of Agricultural Workers."

[71] Quadagno, *Transformation of Old Age Security*, p. 147.

73

and agricultural workers were included in the bill produced by the Southern-dominated conference committee, they had to have been "regularly employed," which would have excluded most cotton pickers.[72] Self-employed workers (a category that still included tenants and croppers) were still excluded as well.

By the 1950s, though, change was on the horizon. In Chapter 6, we describe the developments that led to the disappearance of much Southern opposition to federal spending on welfare programs in the South. The impact of those changes on the Social Security system was striking. As Jill Quadagno notes,

Step by step, southern congressmen released welfare for the aged poor from local government, passing control to the federal government as the burden of maintaining aged blacks surpassed their economic value and as the threat that direct cash payments to an older relative would subsidize an entire family became less critical to a changing plantation economy.[73]

As a result, agricultural laborers were brought under the Old-Age Insurance provisions of the Social Security system in 1950, 1954, and 1956. The strongest supporters of raising the federal share of public assistance to the elderly and the handicapped in 1958 were the Southerners on the House Ways and Means Committee.[74] By the 1960s, the opposition of Southerners to federal welfare spending had been reduced so greatly that when the Nixon administration proposed an expansion of the federal funding and federal oversight of states' Old-Age Assistance programs in 1969, Southern representatives strongly supported the initiative.[75]

But before those changes had taken hold, other federal initiatives, introduced during the New Deal and World War II, threatened the South's system of paternalistic labor relations in the same way as it had been threatened by Social Security. Before we describe the changes that shook Southern agriculture and caused the disappearance of paternalism and of much opposition to federal welfare spending, we turn in the next chapter to consider the battles waged by Southerners to prevent federal efforts at "reforming" Southern agriculture during the New Deal and their efforts to prevent the outmigration of labor from the South during World War II.

[72] Ibid., p. 148.
[73] Ibid., p. 146.
[74] Ibid., pp. 141–2.
[75] Ibid., pp. 149–50.

4

Southern Opposition to the Farm Security Administration

I. Introduction

Because social insurance had great appeal across the nation, it was harder to fight than programs aimed narrowly at reform in agriculture and Southern agriculture in particular. But even after the threat to paternalism raised by the Social Security Act had been defeated, the federal government remained interested in pursuing policies like those of Federal Emergency Relief Administration (FERA) described at the start of Chapter 3 that addressed rural poverty specifically. Though the fight to exclude agriculture from social insurance programs had been won by the South in 1935, the federal government sharpened its focus on rural poverty in 1937. The Farm Security Administration (FSA) represented intervention in Southern labor relations to alter the relative economic power of landowners and laborers, and then to leave them free to contract among themselves.

The history of the FSA provides a clear example of the difficulty the Southern elite faced in preventing federal intervention in the South's system of labor relations, even as the region sought federal dollars. This episode also illustrates the lengths to which the elite would go to preserve the system of paternalistic relations between them and their dependent laborers and the economic benefits the elite derived as a result. The threat that the FSA posed to the South's system of paternalism was the FSA's role as an intermediary between landlords and tenants. But the FSA's exclusive focus on agriculture left it without a broad base of popular support when the Southern rural elite turned to face that threat.

The FSA was created by the Bankhead-Jones Farm Tenancy Act of 1937.[1] The new agency combined many of the programs initiated by the

---

[1] The most comprehensive studies of the FSA are Baldwin, *Poverty and Politics*; and Maddox, "Farm Security Administration." We rely heavily on these works in this chapter.

Southern Paternalism and the American Welfare State

Resettlement Administration (RA), the Federal Emergency Relief Administration (FERA), and the Division of Subsistence Homesteads in the U.S. Interior Department, programs designed to help eradicate the persistent rural poverty that had been exacerbated by more than a decade of depression in American agriculture.[2] But just nine years after its birth, the FSA was dismantled amid charges of rampant inefficiency, political cronyism, and promotion of Soviet-style collectivism. Congress discontinued the most controversial of the FSA's programs and scattered the remainder among the Extension Service, the Farm Credit Administration, and the new Farmers Home Administration.

The FSA, however, was more than just a controversial, short-lived stepchild of the New Deal. It was a highly visible manifestation of the federal government's concern for a class of citizens who had previously endured poverty in isolation. The FSA was described by its proponents as "an historic attempt . . . to exploit the power, the promise, and the possibilities of politics in securing salvation from the human suffering, social injustice, and economic waste of chronic poverty."[3] As such, it posed a particularly potent threat to the viability of the Southern system of social and economic relations based on plantation agriculture and paternalism.

II. The First New Deal and the Resettlement Administration (RA)

Following the Congressional elections of 1934, the Roosevelt administration's emphasis in economic policy shifted from recovery to reform and the First New Deal was superseded by the Second.[4] Policy makers in Washington had become increasingly aware of the chronic rural poverty that had existed before the Great Depression and had been largely ignored in the rush to promote overall recovery.[5]

Two developments in 1934 and 1935 made the need for such a reform program particularly urgent. First, the New Dealers feared that any com-

---

[2] Though the agricultural sector was not universally depressed in the 1920s as it was in the 1930s, farm foreclosures were at record highs in the 1920s. See Alston, "Farm Foreclosures"; and Alston, Grove, and Wheelock, "Why Do Banks Fail?"

[3] Baldwin, *Poverty and Politics*, p. ix.

[4] Schlesinger, *Politics of Upheaval.*

[5] The WPA and PWA put millions to work, but most were in the nation's cities. Some tentative steps were taken by FERA in the rural areas, but the lack of opportunities for government-made work in the country meant that most of FERA's work involved simple direct relief, at least through March 1934, when the first rudimentary "rural rehabilitation" program had begun; Maddox, "Farm Security Administration," pp. 9–10.

prehensive economic reform they might propose would be successfully preempted by more radical proposals, such as the panaceas offered by the likes of Senator Huey Long of Louisiana and Father Charles Coughlin.[6] The second reason for concern was the adverse effect of the few administration initiatives in this area. The programs of the Agricultural Adjustment Administration (AAA) to raise rural incomes had perversely resulted in increased rural poverty as landlords were implicitly encouraged to employ fewer agricultural workers overall and relatively more wage hands among the remainder.[7]

The result of this concern was the creation of the Resettlement Administration in May 1935. Under the guidance of Rexford G. Tugwell, the New Deal's "house radical," the new agency consolidated a number of programs begun under FERA and the Division of Subsistence Homesteads in the U.S. Interior Department. Tugwell's new agency did more than merely combine a few previously disparate initiatives, though. The RA focused those programs more on the plight of the rural poor. The agency operated on the premises that something fundamental could actually be done about rural poverty and that the government should be significantly involved in such an enterprise.

In the field, the RA managed three programs designed to strike at the causes of rural poverty: (1) production on overused, unproductive, marginal land; (2) a lack of opportunities for off-farm employment; and (3) a crushing, rapidly cumulating burden of debt. The first of these was attacked by purchasing and retiring submarginal land. It was argued that such lands, if kept in production, would have been parceled out to the poorest of tenants, who would have simply been pushed further into poverty by their inability to wring a profit from the overworked, mineral-poor soil. The establishment of rural–urban model communities through the resettlement of destitute farmers and industrial workers was an attempt to improve the off-farm employment opportunities of the former and the self-sufficiency of the latter. Under the RA, neither of these two programs aroused much criticism in the South, because they were operated on a very limited scale. Planters viewed the programs as visionary and utopian but harmless.

The third of the RA's programs, however, was received with much less equanimity in the South. Using loans and outright grants, the RA attempted to "rehabilitate" tenants who had become overburdened with debt. It was thought that, with careful supervision and the breathing space afforded by a rehabilitation loan or grant, these tenants could

---

[6] Baldwin, *Poverty and Politics*, pp. 85–6.
[7] Ibid., pp. 76–8; Alston, "Tenure Choice"; Whatley, "Labor for the Picking."

eventually pay off their debts and attain a measure of independence.[8] Needless to say, this strategy soon ran afoul of the complex set of social and economic relations we have described as characterizing the rural South. Rehabilitation represented a challenge to the status quo in the South: It made the federal government a party to the landlord-tenant agreement and substituted a degree of outside supervision for planter supervision.[9] In short, rehabilitation threatened to undermine some of the dependency inherent in Southern paternalism. The desperate tenant could now turn to the RA for help, whereas previously he had to turn to his landlord.

Much of the initial opposition to rehabilitation, in the South and elsewhere, came from the agricultural establishment: the Extension Service, the Farm Bureau, the state extension services, and the county agricultural agents.[10] These agencies were controlled by the large landowners and tended to represent their interests. The importance of this opposition, however, should not be overestimated. Though opposition was evident in most agricultural regions of the country, it appears to have represented, at least initially, little more than an attempt by the agricultural establishment to preserve its hegemony in local affairs in the face of increasing government intervention. In addition, large landholders themselves gave some support to rehabilitation initially, even in the South. In an FSA survey of attitudes toward RA loans to help needy farmers get on their feet, Southern owners responded favorably nearly as often as croppers and renters. Though owners in the South were roughly three times as likely to respond negatively as croppers or tenants, they were less opposed than Northern owners (Table 4.1).

This apparent lack of Southern planter opposition seems anomalous, but it is somewhat less so in view of the limited scope of the RA loan program and the very small degree of supervision it attempted to exercise over loan recipients. When the FSA was lending 60 percent more and serving perhaps one and a half times as many client families and offering more supervision, advice, and methods for needy tenants to help themselves, planter opposition quickly appeared.[11]

Planters had more to gain than the county agents or the Extension Service of the Department of Agriculture if rehabilitation proceeded on

---

[8] Though promotion of cooperatives and attempts at debt adjustment and tenure improvement were also part of the rural rehabilitation program, these assumed much greater importance under the FSA. We shall consider their effects on paternalism when we discuss the entire FSA agenda below.

[9] Baldwin, *Poverty and Politics*, pp. 120-1.

[10] Ibid., p. 115.

[11] Ibid., pp. 108, 296; U.S. Congress, House, Committee on Agriculture, *Agriculture Appropriation Bill Hearings* (1942), pp. 148-50.

Table 4.1. *Attitudes of farmers toward*
Resettlement Administration
Rehabilitation Loan Program, by tenure
status (1937)

Region and tenure status	Favor (%)	Oppose (%)
Northern		
Owners	68.2	8.7
Tenants	76.4	5.7
Laborers	76.8	4.3
Southern white		
Owners	64.3	6.3
Renters	65.8	2.5
Croppers	62.5	1.2
Laborers	71.7	7.5
Southern black		
Owners	55.0	4.7
Renters	43.9	0.8
Croppers	47.8	0.0
Laborers	32.6	0.0

Source: Schuler, "Social Status and Farm Tenure," pp. 82–3

a very limited scale. A planter renting to a heavily indebted tenant gains something in the form of loyalty in return for continually rolling over the tenant's debt, but he loses something at the same time if the tenant is never able to repay that debt. Conversely, a planter renting to a tenant being financed by a rehabilitation loan loses some tenant loyalty but gains immediate access to funds previously advanced to the tenant. Given an appropriately high rate of discount, planters may well have opted for support of a severely circumscribed program of rehabilitation in the short run.[12]

In such circumstances, the interests of planters may have diverged slightly from those of the agricultural establishment that otherwise represented them. The transfer in 1937 of the RA from FERA to the Department of Agriculture, where the establishment exerted greater control, may have represented an attempt by policymakers to recon-

---

[12] Because the county agents, Farm Bureau officers, and the Extension Service agents would lose some influence over tenants in their jurisdictions but receive no corresponding benefits, their cost–benefit calculus would have pointed to opposition to rehabilitation as the rational course of action regardless of the size of the program.

cile these interests. It also represented an attempt to avoid the equation of rehabilitation loans with relief in the same way that the Social Security Board had been wrested from FERA (at the insistence of Southerners in Congress) to avoid the equation of Old-Age Assistance with relief.[13]

III. The Birth of the Farm Security Administration in Congress

Here matters stood in 1937. In that year, the Bankhead-Jones Farm Tenancy Act of 1937 affirmed the federal government's commitment to the preservation of the family farm and the reduction of farm tenancy. The bill's initial prospects were unpromising in both houses of Congress. The House Agriculture Committee included two members who were owners of large cotton plantations – Representatives Hampton Fulmer of South Carolina and Richard Kleberg of Texas – and three others who were "agents or advocates of cotton and tobacco interests" – Representatives Wall Doxey of Mississippi, John Flannagan of Virginia, and Emmett Owen of Georgia.[14]

Because the bill clearly focused on the problems of the South, representatives from the Midwest and the Great Plains were also apathetic to the overtures of Marvin Jones. That apathy was later transformed into outright hostility as the FSA began to grow and usurp many of the functions of the national agricultural establishment and focus on problems that extended beyond the borders of the South. That hostility was later a boon to Southerners who opposed the FSA because of its effect on agricultural labor costs and the Southern social system as well as because of the threat it posed to the Southern agricultural establishment. Southerners could count on the support of their brethren from the Western and Midwestern agricultural states in the coming years as Southern opposition to the FSA grew. But in 1937, the Bankhead-Jones Act succeeded in papering over these differences, at least for a time.

The national agricultural establishment had been alienated by the autonomy of the RA. The support of large landholders in areas like the South was possible only if the scope and scale of initiatives like the rehabilitation loan program were strictly limited. To ensure passage of his bill in the House, Representative Jones was prepared to make concessions on both fronts. He offered significant local control to prevent disruption of "established relationships," and he introduced a revised bill that reduced by 76 percent the three-year appropriation for loans to help

---

[13] See Chapter 3.
[14] Baldwin, *Poverty and Politics*, p. 179.

tenants buy their farms and eliminated entirely the explicit two-year $150 million appropriation for rehabilitation loan programs.[15]

The compromise succeeded in Congress. In the final vote in the House, Southern opposition was limited to Representative Kleberg of Texas, while the bill passed the Senate on a voice vote over the objections of a lone Southerner, Senator Stephen Pace of Georgia. Senator Bankhead credited the efforts of Senator Russell for the support of the bill.[16] Russell was chairman of the Agriculture subcommittee of the Appropriations Committee and was thus in a position to swing votes. Since arriving in Congress and throughout his career Russell was a supporter of the small farmer.[17] The compromise was less well received by the agricultural establishment and Southern planters, both of whom were disturbed by the refinement and expansion of the RA's programs undertaken by the FSA.

IV. The Farm Security Administration in Practice

The potential effect of the FSA's programs on the South's social and economic arrangements was clearly the point at issue. But how would those programs affect that system? The FSA was more clearly committed to reducing tenancy than its predecessor had been. It included, in addition to the more familiar rehabilitation and resettlement programs carried over from the RA, a program to help tenants purchase their farms. This program was bound to be a source of some difficulty in the South. The program provided credit and technical assistance to families chosen to participate and thus interfered in two of the most visible aspects of paternalism: planter control over the dependent's finances and farm operations.[18]

One of the most marked differences between landlord-tenant relations in the corn and cotton belts was the much greater extent of landlord control over operating credit in the South. A nonowner in the South was some five to ten times more likely to have his credit controlled by his landlord than was a Northern nonowner; for Southern blacks, the difference was even more striking (Table 4.2).[19] Landlord involvement in the

[15] Ibid., pp. 180–3. The Secretary of Agriculture was empowered to allocate funds for this purpose from appropriations previously made for work relief.

[16] Fite, *Richard B. Russell, Jr.*, p. 153.

[17] In 1935 Russell introduced an amendment to a work relief bill that gave the president discretion to use the funds for loans to farmers to purchase land and equipment. On the basis of the Russell amendment, President Roosevelt established the Resettlement Administration. Ibid., pp. 152–3.

[18] The choice of who was to do the choosing was later a source of some contention, as is discussed below.

[19] This comparison demonstrates the extent to which race influenced paternalism; the comparison between Northern and Southern whites shows that differences in the paternalism practiced in the two regions existed independently of race.

Table 4.2. *Nonowners reporting landlord to have
control over nonowners' operating credit (1937)*

Region and relationship to landlord	Nonowners reporting landlord control of credit (%)
Northern	
Related to landlord	6
Unrelated to landlord	2
Southern white	
Related to landord	32
Unrelated to landlord	26
Southern black	
Related to landlord	61
Unrelated to landlord	66

Source: Schuler, "Social Status and Farm Tenure," p. 172

South did not stop there, however. As we would expect in such a system of dependency, the tenant received a benefit, perhaps one not readily obtained elsewhere, in exchange for acceding to control by his landlord. While the Southern landlord controlled his tenants' credit, he was also more likely than a Northern landlord to "stand good" for their debts (Table 4.3).[20] This element of *quid pro quo* is clearly "evidence of the paternalistic side of the landlord-tenant relationship, . . . a pattern of obligations often assumed by the landlord, deriving largely from historical antecedents."[21]

In regard to supervisory control over their tenants, Southern landlords also differed from their Northern counterparts. They were far more likely to have a close relationship with their renters, croppers, and laborers and were therefore more likely to be suspicious of government initiatives that interfered in that relationship. Southern landlords visited their tenants on a daily basis roughly twice as much as Northern landlords did (Table 4.4). Laborers were closely supervised in both areas and consequently received daily visits in both the North and South. Again, the figure for black tenants is much higher, indicating both a greater "demand" by blacks for paternalism as well as a greater "supply" of paternalism by plantation landlords.

Southern landlords did not merely appear more often than Northerners. They exercised much wider powers of supervision during those visits. When asked "What do you have to say about the farming operation

[20] Because landlord control over credit was negligible in the North, this comparison was done only for Southern tenants.
[21] Schuler, "Social Status and Farm Tenure," p. 173.

Table 4.3. *Southern landlords reported by*
nonowners to "stand good" for nonowners'
debts (1937)

Tenure status	Landlords who "stand good" for debts (%)
Southern white	
Renters	54
Croppers	54
Laborers	55
Southern black	
Renters	69
Croppers	79
Laborers	60

Source: Schuler, "Social Status and Farm Tenure," p. 172

of your tenants or employee?" five times as many Southern white land-lords as Northern landlords reported giving strict orders. The proportions are nearly reversed for the response "I leave decisions entirely up to him." Schuler concluded that these "figures point to a fundamental difference in living social relationships . . . out of which have grown fundamentally different organic social structures."[22] At the very least, these comparisons demonstrate the extent to which the FSA's tenant purchase program represented a distinct departure from established practice. Outside supervision of credit and operations was more likely to be seen as unwarranted and dangerous interference.

The rural rehabilitation program the FSA inherited from the RA was, as we have noted above, opposed by the agricultural establishment but tolerated by planters so long as it was not greatly expanded. Under the FSA, the program was expanded; spending on rehabilitation loans alone rose from $78 million under the RA to $125 million under the FSA,[23] while other rehabilitation methods potentially even more damaging to Southern paternalism were being tried.[24] Planter support, as we shall see,

[22] Ibid., p. 34.
[23] For sources of figures, see Baldwin, *Poverty and Politics*, pp. 180–3.
[24] This happened despite Representative Marvin Jones's promises to Southern Congressmen. Jones kept part of his deal: Funding of rehabilitation programs was to be at the discretion of the Secretary of Agriculture (though he turned out to be quite generous), and some local control was maintained (though only in the area of debt adjustment; see below). Jones promised discretion and local control; he never set limits on how much discretionary funding could be authorized and never promised local control over specific programs.

83

Table 4.4. *Frequency of landlord's visits as reported by tenants*
(1937)

Frequency of visits	Northern (%)	Southern white (%)	Southern black (%)
Daily	5	27	38
Several times per week	4	19	21
Weekly	5	11	16
Every two weeks	3	3	4
Every three weeks	1	2	1
Monthly	9	8	10
Several times per year	49	19	9
Never	24	11	1

Source: Schuler, "Social Status and Farm Tenure," p. 172.

quickly collapsed. Landlords soon joined the chorus of agricultural establishment figures clamoring for the dismantling of these rehabilitation programs. What was the source of this opposition and how did the FSA rehabilitation program differ from that under the RA (which, as we have seen, enjoyed at least a modicum of support in the South)?

Rehabilitation under the FSA consisted of the use of standard rehabilitation loans, the distribution of grants for coping with natural disasters, the promotion of group services, cooperatives, and neighborhood action groups, and efforts to reschedule tenants' debts and improve the condition of their tenancy. Each of these devices contained something that might have aroused concern among Southern planters interested in maintaining paternalism.

The loan program could have enjoyed at least some landlord support in the South if it had been limited. When the program was expanded under the FSA, the same sort of cost–benefit analysis that had prompted support of a limited program was more likely to provoke opposition. Opposition would arise in those areas where the loans would interfere significantly with the supply of labor, most likely the plantation areas. In other areas of the South there was support for loans to help small family farmers acquire their own farms, particularly white farmers.[25]

FSA grants for disaster relief may at first also seem likely to have provoked planter opposition. Such grants would have replaced the landlord as the source of aid in emergencies. Previous experience with disas-

---

[25] As noted earlier, Senator Russell (GA) was an ardent supporter of the loan program throughout the history of the FSA; Fite, *Richard B. Russell, Jr.*, pp. 149–57.

ter relief, however, indicated that planters were not averse to their tenants' receiving such assistance if planters themselves were unable to provide it and if such assistance was explicitly defined as temporary. Disaster relief represented a nuisance to planters at worst, and perhaps a great convenience for them if some of their own resources had been wiped out in the disaster.[26]

The promotion of group activities and cooperatives, on the other hand, would have posed an unambiguous threat to paternalism, regardless of how such organizations might be structured or controlled. First and most directly, such enterprises took money out of the pockets of the country merchants, who were often allied with the large planters when not in their direct employ. Planter control of tenant credit and willingness to guarantee the debts of tenants meant that the local country or plantation store was the only place where the tenant could shop. When the country store was the only option and the planter would supply credit there, the tenant was reasonably happy to shop there. Cooperatives would give the tenant another option and make the country store a less appealing alternative even if the landlord continued to provide credit there.

A second and perhaps more subtle way that cooperatives struck at paternalism was by demonstrating to tenants that they could help themselves. They did not need the planter to intercede at the store or in the marketing of the crop or in the legal system if they had cooperative organizations. Tenant cooperatives to buy supplies, sell cotton, and provide group services such as legal counsel would have made some planter-supplied benefits redundant. If they could secure these things themselves, tenants would have been disinclined to get assistance from their landlords, paying for it over time in deference, loyalty, and hard work.

Cooperatives also represented a potent threat to the Southern social system *qua* system. The amount spent by the FSA on these ventures was only a trivial share of the agency's total budget, yet this aspect of the rehabilitation program soon provoked virulent opposition in the South and directly contributed to the eventual downfall of the FSA.[27] The threat to the Southern social system, and the planter domination thereof, posed by FSA cooperatives was clearly at least as important to planters as the direct effect of such ventures on the profitability of their country stores or the money wages they paid to their agricultural labor.

The last method employed by the FSA in rehabilitating tenants was direct intervention in the landlord-tenant relationship, by negotiating

[26] Raper, *Preface to Peasantry*, pp. 256–7.

[27] Senator Russell, though a staunch supporter of the FSA, was opposed to the use of funds for cooperatives; Fite, *Richard B. Russell, Jr.*, pp. 156–7.

Table 4.5. *Tenants dissatisfied with present agreement who suggest specific changes (1937)*

Suggested change	Northern tenants (%)	Southern white		Southern black	
		Renters (%)	Croppers (%)	Renters (%)	Croppers (%)
Written rental agree-ment	2.9	21.2	15.5	18.9	27.8
Longer lease	50.7	28.8	11.1	25.8	16.1
Better division of in-come w/landlord	—	1.5	2.2	0.8	1.4
Change mode of rent payment	1.4	10.6	2.2	3.8	1.9
Better credits ar-rangements	1.4	1.5	—	4.5	5.7
Fairer treatment or settlement	—	—	—	—	5.2

Source: Schuler, "Social Status and Farm Tenure," p. 164

better terms for the tenant's debt and promoting more equitable, standardized rental agreements. Again, the FSA was getting itself into a very delicate area. Direct intercession on the tenant's behalf did more than just show the tenant that he could turn to someone other than his landlord for help; it opened to negotiation and outside scrutiny what had previously been a process steeped in tradition and unspoken but implicitly understood mutual obligations. In attempting to mediate this process, the FSA was opening a true Pandora's box.

Southern tenants and landlords made oral rather than written leases more often than their counterparts in the North, despite some dissatisfaction with this custom in the South. This dissatisfaction is indicated by the differences in the proportions of Northern and Southern tenants who indicated a desire for a written lease (Table 4.5). Most Northerners already had written agreements. Only half as many Southern as Northern landlords reported written leases with tenants.[28] Southern landlords favored the oral or traditional lease because it fostered paternalism by making the landlord-tenant relationship less businesslike. Landlords liked to believe that they were not exploiting their tenants but instead looking out for their interests and preventing their exploitation by others. There was consequently no need for a written lease.

[28] Schuler, "Social Status and Farm Tenure," p. 161.

The FSA debt adjustment and tenure improvement program would have changed this situation by requiring the landlord to put the terms of the lease in writing. This change would have made the relationship more businesslike and given the tenants the chance to put on the table a long list of grievances that it was pointless to voice when the lease was oral and lacked third-party observation. Tenants in the South wanted a more equitable division of income with the landlord, a different mode of payment, a fairer settlement, and better credit arrangements (Table 4.5).

V. The Impact of the Farm Security Administration

Thus did the FSA threaten the system of paternalism. A wealth of evidence seems to confirm the worst fears of Southern landlords and planters. Where the FSA made noticeable inroads, tenants and farm laborers did transfer from their landlords to the FSA the loyalty that was the raison d'être of paternalism. A few examples will show this effect and at the same time characterize the qualitatively different labor response elicited by provision of in-kind benefits – in this case, the new government paternalism provided by the FSA – that we have argued was the source of that loyalty.

In a study of a black belt plantation, Rubin found that blacks receiving government benefits viewed the benefits as a sign that "someone way off yonder" cares for them.[29] This attitude on the part of benefit recipients manifested itself in loyal behavior toward the agency and its representatives. In practice, such loyalty translated into a willingness to render service over and above the expected norm because the FSA was seen as either "good" to its tenant–clients or willing to be "good" in exchange for those tenant–clients' "good" behavior.

As a result of these loyal feelings engendered by the perception of FSA concern, tenants were more diligent, conscientious, and hard working under the FSA than they otherwise would have been. In Texas, the FSA observer noted: "There are indicators that the placating attitude that had been used toward a landlord or merchant is sometimes transferred to the supervisory personnel. Some families feel that they are doing something to please the supervisor rather than thinking of a practice as helping their own welfare."[30] This attitude was shown by a woman admonished by an FSA official for a minor violation of the terms of their agreement. She responded, "Why, I've canned 200 quarts of green vegetables for you!" In the same way, to show his gratitude toward the FSA, another

[29] Rubin, *Plantation County*, p. 185.
[30] Larson, "Ten Years of Rural Rehabilitation," p. 338.

recipient told the local supervisor, "I try to reason with my neighbors that they ought to *show their appreciation to the government* by attending meetings [with the FSA representatives]."[31]

To ensure that they rather than the FSA would benefit from such loyal responses to the provision of paternalism and continue to receive deference from their workers, landed interests in the South were willing to expend considerable resources. We now turn to the battle they waged against the FSA.

VI. Opposition to the Farm Security Administration Takes Shape

The FSA had been in operation for just over a year in 1938. Yet even at that early date, the FSA's Director of Information, John Fischer, could report that "within the last few months . . . powerful opposition has been encountered in areas where the work of the FSA runs counter to the established economy."[32] Nowhere were the programs of the FSA more at variance with the "established economy" than in the South.

Southern opposition to the FSA intensified steadily after 1938. Increased opposition, however, was also apparent in other regions, as a result of the expansion of FSA programs and continued FSA usurpation of the powers of local agricultural establishments. This development was clearly part of the story behind rising Southern opposition; but given the modesty of the expansion in FSA programs and funding relative to the tenacious opposition the agency aroused in the South, it was clearly but a very small part of that story.

A more important reason for increasing Southern opposition to the FSA over time was the mounting conflict between the philosophy of the FSA and the Southern social system that rested upon paternalism, deference, and cheap labor. Opposition had undoubtedly been muted in the early years of the FSA's existence, when many big planters were struggling for their survival. By 1938, when planters had begun to get back on their feet, their concern for the Southern social order prompted them to take an increasingly hard look at what the FSA was saying and doing.

This trend was part of a more general shift toward conservatism that occurred throughout the nation in the late 1930s and early 1940s as the recovery progressed. At many New Deal agencies, this political shift led to a retrenchment of some programs and a rethinking of some goals. The FSA, however, was unwilling to bow to these pressures. The agency refused to bend to the new political winds blowing across the country

---

[31] Ibid., p. 339; emphasis added.
[32] Baldwin, *Poverty and Politics*, p. 263.

by 1940. As a result it was increasingly seen as radical, at least in the South, where the FSA program had always represented a distinct departure from the established order.

This reception contrasts markedly to that of the AAA at roughly the same time. The AAA made every effort to accommodate planters and large landowners and to avoid upsetting the existing social order, particularly in the South. One evaluation of the AAA's performance concluded:

> The AAA was never conceived for the purpose of equalizing income or restoring freedom of initiative and equality of opportunity among different tenure classes within the farm population. That a problem of this sort exists in acute form in certain sections, and particularly in the South, was recognized by sponsors of the act; but solution of this problem was not included as an objective of the AAA.[33]

The FSA attempted to deal with just these problems and continued to do so even as opposition to such reforms was increasing.

The FSA was thus increasingly viewed as a radical, disruptive force, just when the political climate in the nation, and in the South especially, was becoming less tolerant of such forces. With the start of the nation's preparations for war after 1939, a general economy drive in Congress provided further justification for Southern opposition. Southerners, taking advantage of the climate of austerity conditioned by the country's preoccupation with the war, could give vent to their opposition to the FSA. The result of the Southern perception of the FSA's radicalism was strident, stinging Southern rhetoric that condemned the agency as "un-American" and a threat to the Southern way of life. As the preparations for war proceeded and Southerners gained a Congressional forum for their views, they successfully transformed their rhetoric into actions.

Even earlier, though, Southerners had actively worked to control the FSA's damage to their system. Because the FSA enjoyed at least some support in areas where it was not so disruptive of local socioeconomic relations as it was in the South, Southern opposition initially expressed itself in the field where the FSA operated.

Opposition in the Field

The negative effects of some FSA programs on paternalism in the South could have been greatly mitigated if landlords and the agricultural establishment had been able to obtain some control over them. The erosion of paternalism these programs would otherwise have caused might have been prevented if loans to allow tenants to purchase their farms had to

---

[33] Nourse et al., *Three Years*, pp. 348–9.

be approved by the big local planters or if the rescheduling of tenants' debts was done at the discretion of the local county committee. For example, if a county committee controlled by the large planters in the area had to pass upon FSA loan applications filed by tenants, those tenants would have had to continue their loyal behavior to secure the loan. Likewise, if such a committee was responsible for debt adjustment, tenants would have had to do the same to obtain favorable terms. In both cases, loyalty to the planter would persist. Further, such planter control might not merely prevent the erosion of paternalism; it might actually buttress it. Such buttressing would have occurred where planter control allowed them to mete out FSA-supplied benefits and receive in return the loyalty that recipients would feel toward their benefactors.

The first form that opposition to FSA initiatives in the South assumed, then, was the attempted co-optation of the loan programs and the debt adjustment process. Some of this co-optation was probably inevitable: Because they lived and worked and dealt with the people in an area, it was only natural that "many of the county supervisors [of the FSA] tended to mirror the established pattern of community leadership."[34] Southern planters and their agricultural establishment also shaped FSA policy more actively at the local level. In fact, "the seduction of their supervisors by extension officials and county agricultural agents" was a source of constant concern to FSA officials.[35] Though such seduction could have happened wherever the FSA went into a new community, it presented a particularly vexing problem in the South, where the established community leadership had a greater stake than most in seeing that the FSA reflected the values of the community.

The subtle and almost natural co-optation led in the South to a reluctance by FSA representatives to pursue policies that might upset community leaders. Big planters enjoyed an implicit veto power over the decisions of the local FSA administrator. In administering the tenant purchase and rural rehabilitation loans, though official FSA policy directed that such assistance be extended to all regardless of tenure status, "many county and district supervisors 'skimmed' the cream."[36] Assistance was given to those farther up the agricultural ladder, to tenants more likely to be able to make it on their own. In the South, this selectivity meant that those most dependent on their landlords (poor black croppers, for instance) were frequently denied assistance and left to obtain such help from paternalistic planters.

FSA leaders in Washington were well aware of the opposition they

[34] Baldwin, *Poverty and Politics*, p. 260.
[35] Ibid., p. 253.
[36] Ibid., p. 260.

might provoke in the South. In attempting to adjust to such realities while seeing that necessary credit was extended, the FSA formalized the seduction of its local representatives by countenancing significant landlord control over the terms of its loans:

> In situations where many of the program objectives were opposed, but where the credit facilities were needed, an accommodation was sometimes arrived at. Landlords might encourage their tenants to apply for a loan, but they might also negotiate the loan, make out the farm plan, and adjust the home plan to coincide with the customary "furnish"; or the landlord might set aside a plot for garden although the tenant might not have time to work it.[37]

The effect of such an accommodation in the South was to remove the FSA from the picture almost entirely. The planter could provide funds to his tenant and appear to do so of his own volition and in conformity with traditional arrangements. The landlord could continue to be seen as the protector by his tenant and enjoy that tenant's continued loyalty in return.

These arrangements for Southerners were frequently informally ratified in Congress through "regional treaties . . . negotiated in the Capitol cloakroom and in the privacy of committees. . . ."[38] Such was the case with FSA programs like tenant purchase and rural rehabilitation loans that did not immediately endanger paternalism if carefully managed and planter controlled. Programs less amenable to adjustment such as the promotion of cooperatives and formalized leases were dealt with less subtly.

The final area of co-optation involved the exercise of what little local control had actually resulted from the compromise over the original Bankhead-Jones Act. The one FSA program that explicitly provided for oversight by members of the community was the FSA's debt adjustment effort. Here the local county committee had responsibility for negotiating a new schedule for the tenant's debts.[39] In the South, where large planters usually dominated these committees, this arrangement left the tenant dealing with many of the same planters as he had dealt with before the FSA arrived. There was no impartial third party deciding upon a more equitable debt burden and thus no threat to paternalism.

The tenant might have actually looked more favorably upon his landlord if some small adjustments were made and seemed to result from the landlord's generosity. The FSA recognized this dynamic of local control: "Once an adjustment had been made according to the recommendations

---

[37] Larson, "Ten Years of Rural Rehabilitation," p. 338.
[38] Baldwin, *Poverty and Politics*, p. 258.
[39] Larson, "Ten Years of Rural Rehabilitation," p. 7.

of a local group, the farmer whose debts have been adjusted is more likely to look to this group for financial advice in the future. This provides a basis for a measure of continuing informal supervision by local people."[40]

Maintaining the status quo in the South in the face of other FSA programs was more problematic. Certain programs threatened paternalism regardless of how they were managed. For example, tenure improvement was aimed at formalizing the landlord-tenant relationship. It would have greatly limited the scope for the informal give-and-take and the unspoken agreements that were the very essence of paternalism in the South. Promotion of cooperatives was similarly inherently subversive of planter control as such enterprises provided viable substitutes for planter paternalism. Southern opposition to these programs had a much more aggressive character: Co-optation was abandoned in favor of outright coercion of tenants and the manipulation of public opinion.

Opposition to tenure improvement was apparent from the very outset. Planters put numerous impediments in the way of the program's implementation. These problems were readily admitted by the FSA:

Landlord objections to provision for dividing Government benefit payments with tenants were reported. Not uncommonly, the lease was considered just "another form" which was a condition for the loan and was not read, nor taken seriously by either landlord or tenant. . . . Basically, where the lease was a threat to landlord control [as it most certainly was in the South], it might be disregarded by tacit agreement or through coercive measures.[41]

In short, landlords often could prevent FSA interference by both making the lease-writing process difficult and ignoring its results.

The FSA's cooperative programs met still more virulent opposition in the South. That opposition, though, was not confined to the actions of planters trying to subvert the programs in the field. It extended to editorials in the Southern press and resolutions in the Southern legislatures. Planters' willingness to use these other means in their struggle with the FSA (and the willingness of these instruments to be so used) indicates the extent to which this particular program ran against the Southern grain.

A representative editorial, in the Birmingham, Alabama, *Age-Herald*, after voicing some support for the tenant purchase program, charged that the FSA "has gone beyond the two things it was created to do [promote the family farm and reduce tenancy] and in directions of a collectivism exactly contradictory to the ideal of its creation . . . promoting socialistic dreams, dreams of things nearer revolution than reform,

[40] Ibid., p. 261.
[41] Ibid., p. 267.

dreams of a governmental paternalism that goes beyond good sense or good policy."[42] The crux of the matter, then, was this new "governmental paternalism" that was likely to undermine the foundations of Southern society.

Opposition in Congress

The fight against the FSA in Congress had two distinct components. As noted above, the most important was the attempt, led by Southerners, to limit FSA appropriations after 1940.[43] A slightly less well-known form of opposition appears to have been the attempt to alter in small ways, either through legislative or administrative measures, the rules under which the FSA would operate.

A number of such seemingly minor changes were made even before the larger battle over FSA appropriations opened in 1940. We have discussed the shift in responsibility for rural rehabilitation from FERA to the U.S. Department of Agriculture. This was more than just a change in the location of the FSA's offices. It indicated "a shift from being administered by a public assistance agency performing a relief function for rural people . . . to being administered by an agency carrying out primarily an agricultural program with social welfare objectives."[44] The difference signals the direction in which Southerners hoped to move the agency if they could not yet dismantle it.

The county committees had initially been given no more than an advisory role in programs other than debt adjustment. A combination of legislative and administrative actions gave them a great deal more power after 1937. In the rural rehabilitation and tenant purchase loan programs, they came to exercise "certain administrative control functions through passing upon the eligibility of applicants and deciding the action to be taken on cases active 3 or more years."[45] As planters in the South controlled such committees, this action further formalized the accommodation previously reached with them in this area.

This seemingly minor change also signaled a much larger shift with important ramifications for the success of the entire FSA agenda in the

---

[42] Quoted in Baldwin, *Poverty and Politics*, p. 284.

[43] Senator Russell appears to have been an outlier with his continued support. However, he supported agriculture in general and fought and won to save appropriations for parity payments and soil conservation; Fite, *Richard B. Russell, Jr.*, p. 156. One interpretation is that Russell "gave in" behind the scenes on the program that mattered to him the least.

[44] Larson, "Ten Years of Rural Rehabilitation," p. 7.

[45] Ibid.

South: "increased delegation of judgment determinations to the lower administrative levels, and provision through such means as the 'agricultural area' administrative level and special area programs to meet localized needs."[46] Recognition of such "localized needs" played right into the hands of Southern planters.

A final change in this area might seem the most insignificant of all: a shift from the use of both cash and in-kind loans and loan repayments in work, kind, or cash to an exclusive reliance on loans and repayments in cash.[47] Cash loans and repayments were certainly easier to administer than in-kind accounts. Some of the motivation for such a change may thus have been a desire for administrative simplicity and accountability. But the importance of noncash exchanges between planters and tenants in the South may have provided another motivation: a desire to distance the FSA loan program from planter paternalism. Under the new rule, the tenant in receipt of an FSA loan could no longer help to pay back the agency by canning some vegetables or diligently attending meetings with FSA representatives. The loan would have to be a straight business transaction, paid and repaid in cash. Tenants intimidated by the impersonality of such an exchange were left free to seek help from their landlord, who would gladly accept repayment in kind or in hard work.

That these minor changes and adjustments had the effect of turning back some of the FSA's attack on paternalism is not in doubt. That they were solely the work of Southern landholders and their agents cannot be proved. These actions nonetheless bear the unmistakable stamp of Southern influence.

As we have seen, the early Congressional battles over the fate of the FSA amounted to minor skirmishes: changes in rules or administrative procedures, worked out in the Agriculture committees, where Southerners wielded great power. With the start of America's involvement in World War II, however, Southerners gained an opportunity to open hostilities on a new and much more promising front, the appropriations process. Though Southerners were in the minority on the House and Senate Appropriations committees, the preparations being made everywhere for war and the support they received from representatives of other regions where FSA encroachment upon the bureaucratic prerogatives of the local agricultural establishment was feared gave Southerners the chance to voice anew their criticisms of the FSA. The *Atlanta Constitution* reported that the fight to cut the agency's funding was the work of "organizations of large owners and producers."[48]

[46] Ibid.
[47] Ibid., p. 8.
[48] Quoted in Baldwin, *Poverty and Politics*, p. 360.

The crucial difference now was that the appropriations committees could delete funding for all FSA programs, whereas the agricultural committees had to content themselves with merely tinkering with the rules under which the FSA operated. Moreover, the charges of waste, inefficiency, and socialization took on a new urgency after 1940, because even representatives from outside the South and the agricultural establishment were now prepared to listen in the interest of helping the war effort by weeding out such profligacy.

From 1940 to 1942, one of the most prominent Representatives in the drive to cut FSA funding was Malcolm Tarver of Georgia. At various times, he described rural rehabilitation as "morally bad" for needy farmers because it raised their standard of living "too rapidly"; he criticized FSA supervisory activities as detrimental to farmers' self-reliance; and he characterized resettlement projects as "colonization and un-American."[49] He sponsored an amendment to the FSA appropriation for 1941 – the Tarver amendment – that greatly limited the scope of the tenant purchase program. Other Southerners prominent in opposing the FSA through the appropriations process were Clifton Woodrum of Virginia in the House and Carter Glass and Henry Byrd of Virginia, Kenneth McKellar of Tennessee, and Ellison Smith of South Carolina in the Senate.[50]

The ammunition these Southerners used against the FSA was usually supplied by the parade of anti-FSA lobbyists that came before the Appropriations committees, lobbyists either directly employed by the cotton interests of the South or representing national organizations such as the American Farm Bureau Federation (AFBF), which, as we have seen, had their own reasons for opposing the FSA and were generally quite sympathetic to the views of their Southern members on this issue. Oscar Johnston, president of the National Cotton Council and a major cotton planter, and the leaders of the Southern farm bureaus were vocal in opposition to FSA programs even before 1940.[51] After 1940, they were joined by Ed O'Neal and the AFBF. O'Neal was also a cotton planter in Alabama, so although his organization represented farmers in every state it is not surprising that he felt particularly close to the Southerners on this issue.[52]

[49] Ibid., p. 340.
[50] Ibid., p. 318.
[51] Ibid., p. 292.
[52] See McConnell, *Decline of Agrarian Democracy*, pp. 112–25. McConnell, however, tends to underestimate the extent to which the FSA "constituted a serious economic threat to established interests" (p. 125), particularly in the South. He therefore sees the Cotton Council as having been recruited into opposing the FSA by the AFBF, rather than having had its own reasons for opposing the agency. In fact, Southerners

The findings of a "painstaking and thorough" investigation of the FSA's activities in the South, commissioned by the National Cotton Council and presented as part of the testimony by its president, Oscar Johnston, best summarize the various charges leveled against the agency by these lobbyists (and given a sympathetic hearing by the Southern representatives):

[The FSA] is so functioning and so conditioning its activities as to promote gross inefficiency in the matter of culture and production of cotton and cottonseed; to seriously impede the cost of production of cotton and cottonseed; to lower the morale of farm workers engaged in the production of the commodities under consideration; to threaten, disturb, and disrupt economic and social conditions and relationships throughout the Cotton Belt; to threaten those who produce cotton and cottonseed on a commercial basis; to depress the morale of cotton farmers throughout the belt, and ultimately to destroy the business of farming as a free enterprise and a respectable means of earning social and economic security by American farmers.[53]

The most serious charges, therefore, were waste and the erosion of the American free enterprise system, both potentially volatile issues as the United States was preparing for war. These charges were echoed throughout the hearings on the FSA appropriation each year after 1940.

Often the indictment was straightforward. The FSA was performing many of the functions of the Agriculture Department's Extension Service and such duplication was costly. FSA activities therefore should be transferred to the Agricultural Extension Service and its loan programs assumed by the Farm Credit Administration.[54] But frequently the broadsides of FSA opponents combined all three themes: waste, socialization, and the need to concentrate on the war effort rather than such programs as the FSA was operating. A letter introduced by Senator Richard Russell of Georgia, addressed to Senator Glass of Virginia by one of his constituents, used this shotgun approach. It reads in part: "I am writing to say that I hope you will use your influence to uphold the action taken by the House [cutting off FSA funding]. Surely in fighting such a war as we are now fighting, all such socialistic matters should be stopped."[55] Virtually

had all the reasons for opposing the FSA that large planters from other areas represented by the AFBF had; but Southerners also had additional reasons for opposing it. The prominence of Southerners in the fight to kill the FSA is thus not surprising; they successfully drew on the hostility to the FSA embodied in the AFBF and turned it to their advantage.

[53] U.S. Congress, House, Committee on Agriculture, *Agriculture Appropriation Bill Hearings* (1944), I, p. 1619.

[54] Ibid., pp. 412–13, 510.

[55] U.S. Congress, Senate, Committee on Agriculture, *Agriculture Appropriation Bill Hearings* (1944), II, p. 667.

the only thing that this letter and others like it did not do was accuse the FSA administrator, C. B. Baldwin, of being a Communist and his associates of being sympathizers. This task fell to Senator McKellar of Tennessee.[56]

For the most part, however, the debate over the FSA was far less focused than we have suggested. The hearings generally proceeded with Southern lobbyists like Johnston and O'Neal free to rail against the failings of the FSA either real or imagined, with sweeping generalizations and allegations from sources unnamed.[57] When Baldwin appeared before the committee, he was usually queried on alleged irregularities in one or two of the FSA's estimated 700,000 cases, rather than allowed to respond to these general charges.[58] The supporters of the FSA on these committees were less persuaded by these one-sided presentations, which the Southerners engineered, than they were worn down by them year after year.

Finally, after the third full year of these attacks, FSA supporters either gave in or lost: On April 13, 1943, the House Appropriations Committee voted to abolish the FSA. The full House followed suit a week later. Though the Senate took less drastic action by reducing total FSA funding by 5 percent – most likely the result of Senator Russell's support – the final conference report produced what came to be known as the "death appropriation bill." Rural rehabilitation funding was slashed 43 percent, promotion of cooperatives and land leasing by the agency were outlawed, and severe restrictions were placed upon the few remaining loan programs.[59]

The FSA limped on for another three years, but on August 14, 1946, President Harry Truman signed into law the Farmers Home Administration Act of 1946. The Act officially abolished the FSA, amended the original Bankhead-Jones Act, and transferred the FSA tenant purchase program to the new Farmers Home Administration. The FSA was dead at last.

Looking back on the battle in the field and in the Congress, one former FSA official was not entirely surprised by the extent of the Southern opposition:

Those Southerners who were bitterly opposed to us were opposed for understandable reasons. We were in many ways subversive of the *status quo*. . . . The

[56] Baldwin, *Poverty and Politics*, pp. 357–8.
[57] U.S. Congress, House, Committee on Agriculture, *Agriculture Appropriation Bill Hearings* (1943), pp. 770–1.
[58] Representatives Tarver and Cannon were particularly fond of this tactic; ibid., pp. 772–88.
[59] Baldwin, *Poverty and Politics*, pp. 385–94.

programs of the FSA represented a serious threat to the dependence of the farm tenant and sharecropper on his landlord, the store-keeper, and the court-house gang. . . . It didn't take many FSA clients in a Southern county to prove the fact that the FSA was real, that it was there, that the poor farmer need not be so entirely dependent on the rules of this community.[60]

The opposition of the Southerners, then, was expected. But by the late 1950s and early 1960s, former supporters of the FSA may have been surprised to see Southerners speaking up in support of expanded funding for the FHA, even as that new agency was beginning to support cooperatives and emerge as the rural cornerstone of President Lyndon B. Johnson's Great Society. By that time, however, a tenacious defense of paternalism no longer made sense to Southern landed interests. As we shall see in Chapter 6, mechanization had come at last, and with it the demise of plantation paternalism, a socioeconomic system that had endured the better part of a century.

[60] Ibid., p. 282.

5

The Bracero Program and Wartime Farm Labor Legislation

I. Introduction

The South's system of paternalism and social control was threatened, as we have seen, by federal programs like Social Security and the initiatives of the Farm Security Administration that involved direct government intervention in the relationship between landlords and their tenants and workers. But the system was vulnerable in another respect: If workers perceived that they had better prospects elsewhere, the option of migration out of the South would have made workers less willing to accept paternalistic arrangements. The increased demand for labor during the Second World War created just such an option. Much of the labor legislation enacted during the war, particularly the Bracero Program for the importation of Mexican laborers, reflects the influence of Southerners eager to prevent migration out of the South and maintain the viability of paternalism and social control.

The Second World War was a time of unprecedented dislocation in all sectors of the U.S. economy. The federal government transformed whole industries overnight, mobilized civilian armies of workers to man them, and imposed a system of price controls and rationing that prevented the price mechanism from allocating many resources.[1] One result of such wrenching change was that sectors of the economy that stood to lose under such a regime resorted to nonmarket means to protect their interests. The South was no exception and, as we discussed in Chapter 2, also had the political clout to limit intervention in its labor markets.

In this chapter we discuss the efforts of the agricultural interests in the South and the Southwest to ensure the availability of a supply of cheap labor. Through a variety of legislative initiatives, these agricultural inter-

---

[1] The most comprehensive source on the mechanisms and effects of wartime price controls is Rockoff, *Drastic Measures*.

ests initially fought to protect a status quo in the agricultural labor market based on cheap labor and paternalistic relations with workers. Their later goals and victories went well beyond that status quo, however. The result of their actions was a farm labor program that helped assure the continued viability of low-wage agriculture in the South and Southwest into the early 1960s.[2]

Farm labor legislation during the Second World War served specific regional needs through the restrictions it placed on labor mobility. Legislation limited the movement of workers from labor surplus regions into either the armed forces, war industries, or higher-paying farm employment in labor deficit regions. This occurred despite convincing evidence of a considerable excess supply of labor in some regions: In a report to Congress in March 1940, a Congressional committee concluded that the nation's agricultural sector harbored a reserve of at least five million workers who were either "unused or inefficiently used," roughly half unemployed and half underemployed.[3] Subsequent legislation was apparently designed, at least in part, to limit the reallocation of unemployed and underemployed workers across regions.

By the spring of 1942, only a few months after the official entry of the United States into the war and only two years after the Congressional study finding a surplus of farm labor, warnings were sounded in Congress (often by representatives from the relatively labor-rich Southern region) of the dire consequences that would follow from a failure to address a farm labor shortage. Though much wartime labor legislation was enacted in the name of alleviating this supposed shortage of agricultural workers and assuring a continued supply of crucial foodstuffs and non-food commodities such as cotton, the crisis may not have been as severe as Congressional critics contended.

Given the prewar distribution of unemployed and underemployed farm workers, it is unlikely that the extent of labor depletion that existed in fact was either as uniform across regions or as great as the proponents of wartime labor legislation maintained. Even if we concede that their description of the farm labor situation was accurate, however, the solution offered in most of the legislation enacted early in the war – virtually

---

[2] U.S. Congress, House, *Destitute Citizens*, p. 403. See Wright, *Old South, New South*, for more on the results of the continued dependence on low-wage agriculture in the South. Though he dates the onset of recent Southern economic development earlier than we have, Wright suggests as we do that the end of the region's dependence on cheap labor was a key step in that development.

[3] Kaufman, "Farm Labor," provides an invaluable discussion of the issues raised in this report, and indeed of the entire farm labor "problem" as described here. Kaufman was the first to note the discrepancy between the figures used by politicians to justify many farm labor programs during the war and the true magnitudes of those numbers.

Table 5.1. *Unemployment by region (1940)*

Region	Labor force	Number unemployed	Percent unemployed
New England	788,733	106,461	13.5
Mid Atlantic	2,368,712	378,220	16.0
E.N. Central	3,269,224	441,859	13.5
W.N. Central	2,691,796	322,932	12.0
S. Atlantic	3,796,419	386,451	10.2
E.S. Central	2,512,384	283,392	11.3
W.S. Central	2,615,111	337,651	12.9
Mountain	831,046	144,891	17.4
Pacific	1,302,405	200,457	15.4
Total U.S.	20,175,830	2,602,314	12.9

Source: U.S. Census Bureau, *Sixteenth Census*, III, Tables 17 and 18

blanket deferment for farm workers – would not have been helpful unless all farm products were equally important to the war effort. The remedies they offered appear to have been designed less to promote a more efficient allocation of scarce labor resources in agriculture than to preserve the existing regional distribution of farm workers.[4]

This is not to say that the sole or even principal goal of those who supported these programs was to assist large planters in the South and Southwest in maintaining their regional economic hegemony. On the contrary, we suspect that many people were quite sincere in their belief that agricultural labor was desperately scarce in some areas, and that any reasonable plan for national wartime mobilization should address such problems of scarcity. At the same time, however, an understanding of the extent to which these programs served the economic interests of the Southern elite is additional evidence of the importance of cheap and dependent labor to Southern landlords.

II. The Farm Labor Shortage

As can be seen in Table 5.1, rural unemployment varied across regions: In the Southern states it was slightly below the national average of 12.9 percent in 1940, while in the Mountain and Pacific states it was well

[4] This has been pointed out in great detail in Kaufman, "Farm Labor." Both Rockoff, *Drastic Measures*, and Higgs, *Crisis and Leviathan*, also note the power of the farm bloc in winning disproportionate concessions from the government during the war, particularly from the Office of Price Administration.

above the average. These figures, however, understate the amount of available labor to the extent that underemployment existed.[5]

Though it is difficult to estimate the extent of underemployment, one useful measure is average wages, which were lowest in the South. A second measure, suggested in a 1942 study, is the fraction of full-time farmers with gross farm income of less than $1,000.[6] The labor necessary to produce $1,000 in farm products was considered to be less than the labor required in a full-time nonfarm job. Using 1940 Census figures and 1939 earnings data, the Hammer and Buck study found the greatest underemployment by this measure was in the South (See Table 5.2). A measure of available labor that could take account of both unemployment and underemployment would probably rate the South, where underemployment was presumably greatest, and parts of the Southwest, where unemployment exceeded the national average as regions best able to contribute manpower to the war effort and at the same time to maintain or increase agricultural output.

Though a large reserve of unemployed and underemployed workers was initially available, that reserve was depleted over the war years, as the farm population fell and wage costs rose considerably. For the U.S. as a whole, the farm population fell by five million (17 percent) from 1940 to 1945 and farm wages in 1946 stood at two and three quarters times their level in 1939.[7] The greatest percentage decline in the farm population came in the West South Central region, while the greatest increase in wages occurred in the Great Plains states.[8]

The increasing tightness of the farm labor market through 1942 explains much of the subsequent wartime farm labor legislation. When labor markets heated up, support for controlling wages and migration emerged. That support was strongest in the South, where wages had been the lowest before the war. The rising direct wage costs of production in labor-intensive agriculture and the indirect effect of tightening labor markets on the cost of supervising agricultural workers motivated opposition from agriculture to the free mobility of farm labor during the war. Labor mobility probably concerned Southern employers more than employers elsewhere because Southern employers used more labor-intensive production techniques, so wages and supervi-

[5] By "underemployment," we mean the employment of workers where their productivity at the margin was well below the economy-wide average.
[6] Hammer and Buck, "Idle Man Power."
[7] Walter W. Wilcox, *Farmer in the Second World War*, pp. 46 and 99.
[8] Despite the dramatic increase in wages, the war years were good times for farmers: The index of prices received to prices paid increased nearly 50 percent; U.S. Census Bureau, *Historical Statistics*, p. 489.

Table 5.2. *Full-time farmers with gross earned farm income below $1,000 by regions (1939–40)*

Region	Number	Percent of full-time farmers
West	97,607	4
Great Plains	190,038	7
Midwest	474,520	17
Northeast	124,839	5
South	1,829,793	67
Total U.S.	2,716,793	56

Source: Hammer and Buck, "Idle Man Power"

sion costs were a larger percentage of total costs in the South than elsewhere.

III. Early Wartime Farm Labor Legislation

Worker mobility during the war could have resulted from the induction or enlistment of workers into the armed forces, their migration to sites of war industries, the reallocation of farm workers by the government, the recruitment of workers by agents from labor-deficit regions, or the self-initiated movement of workers to labor deficit regions in response to higher wages. Farm labor programs during World War II addressed all of these possible sources of labor depletion.

The induction of farm workers into the armed forces or their easy migration to sites of war industries was largely foreclosed by the passage of the Tydings amendments in 1942. Introduced by Democratic Senator Millard Tydings (MD) as an amendment to the Selective Service Act of 1940, this legislation provided deferments to everyone found by their Selective Service Board to be "necessary to and regularly engaged in an agricultural occupation or endeavor essential to the war effort" for as long as those persons remained so employed in agriculture. A great deal of discretion was left in the hands of the local Selective Service Boards, however, since they were left to determine whether one's work was "essential" to the war effort. Especially in the South, these boards were dominated by the rural agricultural elite, which had an obvious interest in seeing as many of its workers as possible excused from military service.[9]

[9] The elites in the South also dominated the Farm Bureau and the Agricultural Extension Service and, as we shall see below, they were instrumental in securing the passage of further wartime farm labor legislation.

The Senate passed the Tydings amendments as part of a package of amendments to the Selective Service Act of 1940. The amendments survived a conference with the House of Representatives, and became Public Law 772 on November 13, 1942. In the following months, the Selective Service Administration issued a series of guidelines to assist local draft boards in determining whether a farm worker was in fact essential.[10] Each worker's potential contribution to the war effort was measured in "war units," with one unit corresponding to the labor required "for the care of one milk cow or an equivalent amount of work on crops or other livestock."[11] The original guideline used for determining whether a worker was "essential" was sixteen war units. Though this was quite low by the standards of most regions, it was considered too high in the South, because of the large number of underemployed farmers. As a result, Democratic Senator John Bankhead (AL) advocated both changing the war unit standard from a requirement to a goal and lowering the minimum standard to eight units. This was accomplished in January 1943.[12]

Though these guidelines allowed even the least productive agricultural workers to secure deferments, some politicians thought the criteria were still too stringent. Consequently, a further amendment was proposed in 1943 which would have considerably relaxed the loose criteria for deferment contained in the original Tydings amendments: the continued employment of a worker in agriculture would only have to be deemed "in the best interest of the war effort" rather than "essential to the war effort" in order for the worker to secure a deferment.[13] Though this 1943 amendment never passed in the House of Representatives, it passed easily in the Senate (by a vote of 50 to 24) under the guidance of Senator Richard Russell (GA).

From 1943 to the spring of 1945, Congress did not attempt to change the criteria for deferment. However, Congress moved to reinforce farm deferments following a review ordered by the Director of the Selective Service on January 3, 1945 which resulted in the drafting of many previously exempt farm workers.[14] In the Senate on March 2, 1945, Senator

---

[10] A summary of the guidelines is contained in U.S. Selective Service System, "Selective Service," pp. 111–18. Evidence of the laxness of these standards is contained in Kaufman, "Farm Labor," pp. 135–6.

[11] Benedict, *Farm Policies*, p. 438.

[12] Wilcox, *Farmer in the Second World War*, pp. 85–6.

[13] The proposed amendment, as well as a survey of county extension service agents that purports to show the severity of the shortage of agricultural workers resulting from migration and induction, can be found in U.S. Congress, Senate, Committee on Military Affairs, *Report on Deferment*.

[14] The information contained in this paragraph all comes from Rich, *U.S. Agricultural Policy*, p. 77.

The Bracero Program and Wartime Farm Labor Legislation

Tydings inserted language into the Military Manpower Bill (HR 1752) which strengthened farm deferments but the bill died on April 3, 1945. Earlier in the spring Tydings had proposed an amendment that would have imposed $10,000 fines and five-year prison sentences on deferred farm workers who left their jobs without the approval of their draft boards. The amendment passed the Senate Military Affairs Committee but Tydings withdrew the amendment. A bill reinforcing the farm worker draft deferment (House Joint Resolution 106) passed on February 27, 1945. The original bill would have frozen farm workers in their jobs even if they were not eligible for the draft but Republican Representative Charles Halleck (IN) proposed an amendment striking out such a measure. Following Senate and conference action the bill was sent on to President Truman, who vetoed the resolution on May 3, 1945.

The reallocation of farm workers across regions through the operation of government programs was effectively barred by the Pace amendments, which prevented the expenditure of federal funds for the transportation of agricultural workers out of a county without the permission of the county agent.[15] Democratic Representative Stephen Pace (GA) proposed these amendments to the Farm Labor Act of 1943 (Public Law 45), and Senator Richard Russell and Democratic Senator Alben Barkley (KY) shepherded them through the Senate.[16] Like the Tydings amendments, the Pace amendments received the backing of numerous representatives from New England and the North Central states, but the principal regional beneficiary was the South. As one observer has noted:

[The amendment] was designed to hold labor in the South where underemployment was common and wage rates notoriously low. Both the short-term and long-term national interest lay in moving some of the labor out of such areas, but such outmovement was not looked upon with favor by employers in the areas that would thus be deprived of part of their labor supply.[17]

The remaining motivations for the migration of agricultural workers were recruitment by private agents or the lure of higher wages. A number

[15] The programs operated by the federal government that affected farm labor and were the target of these amendments are described in Rasmussen, "Emergency Farm Labor." Rasmussen also provides a good introduction to the informal arrangements with the Mexican government that evolved into the bracero program.
[16] The bill to which the amendments were attached was an early attempt to rein in the Farm Security Administration (FSA), which many representatives of agricultural landowners felt was overly concerned with the welfare of farm labor. This attitude was characteristic of the Farm Bureau Federation (which actually wrote the Pace amendments and much of the rest of the bill) and representatives in Congress from the South and California.
[17] Benedict, *Farm Policies*, p. 439.

of state emigrant agent laws (and the stricter enforcement of existing statutes in the early 1940s) required that agents employed to recruit workers from one state to work in another state be licensed by the state from which the workers would be removed; violation could result in steep fines and prison terms for the offending agent. Of the twelve states with such laws on their books in 1942, eleven were in the South.[18] As Kaufman has noted, "these laws . . . were presumably enacted in order to regulate the recruitment of labor for use outside the state. But, with the exception of Pennsylvania, they were obviously intended to discourage the movement of labor outside the state."[19]

Legislation to keep agricultural labor in the South cheap and available was only partially successful. Wages in the South rose, but except for Florida, Oklahoma, and Texas, they rose less than the national average. Moreover, Southern wages started at a lower level than elsewhere, so the North-South wage gap increased.[20] In absolute numbers, more agricultural workers in the South received deferments than elsewhere but this was a reflection of the labor intensity of the South. In terms of deferments per number employed, the South fell below the rest of the nation, reflecting greater underemployment at the start of the war.[21] Another indicator that the South's success was only partial is reflected in the decline in cotton production over the war years.[22] Nevertheless, despite the mixed impact of legislation, the South still emerged from the war as a low-wage, labor-intensive region.

The wartime programs discussed so far directly curtailed much out-migration of labor from agriculture. The effect of these programs was to leave but one avenue through which farm workers eligible for the draft could leave employment in a state without risking induction into the armed forces: self-initiated migration to another agricultural region. The bracero program effectively closed this last avenue. Unlike the other direct controls on labor mobility, however, the legal importation of Mexican labor, though begun during the war as a temporary measure, continued for nearly two decades after its inception.[23] The political history of

---

[18] The twelfth, Pennsylvania, charged only a nominal licensing fee and provided no penalty for violation. For a discussion of the particular provisions of the various state laws, see Kaufman, "Farm Labor," pp. 139–40. For a discussion of the origin of the emigrant agent laws see Roback, "Southern Labor Law."

[19] Kaufman, "Farm Labor," p. 139.

[20] Wilcox, *Farmer in the Second World War*, p. 96

[21] Ibid., p. 87.

[22] U.S. Department of Agriculture, "Statistics on Cotton," p. 81.

[23] Throughout, we will refer to any legal arrangement by which Mexican labor was permitted into the states as the bracero program. Some scholars use the term "bracero program" only for the legislated program from 1951 to 1964.

the bracero program is further evidence of the South's economic incentive and political ability to maintain cheap labor in the South.

IV. The Bracero Program, 1942–1964

The arrangement for the importation of temporary Mexican farm laborers – the bracero program – that began in 1942, limited the last avenue by which labor surplus regions could lose workers – self-initiated migration. But, unlike the other wartime initiatives, the bracero program continued for nearly twenty years after the war. The program was initiated at the behest of cotton growers in the South and Southwest in response to purported farm labor shortages.[24] By bringing Mexican workers into areas where domestic labor was scarce, this program greatly reduced the range of choices confronting farm workers in labor-surplus regions and made their migration less likely.

A Brief Legislative History of the Bracero Program

The bracero program began as an international agreement between the governments of Mexico and the United States on August 14, 1942. The initial statutory authority for the 1942 treaty came through the discretionary authority of the Commissioner of Immigration to waive the provision of the Immigration Act of 1917 that excluded contract labor. There was a large flow of Mexicans into the U.S. agricultural labor market in the 1920s. Unemployment in the 1930s, and the enforcement by the Commissioner of Immigration of the literacy test, head tax, and contract labor provisions of the Immigration Act of 1917, prevented the use of Mexican labor throughout the 1930s and early 1940s.[25]

The new international agreement did not permit open migration, however. U.S. agricultural employers recruited Mexicans, but the contract was between the individual Mexican and the U.S. government. The United States considered any Mexicans entering the United States during this period without a contract as illegal aliens. The Mexican government's role was to supervise the program and bring grievances to the attention of the United States. The agreement forbade Mexicans from making contracts in any state, such as Texas, where they were subject to discrimination.

---

[24] For background on the initiation of the Mexican labor program see Rasmussen, "Emergency Farm Labor," p. 200; Scruggs, "Mexican Farm Labor"; and Craig, *Bracero Program.*

[25] Scruggs, "Mexican Farm Labor," p. 141.

Southern farm interests played an early role in the bracero program, by voicing their demands to their representatives and the Commissioner of Immigration. In June 1941, Representative Kleberg of Texas wrote to President Roosevelt advocating the importation of Mexican laborers.[26] Other Southwestern legislators followed suit, so that by the time of the negotiation of the treaty, the South and Southwest were firmly aligned in support of a bracero program.

At Mexico's request, the initial importation of Mexican laborers was done under the auspices of the Farm Security Administration. As discussed in Chapter 4, farm interests in the South and Southwest were opposed to the prolabor attitude of the FSA, and consequently they lobbied and succeeded in shifting the administration of the program to the War Manpower Commission in June 1943.[27]

The initial agreement with Mexico was given legislative approval in 1943 when Congress passed Public Law 45, which allowed the government to admit temporary agricultural labor from Central America, South America, and islands in the Caribbean. The bracero program was conceived strictly as a wartime measure, but through a series of bills it was extended until December 31, 1947. The farm bloc's continued demand for cheap reliable labor seems to have been the primary motivation for extending the program beyond the end of the war.

With the expiration of wartime legislation, the only statutory authority for the admission of Mexican labor from 1948 to 1951 was the Immigration Act of 1917. Immigration was restricted and regulated by international agreements made in 1947, 1948, and 1949.[28] Permission for workers to enter the United States was required from the U.S. Employment Service. The lack of a formal agreement between Mexico and the United States during this period is not a sign of the weakness of the farm bloc. In fact, agricultural employers favored the stipulations of the Immigration Act to those of the wartime bilateral agreement with Mexico.[29] The agricultural employer was now considered the contractor as opposed to the U.S. government.

The direct recruitment of Mexicans by U.S. employers under the Immigration Act was criticized by the governments of both Mexico and the United States. A report by the U.S. President's Commission on Migratory Labor (1951), coupled with an increase in the demand for labor due to the Korean War, prompted further action in Congress. In January 1951, the United States sent a delegation to Mexico to discuss creation of a

---

[26] Ibid., p. 143.
[27] Craig, *Bracero Program*, p. 47.
[28] Ibid., p. 53.
[29] Ibid.

The Bracero Program and Wartime Farm Labor Legislation

program acceptable to both sides. The Southern farm interests were well represented in the delegation by Democratic Senator Allen J. Ellender (LA), Chairman of the Senate Committee on Agriculture and Forestry, and Democratic Representative W. R. Poage (TX) of the House Agriculture Committee.

Following these international discussions, Senator Ellender introduced in February 1951 the legislation that eventually resulted in the passage of Public Law 78 on July 13, 1951, which institutionalized the bracero program. With more or less minor changes, the bracero program remained in effect until 1964. Public Law 78 did not allow open immigration of Mexican labor. Instead, U.S. farmers expressed their demands for labor to the U.S. Department of Labor, which in turn requested labor from the Mexican government which oversaw recruitment in Mexico. Temporary Mexican laborers who did not migrate under the auspices of Public Law 78 (the bracero program) were considered illegal aliens.[30]

In addition to shaping the initial legislation, Southern representatives remained solidly behind the program. In Table 5.3, we list the voting preferences in the House of Representatives by state on the renewal of Public Law 78. Only two Southern states, Arkansas and Texas, were major bracero using states. Yet 97%, 92%, and 79% of all Southern Representatives (including Arkansas and Texas) voted in favor of renewing Public Law 78 in 1953, 1961, and 1963. The corresponding percentages for bracero states (excluding Arkansas and Texas) are only 80%, 72%, and 64%. Initially, no group of states opposed the bracero program, but by 1961 the nonbracero states as a group voted against renewing P.L. 78. In the defeat of Public Law 78 in 1963, both the nonbracero states and other states in the aggregate opposed Public Law 78. But even in 1963, no Southern state had a majority of its representatives voting against the bracero program.

The Motivation Behind the Bracero Program

In the previous section, we argued that Southern and Southwestern farm interests acted out of self-interest in establishing and maintaining a program for the importation of Mexican labor. It is often assumed that this self-interest was a desire for low-wage labor. Worry over the escalation of farm wages (or shortages of farm workers) early in the war no doubt motivated the initial demand for Mexican labor. After the enactment of Public Law 78, however, cheap labor – in terms of wages alone – no

[30] For a detailed discussion of the legislative debate that preceded the passage of Public Law 78, see Lyon, "Migratory Farm Labor."

Table 5.3. *Votes on renewal of P.L. 78 in U.S. House of Representatives (1953–63)*

State	Type	1953				1961				1963			
		T	Y	N	A	T	Y	N	A	T	Y	N	A
Alabama	S	9	8	1	0	9	7	0	2	8	5	1	2
Alaska	N	—	—	—	—	1	1	0	0	1	0	1	0
Arizona	B	2	2	0	0	2	1	0	1	3	3	0	0
Arkansas	S	6	5	0	1	6	6	0	0	4	4	0	0
California	B	30	22	4	4	30	23	7	0	38	21	15	2
Colorado	B	4	4	0	0	4	3	1	0	4	3	1	0
Connecticut	N	6	4	1	1	6	1	5	0	6	0	6	0
Delaware	O	1	0	0	1	1	0	1	0	1	0	1	0
Florida	S	8	8	0	0	8	7	1	0	12	9	3	0
Georgia	S	10	10	0	0	10	9	0	1	10	6	2	2
Hawaii	N	—	—	—	—	1	0	0	1	2	0	2	0
Idaho	O	2	2	0	0	2	2	0	0	2	1	1	0
Illinois	O	25	10	10	5	25	6	19	0	24	6	11	7
Indiana	O	11	9	2	0	11	6	4	1	11	4	4	3
Iowa	O	8	4	2	2	8	4	4	0	7	2	5	0
Kansas	O	6	6	0	0	6	6	0	0	5	5	0	0
Kentucky	O	8	5	3	0	8	4	3	1	7	3	4	0
Louisiana	S	8	8	0	0	8	8	0	0	8	3	3	2
Maine	N	3	3	0	0	3	3	0	0	2	1	1	0
Maryland	N	7	4	3	0	7	3	4	0	8	3	5	0
Massachusetts	N	14	6	6	2	14	2	12	0	12	1	8	3
Michigan	B	18	11	6	1	18	9	7	2	19	10	5	4
Minnesota	O	9	5	4	0	9	7	2	0	8	3	4	1
Mississippi	S	6	5	0	1	6	5	0	1	5	4	0	1
Missouri	O	11	5	4	2	11	5	5	1	10	2	4	4
Montana	O	2	2	0	0	2	1	1	0	2	1	1	0
Nebraska	O	4	3	0	1	4	3	1	0	3	2	1	0
Nevada	O	1	1	0	0	1	0	1	0	1	0	1	0
New Hampshire	N	2	1	0	1	2	1	1	0	2	0	2	0
New Jersey	N	14	5	8	1	14	5	8	1	15	2	11	2
New Mexico	B	2	2	0	0	2	2	0	0	2	1	0	1
New York	N	43	19	21	3	43	14	27	2	41	5	31	5
North Carolina	S	12	12	0	0	12	9	0	3	11	9	0	2
North Dakota	O	2	1	1	0	2	2	0	0	2	2	0	0
Ohio	O	23	14	8	1	23	14	8	1	24	9	13	2
Oklahoma	S	6	6	0	0	6	4	1	1	6	4	1	1
Oregon	O	4	3	0	1	4	3	1	0	4	3	1	0
Pennsylvania	N	30	11	14	5	30	6	23	1	27	3	22	2

Table 5.3. (cont.)

State	Type	1953				1961				1963			
		T	Y	N	A	T	Y	N	A	T	Y	N	A
Rhode Island	N	2	0	2	0	2	0	2	0	2	0	2	0
South Carolina	S	6	5	0	1	6	6	0	0	6	6	0	0
South Dakota	O	2	2	0	0	2	1	1	0	2	2	0	0
Tennessee	S	9	7	2	0	9	5	3	1	9	3	4	2
Texas	S	22	22	0	0	22	18	3	1	23	13	6	4
Utah	O	2	1	0	1	2	2	0	0	2	2	0	0
Vermont	N	1	0	0	1	1	1	0	0	1	0	1	0
Virginia	S	10	8	0	2	10	9	0	1	10	10	0	0
Washington	O	7	6	1	0	7	4	3	0	7	3	4	0
West Virginia	O	6	1	5	0	6	0	6	0	5	0	5	0
Wisconsin	O	10	5	4	1	10	5	5	0	10	3	6	1
Wyoming	O	1	1	0	0	1	1	0	0	1	1	0	0
Total		435	284	112	39	437	244	170	23	435	183	199	53

Notes: Each state is placed in one of four categories: Bracero states (B): The seven states that employed over 10,000 bracero months during any year between 1954 and 1964 inclusive. The number of bracero months in other states falls off quite rapidly after these seven states. Montana was the next largest user of braceros and averaged 3,000 bracero months a year. Southern states (S): The twelve states of the old Confederacy plus Oklahoma. Nonbracero states (N): The fourteen states that employed no braceros between 1954 and 1964 inclusive, excluding Southern states in the above category. Other states: The twenty non-Southern states which do not fall into the above categories. All of these states employed some braceros between 1954 and 1964 inclusive, although not enough to be considered a major bracero using state. The votes were based on compilations in the *Congressional Digest*: Yes (Y) if the Representative voted yea upon, paired for, or announced for; No (N) if the Representative voted nay upon, paired against, or announced against. An abstention (A) was recorded if the Representative voted a general pair or was absent for the vote. Vacancies were also counted as abstentions. The total number of votes cast by the state's delegation is also shown (T). The total vote in 1961 was 437 because, with the entrance of Alaska and Hawaii into the U.S., the size of the House of Representatives was allowed to increase temporarily from its maximum of 435. After reapportionment for the 88th Congress (1963), the size was again reduced to 435.
Source: Votes are from *Congressional Digest* (various issues, 1953–63); data on bracero hours are from U.S. Department of Labor, Bureau of Employment Security, *Farm Labor Market Developments* and *Farm Labor Market Development: Employment and Wage Supplement,* yearly issues

longer seemed to be the only motivation for support of the bracero program, because the total cost of bracero labor exceeded that of domestic
farm workers and most likely the cost of illegal Mexican workers.[31] If
direct labor costs did not motivate Southern and Southwestern support
for the program, what did?

In the eyes of agricultural growers, Mexican labor differed from domestic labor in their willingness to work harder. What differentiated the
braceros from illegal Mexican workers was the dependability of the braceros. Both attributes are desirable in agriculture because of the high
supervision costs associated with agricultural labor and the importance
of timing in the harvest. Braceros were more dependable than illegal
Mexican workers almost by definition. With illegal workers, it was difficult to negotiate contracts prior to their arrival. Moreover, employers
were never certain if and when the U.S. Immigration Service would crack
down on illegal entrants.

It has been suggested that Mexicans worked harder than domestic
laborers because they were more accustomed to stoop labor and long
hours in Mexico.[32] This may be in part true, but a better explanation for
their greater willingness to work hard was that the opportunity cost for
Mexicans of losing their jobs in the United States was greater than that
for domestic laborers. For Mexicans, the bracero program represented
an opportunity to earn enough money to purchase land in Mexico. The
fact that the number of Mexicans who wanted to be braceros exceeded
the number of available positions suggests that Mexicans were not indifferent between domestic and U.S. wages. Hancock estimates $5.80 as the
daily bracero wage in 1957 and sixty-three cents as the daily wage for
similar work in Mexico.[33] Thus bracero wages were nine times greater
than what a Mexican could earn at home.

The above arguments suggest that support for the bracero program
should have come from Representatives of states that used braceros. This
was the case, but as noted above, solid support also came from the
South, where few braceros were employed. In 1959, for example,
twenty-four states used braceros, but 94 percent of them were employed

[31] Craig, *Bracero Program*, p. 80. This is true on the margin for an individual
employer, but in the absence of a bracero program, wages for domestic workers most
likely would have been considerably higher. There is still some debate as to whether
braceros received direct cash wages equal to the cash wages paid to domestic workers.
Galarza, *Strangers in Our Fields*, argues that braceros were paid less than domestics,
but he does not include the cost to employers of providing Mexican labor with transportation, housing, and work guarantees.
[32] Craig, *Bracero Program*. In the 1950s and 1960s Californians, in areas employing
braceros, believed that braceros were farm employers in Mexico. We thank Clark
Nardinelli, a native Californian, for this anecdote from his youth.
[33] Hancock, *Role of the Bracero*, p. 29.

in Texas, California, Arkansas, and New Mexico.[34] Of the Southern states, only Texas and Arkansas employed many braceros, yet Representatives from other Southern states consistently supported the program.

Support for the program from Representatives of the Southern states that did not use braceros appears to have been the result of a desire on the part of agricultural interests in those states to protect their own local sources of farm labor. Given that the Deep South had a labor force experienced in cotton cultivation, Southerners may have feared that in the absence of a bracero program, the expanding cotton regions of the Southwest and California would draw away their labor and bid up wages. Their fear may have been well-founded. Musoke and Olmstead have shown the close integration of the national market for cotton-picking labor. They find that from the mid-1920s to the mid-1950s, wages for cotton picking moved together across all cotton-picking states.[35] In response to the fear of losing their labor to the Southwest, Southerners became and remained strong supporters of the bracero program.[36]

Though economic interest motivated grower support for a program of importing Mexican laborers, landowners preferred a program that did not entail much participation by the governments of Mexico and the United States. One manifestation of this desire was the continuing attempt to place control of the program in agencies sympathetic to agricultural grower interests, rather than in the FSA, where it had originally been placed. From 1951 to 1964, the Department of Labor was in charge of the bracero program, yet there were periodic attempts in Congress to shift some or all of the authority for the program to the Department of Agriculture which was much more sympathetic to the interests of growers.

The U.S. government wanted a hand in the program in order to appease domestic labor interests, but more importantly for diplomatic reasons: Mexico argued that it wanted the U.S. government's active participation to safeguard Mexican workers from exploitation. The Mexican government was the most vocal proponent of a formal intergovernmental program. What did Mexico gain from the program? Whether the program required the participation of the two governments, Mexico might have benefitted from the financial and human capital and foreign

[34] Craig, *Bracero Program*, p. 130.

[35] Musoke and Olmstead, "Rise of the Cotton Industry," pp. 397–8. In addition to showing the regional integration of the labor market for cotton, the data presented by Musoke and Olmstead indicate the tremendous impact of World War II on wages for seasonal labor. Over the course of the war cotton-picking wages increased threefold; p. 398.

[36] Naturally, all employers would like to limit job mobility and prevent wages from rising, but few have the political power to do so.

exchange brought home by returning braceros.[37] Hancock estimates that braceros brought back into Mexico no less than $120 million annually in the late 1950s.[38] In addition, the program generated a steady stream of bribes to the Mexican bureaucrats who oversaw the program.[39]

Bribes resulted from the fact that the supply of braceros exceeded the demand. This comes as no surprise given the ninefold differential in wages. Bribery, or *mordida*, most likely amounted to at least $7.2 million in 1957.[40] Aspiring braceros paid approximately 7 percent of their net income in bribes.[41] At first blush, this figure may appear rather low, but not when one recognizes that the next best option of braceros was not necessarily work in Mexico but agricultural work in the United States as an illegal worker. The realization of bribes gives a motive for why the Mexican government tried to stem the flow of illegal workers. Officials in the federal government probably did not receive much direct financial reward from the existence of *mordida*, but they may have enhanced their political support by controlling the initial allocation of bracero contracts.[42]

The Longevity of the Bracero Program

Though the bracero program originated as an emergency wartime measure, it remained in existence nearly twenty years after the war ended.

[37] In the initial 1942 agreement between Mexico and the United States, employers withheld 10 percent of bracero wages and deposited them in Mexican banks. This provision was only in effect from 1942 to 1948; U.S. Congress, House, *Admission of Aliens*, pp. 29–35.

[38] Hancock, *Role of the Bracero*, p. 37. Hancock's estimate is based on data for 1957. In 1957 employers hired 440,000 braceros for an average stay of one hundred days. After deducting for expenses, room and board, and days off, Hancock estimates that the average bracero brought back at least $275. This amount times the number of braceros hired for 1957 yields $121 million.

[39] Craig, *Bracero Program*, pp. 13–19.

[40] Ibid., p. 134. On the basis of interviews with braceros, Galarza states that braceros paid between $12 and $25 in *mordida* to obtain their contracts; Galarza, *Strangers in Our Fields*, p. 36. Multiplying the midpoint of this range by 440,000 (the number of braceros hired in 1957) yields $8.14 million in bribes, which is close to the figure estimated by Craig.

[41] The real cost exceeded 7 percent because *mordida* was paid up front. Assuming a reasonable discount factor of 15 percent would raise the cost of *mordida* closer to 8 percent. For our calculation we used the estimate of bracero take-home income of $275.00 in Hancock, *Role of the Bracero*, p. 37, and the midpoint estimate of *mordida*, $18.50, in Galarza, *Strangers in Our Fields*, p. 36.

[42] Federal officials assigned bracero quotas to the Mexican state governors who in turn assigned them to municipalities. In addition to paying a bribe, it was almost a necessary condition that aspiring braceros be registered as voters in the official Partido Revolucionario Institucional (PRI); Hancock, *Role of the Bracero*, p. 66.

The Bracero Program and Wartime Farm Labor Legislation

The program survived the years immediately after the war despite a national concern over unemployment. Part of the reason for this was that there was not a strong political constituency opposing the program. In addition, many returning veterans preferred jobs in the expanding industrial sector to the jobs in agriculture they had left. More importantly, however, the program survived because of the political power of the interests it served.

The bracero program was considered an agricultural issue rather than a labor issue, and therefore came under the jurisdiction of the House and Senate Agriculture committees. Throughout the lifetime of the program, the chairmen of both committees were known supporters of the program, as were most committee members; furthermore, Southerners were the most senior members of both committees.[43] From 1951 through 1964, Democratic Representative Harold Cooley (NC) was the ranking Democrat on the House Agriculture and Forestry Committee, and Senator Ellender (LA) was the ranking Democrat on the Senate Agriculture Committee.

In addition to controlling the committees responsible for bracero legislation, proponents of the program were able to portray the program as being in the national interest. They claimed that the program was good for national defense, would reduce the number of illegal Mexican immigrants, and was good for Mexican-American relations.[44] Whether valid or not, these rationalizations made it easier to logroll votes to assure passage of bracero legislation, particularly in the early years of the program.

Congress extended Public Law 78 six times. Throughout the 1950s, these extensions passed without much difficulty, but they became increasingly difficult to secure after 1960. Several explanations might account for this:

1. By the early 1960s, the bracero program was less important to its advocates than it had been earlier because the demand for agricultural labor in the South was declining with the widespread adoption of the mechanical cotton picker (made possible by the introduction of improved gins and chemical defoliants).
2. Nonmechanized fruit and vegetable growers now had established relations with Mexican workers who would continue to cross the border illegally in the absence of a formal program.
3. The domestic forces opposed to the program, particularly labor groups, gained lobbying strength.

[43] On the importance of Congressional committees in shaping legislation and directing the subsequent course of the bureaucracies it creates, see Chapter 2.
[44] Craig, *Bracero Program*, p. 90.

4. The "national interest" argument became increasingly implausible over time.

5. The Kennedy administration in general was at best indifferent to the program, and the Secretary of Labor was openly opposed.

It is difficult to assess the relative importance of these explanations, but a look at the changing pattern of votes for and against extending the program sheds some light on the issue. Within states, changes in voting behavior could arise from: (1) replacement of a Representative by another from the same party with a different attitude toward the program; (2) replacement of a Representative by another from a different party with a different attitude toward the program; (3) a change of mind by the same Representative; or (4) reapportionment and hence more or fewer total votes within a state.

Between 1953 and 1961, the number of yes votes on Public Law 78 fell by 40, the number of no votes increased by 58, and the number of abstentions fell by 16. The single most important cause of this change appears to be increases in Congress in the number of Democrats from outside the South. Democrats from states outside the South that did not employ many braceros had opposed the bracero program from its inception, while Northern Republicans had aligned themselves with the Southern bloc and the partisan vote in the bracero states in favor of the program. Between 1953 and 1961, Republicans lost 47 seats in the House to Democrats. Of these 47 seats, 41 were lost in the nonbracero states and other states. Of these 41 seats, 10 Republicans had voted no in 1953. Of the remaining 31 yes Republican votes or abstentions in 1953, when party affiliation changed to Democrat in 1961, 26 votes changed to no.

Between 1953 and 1961, Democrats lost 8 seats to Republicans. In nonbracero or other states, they lost a total of 5. Of the 5 seats lost in the nonbracero and other states, in one case the Democrat had voted yes in 1953. In the remaining 4 cases, 3 no votes changed to yes with Republican representation. This suggests that the alliance between Northern Republicans and Southern Democrats held through the 1961 vote.

Between 1961 and 1963, the number of yes votes on Public Law 78 fell by 61, the number of no votes went up 29, and abstentions went up 30. This time the deciding factor was a change of mind by the same representative. For those representatives who changed their minds from yes to no, we present the breakdown by region and party in Table 5.4.[45]

---

[45] This table includes only Representatives present in both Congresses. The difference between the total of thirty-nine votes switching from yes to no in Table 5.4 and the net increase of twenty-nine no votes between 1961 and 1963 in Table 5.3 is

Table 5.4. *Party and state affiliation of Representatives who changed their votes from Yes to No on P.L. 78 between 1961 and 1963*

	Republicans	Democrats	Total
Bracero states	1	2	3
Southern states	0	8	8
Nonbracero states	13	3	16
Other states	8	4	12
Total	22	17	39

Source: Calculated from Table 5.3

Regional support fell along the lines expected: nonbracero states and other states shifted the most. What seems to have happened is that Northern Republicans changed their allegiance. Northern Republicans were not aligned with the Kennedy administration but rather were voting partners with Southern Democrats, in what was known as the conservative coalition. This suggests that change in Southern agriculture was responsible for the change in the Republican votes. With the increased adoption of the mechanical cotton picker, Southern Democrats now valued the program less and were no longer willing to pay the price in terms of logrolling to ensure its passage.[46] In addition, because of increased opposition from unions and the Secretary of Labor, the price of a yes vote for Northern Republicans may have been increasing.[47]

It is suggestive to see how the mechanization of the cotton crop changed over this short period (Table 5.5). In all Southern states, over a third of all cotton was mechanically harvested by 1963. By 1964, more

accounted for by Representatives who switched from no to yes or abstain and by the departure of Representatives who had voted no in 1961 and the arrival as a result of reapportionment of new Representatives who voted yes or abstained in 1963.

[46] Hawley, "Politics of the Mexican Labor Issue," p. 173, argues that as mechanization proceeded the cotton interests became less concerned with braceros. It is instructive to note that in 1963 Senator Ellender, the Senate architect of Public Law 78, declared that he would not support a further extension of the law if the program were allowed to continue for one more year (p. 174). Reapportionment between 1961 and 1963 resulted in no net change in Southern representation, though the states that lost Representatives (Alabama lost one, Arkansas lost two, Mississippi lost one, and North Carolina lost one) were probably more favorably inclined toward the program than Florida, which gained four of the five seats lost by these states. Texas also gained one seat.

[47] Hawley describes the increased strength of the reform bloc in the early 1960s and their efforts to paint the bracero program as immoral; ibid., pp. 172–4. He suggests that the reform bloc had the most impact on urban Congressmen.

Southern Paternalism and the American Welfare State

Table 5.5. *Percentage of upland cotton harvested mechanically (1961–5)*

Year	AL	AR	GA	LA	MS	NC	OK	SC	TN	TX	U.S.
1961	20	51	32	56	48	11	65	23	26	64	59
1962	29	68	39	64	58	27	73	32	41	78	70
1963	37	73	53	75	65	43	75	42	44	81	72
1964	55	75	62	78	68	59	83	63	56	85	78
1965	73	83	78	82	76	65	84	73	70	90	85

Source: U.S. Department of Agriculture, "Statistics on Cotton," p. 218

than half of the cotton was mechanically harvested in each state. The corresponding figure for 1965 is two thirds. In the early 1960s, Mexican labor for the cotton harvest was becoming substantially less important than it had been in earlier years. Braceros accounted for 27 percent of the seasonal labor force used in the cotton harvest in 1958, but accounted for only 2.8 percent by 1963.[48]

The mechanization of cotton should not be viewed as completely exogenous to the bracero program. Beginning in the late 1950s, the Labor Department began rigorously to enforce compliance with Public Law 78.[49] Housing and other conditions of employment were now regularly inspected. In 1962, Secretary of Labor Willard Wirtz, backed by a federal court decision, established and enforced statewide minimum wages.[50] Meeting the now more stringent standards of the bracero program made bracero labor less attractive to some agricultural employers and on the margin would have increased the adoption of cotton pickers. Increased enforcement and the general hostility of the Labor Department to the bracero program naturally made the program less attractive to agricultural interests and reduced the costs of losing the program.

Whether the demise of the bracero program was the result of a decline in the economic benefits of the bracero program to Southerners and Southwesterners or whether it was a result of a loss in political power is difficult to assess. The case of the expansion of the welfare state in the 1960s, which we address in the next chapter, is less ambiguous.

[48] U.S. Department of Agriculture, Economic Research Service, "Termination of the Bracero Program," pp. 17, 21.
[49] Grove, "Cotton Economy."
[50] Hawley, "Politics of the Mexican Labor Issue," p. 174. The enforcement of minimum wages pertained to domestic and foreign labor.

118

6

Mechanization and the Disappearance of Paternalism

I. Introduction

The tenacious opposition of the white Southern elite to interference in its dealings with Southern farm labor was, as we have seen, consistent with a desire to maintain a system of paternalistic relations with those workers. As long as the cultivation and harvest of cotton required a large supply of cheap, dependable laborers, landed interests had a strong incentive to prevent or limit both the government programs that would have been seen by workers as substitutes for the benefits offered by planters and the migration of workers out of the South. But, by the 1960s, many of the programs originally opposed by the Southern rural elite had come into being without solid Southern opposition, and millions of farm workers had left for the cities of the South and North. We believe that mechanization of cotton was the major catalyst for bringing about the rapid expansion of the federal welfare state and the massive outmigration from the rural South.

Mechanization and the appearance of accompanying science-based technology reduced the economic incentive to provide paternalism. The advances in science that accompanied mechanization increased and stabilized yields, making the farm-specific knowledge of tenants less valuable. Because labor turnover was no longer as costly, the benefits of supplying paternalism were reduced. Mechanization also directly reduced the costs of labor and generating labor effort. With millions of farm workers displaced, the threat of unemployment was sufficient to generate work intensity. Furthermore, mechanization directly reduced the costs of monitoring labor by standardizing the production process and reducing the variation in the marginal productivity of labor. Paternalism became an outdated contractual device.

One might think that the mechanization of Southern agriculture that displaced labor prompted changes in the interests of politicians because

119

of changed political constituencies. Then, one could ignore the economic interests of the rural South in explaining the lack of Southern resistance to Great Society welfare programs and look only at the interests of the new urban constituents. Such thinking is erroneous. The displaced workers in the South – many of them black – for the most part did not vote and as such did not form a new constituency, at least not until the Voting Rights Act took effect, and this did not occur until *after* the passage of the Economic Opportunity Act (which we discuss below) – the heart of the modern welfare state. The most influential constituents, the wealthy rural elite, did not disappear. Gavin Wright, discussing the South's receptivity to civil rights legislation in the 1960s, emphasized the importance of the changed attitudes of this elite: He suggests that, though the desire of business interests to market the region to outsiders was important in transforming attitudes toward race, "it is even more important to recognize the basic contribution of the voices that were *not* heard on the other side, the planters and other protectors of the old isolated low-wage Southern labor market."[1] In examining social welfare legislation, we believe that changes in the attitudes of the existing constituency, the white rural elite, were more decisive than the birth of new constituencies. Furthermore, relative seniority in Congress insulated Southern Congressmen somewhat from the changes, if any, in constituent interests. Southern Congressmen who stayed in office after mechanization were on committees that could serve the interests of the rural South, like the Agriculture Committee, and as such most likely continued to cater to the interests of the rural South. Switching committees to serve the interests of a new constituency did not make political sense.

Evidence in support of our view that political constituencies did not change immediately with the onset of mechanization comes from examining the elections of the 86th (1959–60) through 90th (1967–8) Congresses and the revealed preferences of Southerners for committee assignments.[2] Southern Congressmen were not turned out of office wholesale with the onset of mechanization. In the 86th through 90th Congresses, the South elected thirty-two new Democratic Representatives, a rate of turnover lower than that outside the South in the same period. Nor did the new Representatives seemingly cater to a new constituency. Of the newly elected Southern Democratic Representatives, none whose predecessors were on committees most concerned with social welfare and agriculture requested a different committee assignment from his predecessor.

[1] Wright, *Old South, New South*, p. 268; italics in original.
[2] We are grateful to Kenneth Shepsle for providing data on requests for committee assignments by incoming Congressmen.

Mechanization and the Disappearance of Paternalism

To test our hypothesis that mechanization eroded the economic incentive to provide paternalism, we would ideally like a consistent measure of the prevalence of paternalism that we could correlate with the degree of mechanization in agriculture. No such measure of paternalism exists. Instead, we will take a different tack and rely on several pieces of circumstantial evidence, as well as the limited direct evidence that does exist.[3]

The first pieces of evidence are the association between mechanization and tenancy and the association between tenancy and paternalism. If mechanization reduced tenancy because of a decline in monitoring and turnover costs, it is likely that mechanization indirectly prompted a decline in paternalism. The second piece of evidence is a proxy for the extent of social control: perceptions by blacks of race relations. One of the hallmarks of the South's system of social control was a certain form of race relations. Blacks were expected to show deference to whites in general under the system of social control, but in particular to employers who provided paternalistic benefits. If mechanization prompted changes in race relations, these changes would have signaled the erosion of the system of social control. Because paternalism was linked to the system of social control, changes in paternalism would have taken place as a result. The third piece of evidence is the use of Southern political power. If Southern Congressmen retained their dominance in the committee hierarchy and yet the welfare state expanded in ways previously thwarted, this is consistent with the hypothesis that Southerners retained their power to limit welfare measures but chose not to do so. Moreover, if paternalism was still important to the South, the welfare programs of the sixties had a paradoxical bias: they encouraged rural outmigration from the South.

II. Plowing Up Paternalism

The causal connection between mechanization and the decline in tenancy in the South has been established by a number of scholars. As the adoption of the cotton picker climbed – 42% of upland cotton was harvested mechanically in 1960, 82% in 1965, and nearly 100% in 1969 – mechanization caused a continuous decline in tenancy.[4] Tenancy began to fall

---

[3] For a methodological discussion of the role of circumstantial evidence in economic history, see Fogel, "Circumstantial Evidence."

[4] See U.S. Department of Agriculture, "Statistics on Cotton"; Wright, *Old South, New South*; Fite, *Cotton Fields No More*; Kirby, *Rural Worlds Lost*; Aiken, "Decline of Sharecropping"; Street, *New Revolution*; Day, "Technological Change"; Daniel, *Breaking the Land*; Maier, "Adoption of the Mechanical Cotton Picker"; and Whatley, "Impediments to Cotton Mechanization." Tenancy also fell for reasons other than mechanization. The most notable cause was the decline in cotton acreage prompted by government agricultural policy ostensibly aimed at soil conservation but

before complete mechanization. Scholars such as Street and Day contend that partial mechanization (i.e. the introduction of the tractor) caused both a decline in the number of tenants and a decline in the ratio of tenants to wage workers. Plowing with a tractor resulted in less labor demand throughout the season, as significant amounts of labor were now needed only for weeding and harvesting.

As a result, Day argues, the "maintenance of sharecroppers the year round became uneconomic. Instead, a combination of resident wage labor and labor hired from nearby villages was favored."[5] The logical difficulty with this view is that it sees sharecropping as an inflexible arrangement rather than a contractual form in which several margins can be adjusted. For example, just as the share could be adjusted, so too could in-kind benefits such as housing or medical care. Nevertheless, the observation that tenancy fell with partial mechanization is correct. We contend that the rationale for the decline in tenancy with partial mechanization is the same as the rationale in the case of complete mechanization: Monitoring costs fall with standardized techniques and with the increased unemployment or underemployment wrought by a decline in the demand for labor.[6]

Street argues that partial mechanization prompted a variety of changes in contractual arrangements: (1) During the war, when male labor was particularly scarce, females would receive a small sharecrop plot for hoeing and picking, and males, when home from jobs in war industries, would be hired on a part-time wage labor basis; (2) Some landlords continued to use sharecroppers but charged croppers for tractor operations; (3) The landlord's share increased in recognition of his increased inputs; and (4) The labor force was divided into two parts, enough sharecroppers for weed control and the remainder wage workers.[7] For the South as a whole, tenancy peaked in 1930 and fell thereafter. Wage labor also declined from 1930 to 1960 but not by as much as tenancy.[8]

---

actually proposed to raise farm income. See Aiken and Prunty, "Demise of the Piedmont Cotton Region"; Alston, "Tenure Choice"; and Fite, *Cotton Fields No More.* A notable omission from most historical accounts of mechanization is the role played by the importation of Mexican agricultural workers under the bracero program. The bracero program relieved some of the peak labor demand at harvest, encouraging the adoption of the tractor and eroding paternalism through the same mechanism discussed below. The bracero program also appears to have delayed the adoption of the cotton picker in Texas and Arkansas. See Grove, "Cotton Economy."

[5] Day, "Technological Change," p. 439.
[6] Brannen, "Relation of Land Tenure," observed the same effect in reverse in the 1920s: Planters increased the use of tenant contracts in the face of labor scarcity.
[7] Street, *New Revolution,* pp. 218–27.
[8] Aiken and Prunty, "Demise of the Piedmont Cotton Region"; Alston, *Costs of Contracting,* pp. 2–4, and LeRay, Wilber, and Crowe, "Plantation Organization."

Hence there was a relative shift out of tenant contracts and into wage labor.

Street argues, as have others, that sharecrop contracts secure labor better than wage contracts. The argument is that sharecroppers stay through the harvest for their share whereas wage workers are paid by the day, week, or month. But this ignores the fact that some wage workers are contracted for the year. Furthermore, there seems to be no logical reason precluding the withholding of some wages until after harvest – say as a bonus. Furthermore, as Woodman has noted, sharecroppers are legally wage workers paid with a share of the crop.[9] The reason a sharecrop contract holds workers better is because sharecroppers earn more on average than wage workers. Therefore, given that landlords advance subsistence to both wage workers and croppers and withhold the rest until the end of the season, sharecroppers would forfeit more by leaving before the end of the season.[10] In the same way, tenant contracts secure labor better than sharecrop contracts. Though data is scarce on the income of croppers and tenants, Ferleger reports data that is consistent with our view: In 1913, in the Mississippi-Yazoo Delta, sharecroppers earned an annual income of $333 compared to $398 for share tenants and $478 for cash tenants.[11]

Because tenant contracts were for the year and the length of wage contracts varied, a direct comparison between the number of tenants and the number of hired laborers is inappropriate. An alternative is to compare the ratio of tenants to real wages paid. For the cotton South (the former Confederacy minus Virginia and Florida plus Oklahoma) the ratio of tenants to real wages paid fell from 0.0141 to 0.00018 between 1930 and 1960, a decline of nearly 100 percent. The variation across the cotton South in the relative use of tenant contracts also declined between 1930 and 1960.[12] Tenants numbered close to 1.8 million in 1930, fell to under one million by 1950, and then plummeted to three hundred sixty thousand by 1959. In the next decade, the number fell in half again.

The most precipitous drop in tenancy came during the 1950s, the period when scholars contend that outmigration from the agricultural South became dominated by push rather than pull factors. Heinicke disputes the claim that push factors alone were responsible for the rural black migration in the 1950s, but nevertheless concludes that "labor demand in agriculture fell at least as fast (and in the cotton harvest labor

---

[9] Woodman, "Post–Civil War Southern Agriculture."
[10] Alston, "Tenure Choice."
[11] Ferleger, "Sharecropping Contracts."
[12] Alston, *Costs of Contracting*, pp. 1–3.

market faster than) as labor supply."[13] Even if pull factors played a major role in outmigration in the 1940s and 1950s, paternalism was not necessarily a failure in securing labor. We need to know the counterfactual: how much migration would have occurred in the absence of paternalism? We know that planters responded to the tight labor market of the 1940s by individually offering more paternalistic benefits and by collectively fostering state and local government improvements in schools and other social services. For example, the plantation elite were instrumental in encouraging state governments to provide better schools as a means of discouraging outmigration.

It could be, as Day contended, that the initial push off the farm was from rural farm to rural nonfarm.[14] Indeed, between the 1950 and 1960 censuses the rural nonfarm population in the Delta increased by 93 percent while the rural farm population fell by 54 percent.[15] The fact that during the 1950s the nonfarm rural South absorbed some of the farm displacement suggests that planters would not need to rely on paternalism as much as previously. Nevertheless, because displacement varied considerably across the South, and labor supply was not homogeneous, paternalism would still have been important in some regions during the 1950s, especially to secure the most valuable laborers. Though tenancy began to decline in the 1930s, paternalism did not fade away immediately. It appears as if paternalism began to wane in the 1950s with rapid mechanization and the decline in cotton acreage.

Cotton acreage in the South increased by 1.4% from 1940 to 1950 and decreased by 51.8% from 1950 to 1960.[16] Cotton acreage decreased the most in nondelta states. Adoption of the cotton picker on the other hand was negligible in the nondelta Southern states (excluding Texas): The percentage of acreage harvested mechanically did not exceed 8% in any nondelta Southern state (except Texas), while it ranged from 36% in Arkansas, to 38% in Mississippi, and 50% in Louisiana in 1959.[17] Though both the absolute number of tenants and their number relative to the size of the agricultural labor force peaked in the 1930 census,

---

[13] Heinicke, "Black Migration," p. 219. Heinicke, unpublished paper, argues that although mechanization pushed blacks off the farm in the 1950s it can account for at most 24 percent of the black migration from the rural South during the 1950s. Heinicke, "Black Migration," p. 236, argues further that other push factors were at work besides mechanization. Most notable was the decline in cotton production, some of which he argues was caused by tractorization but also by government farm programs, increased production in the Western states, increased production abroad, and competition from synthetic fibers.

[14] Day, "Technological Change," p. 443.

[15] Ibid.

[16] Heinicke, "Black Migration," table 2.8, p. 53.

[17] U.S. Department of Agriculture, "Statistics on Cotton," p. 218.

Mechanization and the Disappearance of Paternalism

there is considerable anecdotal evidence that paternalism was still used in the thirties and the war years. Paternalism did not begin to decline immediately with the decline in tenancy for several reasons: (1) The unemployment that in part led to the substitution of wage workers for tenants was not expected to be permanent and paternalism more so than tenancy represented a long-term contract; (2) the Agricultural Adjustment Act (AAA) that led to a reduction in labor demand and thereby a reduction in tenancy was initially an emergency measure whose future life was uncertain, as demonstrated by the Supreme Court's ruling it initially unconstitutional; and (3) the cost of using paternalism was in part subsidized through the funds of the Resettlement Administration, which the local elites controlled.[18] We present direct evidence on the disappearance of paternalism in the late 1950s and early 1960s at the end of Section III in this chapter.[19]

The decline in the number of tenants and in the ratio of tenants to wage workers prompted a reduction in the provision of a variety of in-kind goods and services to workers – most notably food and housing – because of economies of scale.[20] Previously, if plantation owners provided their workers with food and shelter, they had more contact with them, became more familiar with them, and could thereby provide paternalism at a lower cost. This is because contact and knowledge allowed them to identify "good" workers more easily and provide them with greater paternalism, reinforcing in the minds of workers the causal link between performance and the receipt of paternalism. When fewer in-kind goods were provided, the reduced contact between employers and workers raised the cost of providing paternalism.

We are advancing a supply-side story for the decline in paternalism, but there was no doubt a decline in the demand for paternalism caused by rising income and education levels which would have diminished the value of planter intercession in many commercial transactions and in legal and social difficulties. However, unless one advocates a threshold model for the impact of education and income on paternalism, the steady climb in these factors would have had only a modest impact on the decline in paternalism because education and income had been rising over the course of the twentieth century with little discernible impact on paternalism. An alternative demand explanation for the decline in paternalism is World War II. After seeing how the rest of the world worked, former tenants were reluctant to come back to a system of paternalism

[18] See Chapter 4 on this last point.
[19] The evidence is drawn from a 1968 survey of Humphreys County, Mississippi, published in Dunbar, *Our Land Too*.
[20] Alston and Ferrie, "In-Kind Compensation."

which they found demeaning. We suspect that World War II did change
tastes for some in a way that made paternalistic arrangements less appealing, but this could not be the whole story because many tenants
never had any war experience. The majority of Southern tenants did not
leave the farm for work in war-related industries or military service in
part due to the efforts of Southerners in limiting outmigration through
emigration laws and draft deferments.[21] In addition, returning veterans
from World War I had not ushered in a period of diminished paternalistic relations in Southern agriculture.

The onset of mechanization and declining acreage, that prompted the
rapid decline in tenancy in the 1950s, ushered in a period of relative
labor surplus and with it an increased likelihood of unemployment.[22]
Unfortunately yearly state level unemployment figures are not available.
Nevertheless, the increase in rural nonfarm population and decrease in
farm population is consistent with a relative surplus of labor in Southern
agriculture.[23] Day argued that as mechanization proceeded it first caused
a displacement from farm to rural nonfarm which would have raised
local unemployment rates in agriculture or more likely increased underemployment dramatically. The data on wages is consistent with this; real
cotton harvest piece rates fell during the 1950s whereas real daily wages
increased only slightly.[24] So long as workers were not indifferent between
unemployment and working, then higher unemployment rates enhanced
the monitoring effectiveness of any given wage.[25] Higher unemployment,
by reducing monitoring costs, substituted for tenancy and paternalism,
prompting employers to negotiate wage contracts with their remaining
laborers. Alston found a negative relationship between unemployment
rates and the ratio of the number of tenants to the dollar value of wage
expenditures in a pooled time-series cross-section regression for data
from ten Southern cotton-growing states for the years 1930 to 1960.[26] If
the expenditures on wage contracts went up relative to the number of
tenants, this suggests that paternalism fell, because wage workers were
seldom the beneficiaries of paternalism – paternalism was not necessary,
as wage workers either were closely monitored by human supervisors,
were already monitored by the nature of the technology, or were reluctant to shirk because of the threat of unemployment.

Monitoring costs also fell because mechanization reduced the varia-

[21] See Chapter 5.
[22] Day, "Technological Change," p. 441.
[23] Ibid., p. 443.
[24] Heinicke, "Black Migration," pp. 110–11.
[25] See Bowles, "Production Process"; and Carmichael, "Self-Enforcing Contracts"
and "Efficiency Wage Models"; Shapiro and Stiglitz, "Equilibrium Unemployment."
[26] Alston, *Costs of Contracting.*

tion in the marginal productivity of labor. Machines by their nature standardize work output and limit the scope for shirking. For example, plowing or cultivating with a tractor provides less scope for shirking than plowing with a mule or cultivating with a hoe. With the tractor technology, employers could evaluate labor effort after a given task better than they could with the mule technology. The ability to monitor labor effort ex post reduced supervision costs and thereby part of the rationale for share contracts and paternalism. This created an additional incentive to negotiate wage contracts with the remaining laborers. Using the ratio of tractors to horses plus mules as a proxy for mechanization and supervision costs, Alston found that mechanization was negatively correlated over time and across space with the relative use of tenancy contracts in the ten major cotton-producing states in the South.[27] Monitoring costs may have fallen for another reason as well. Unlike mules, tractors or cotton pickers were seldom owned by workers. When landlords owned the capital equipment, they had an incentive to monitor its use. If they were present for this reason the marginal costs of monitoring labor fell and so too did the incentive for tenancy and paternalism.[28] The fact that paternalism and tenancy went hand in hand and that both were driven by supervision costs implies that if mechanization prompted a shift into wage contracts, then it also reduced the use of paternalism.

So far we have discussed the impact of mechanization on the supply of paternalism by white landowners. But mechanization also affected the demand for paternalism by primarily black farm workers in two ways. Paternalism was an implicit contract between workers and employers: In return for "good and faithful" labor, employers offered protection and other services. The timing of the exchange was important. "Good and faithful" labor came first and then the landlord delivered. This relationship was maintained as long as workers *expected* planters to uphold their side of the bargain. If, during the 1950s, workers foresaw the incentive of planters to renege as mechanization proceeded, the incentive for them to toil in the present diminished as the demand for labor declined. To stimulate work effort, payment had to be made more coincident with labor effort. Paternalism, with its promise of payment in the future, became less effective.

Mechanization also affected paternalism less directly. To be effective, paternalism required a lack of either well-defined and enforced civil rights or government-supplied social services. In such a world, it made sense for blacks (and for that matter poor whites) to obtain a white protector. With the advent of Great Society programs, poor Southerners

[27] Ibid.
[28] See Alston and Higgs, "Contractual Mix."

would have had a substitute for planter paternalism. Mechanization increased the likelihood of Great Society programs in two ways: one via the supply of legislation (which we discuss in greater detail below), and the other via the demand for legislation. By causing outmigration to the urban North, mechanization increased the size of the Northern black constituency.[29] Northern Democrats seized the opportunity to win the augmented urban black and poor white vote by satisfying their demand for Great Society programs.[30] With a new federal safety net in place, black and white workers in the South could do without paternalistic relationships, which may have hastened the demise of paternalism.

III. Tenancy, Deference, and the Provision of Paternalism

For the 1930s, Charles Johnson found that the best indicator of social conditions in the South – education and race relations among others – was cotton cultivation.[31] Our analysis suggests the reason. Under paternalism, in addition to providing "good and faithful" labor, agricultural tenants showed deference to their landlords, whereas the system of social control required that black tenants show deference to whites at large.[32] Employers may have insisted on deference because of its impact on production, even though many tenants detested it: deference may have reinforced the hierarchical relationship between landlords and tenants and increased the effectiveness of authority and supervision.[33] Tenancy facilitated the maintenance of deference and of racial etiquette in general.

In the 1920s and 1930s tenants received much of their income in-kind. Most notable was the purchasing power advanced at plantation stores

[29] See Young, Bernstein, and Higgs, "Demise of Prescriptive Racism," for a discussion of the impact of Northern black constituents on the voting behavior of Senators on civil rights bills in the twentieth century.

[30] See Piven and Cloward, *Regulating the Poor*, pp. 248–82.

[31] Charles S. Johnson, *Statistical Atlas*.

[32] Deference appears to have been (or still is) part of paternalism in a variety of countries around the globe. See Alston and Ferrie, "Social Control." Rubin, *Plantation County*, p. 90, described the deferential behavior of Sam, a black tenant: "By inclining his head, Sam shows the white man that he acknowledges him as superior. He tips his hat to white men and women. He does not look a white woman straight in the eye. Sam treats all whites, from the 'sorriest' poor white to the wealthiest 'high type' white from the plantation, with the same deference. He waits until a white person is disengaged before approaching for conversation.... He says 'sir' or 'ma'am' at all times, punctuating his conversation frequently with these titles of courtesy."

[33] Fenoaltea, "Authority, Efficiency, and Agricultural Organization," describes a similar functioning of authority in medieval England. For documentation of tenants' dislike of displaying deference, see McMillen, *Dark Journey*; Davis et al., *Deep South*; Powdermaker, *After Freedom*; Raper, *Preface to Peasantry*; and Rosengarten, *All God's Dangers*.

or designated stores in the country or town. Black tenants and croppers frequently did not have discretion over where they shopped. To merchants, they were a guaranteed clientele. This enabled merchants to treat blacks differently from whites without cost. For example, merchants did not permit blacks to try on clothing and would even stop waiting on a black customer to wait on white customers who subsequently entered the store.[34]

For black agricultural workers, the decline in tenancy brought with it a rise in cash income relative to kind, both because of a reduction in economies of scale in supplying in-kind goods and because wage workers were generally paid in cash and not given advances. Displaced tenants, if they found employment, got jobs that paid cash wages. In addition, income levels were rising in general, further increasing discretionary cash income.[35] In a cash economy, if treated disrespectfully by a merchant, blacks could take their business elsewhere. Merchants had an economic incentive to make concessions to blacks not only because of economic pressure from blacks who stayed within the South but also because the outmigration accompanying mechanization was causing a scramble for economic survival.

Receiving better treatment in commercial transactions gave blacks increased self-respect that was continually reinforced. As early as the 1930s, Raper noted

[T]he dependent family began to acquire training in personal and family responsibility and in discriminating buying. The family seemed to take on a sense of self-direction: when furnished through a commissary, the head of the house and other members went several times a week to get this or that, each time acknowledging their dependence and usually stressing it in order to get what was wanted. When a cash allowance was given a tenant, he reported to the landlord at the first of the month to get what was his by agreement. With this money he went forth to buy where he thought he was getting the best values for his money, and where he was treated with the most consideration.[36]

As a result, race etiquette and deference to whites at large, which had been enforced in part through tenancy and the absence of cash, were being threatened as tenancy declined.

Better treatment of blacks in commercial transactions prompted de-

[34] Powdermaker, *After Freedom*, p. 50.
[35] Heinicke estimated the percentage change in real rural median black family income from 1950 to 1960. The percentage increase ranged from a low of 31.3 percent in North Carolina to a high of 74.2 percent in Georgia; Heinicke, "Black Migration," p. 261. See idem, "Black Migration," ch. 5, for a discussion of the factors responsible for the increase in median black family income in the 1950s.
[36] Raper, *Preface to Peasantry*, p. 177.

mands by blacks for better treatment in society. Payment of cash and fewer personal dealings with employers divorced somewhat work and social life. Blacks were not independent economically of whites, but the frequency with which they were required to demonstrate dependence through deferential behavior declined as tenancy declined. If this was true, blacks would have perceived race relations as better where tenancy was lower. And they did.

As part of a study of Southern politics in 1961, Matthews and Prothro collected data on the perception of race relations by blacks in communities across the South.[37] Alston used these data to test for the influence of tenancy on race relations.[38] In an analysis controlling for other influences – median black income, degree of ruralness, the ratio of black population to total population, education and exposure to television – Alston found results consistent with the hypothesis that tenancy was correlated with traditional Southern race etiquette: A high level of tenancy was the only variable that was consistently and strongly associated with perceptions of poor race relations. This suggests that as tenancy rates fell, the institution of social control was weakened. Because paternalism was linked to the system of social control, the use of paternalism would have declined as well. Even before the movement for civil rights at the federal level, then, technological forces were working to undermine the South's traditional system of race relations – what we have called its system of social control – and the paternalistic relations that it fostered.

A study of plantation life in the Mississippi Delta in 1968 documents many of the changes we contend were occurring throughout the South in the late 1950s and early 1960s.[39] The study states that

For the most part, the plantation system and the relation of tenant to planter remained basically the same from its beginnings until the late 1950s. Then, the forces of the first hallelujahs of the civil rights movement, of a northward migration, and of a new idea in agricultural efficiency – mechanization – converged on the plantation country and began to alter the system in such a way that some day its back will be broken.[40]

The important underlying change that occurred with mechanization was the destruction of the dependent relationship between the plantation owner and his tenants and workers. When mechanization arrived, planters began to treat their workers more as workers than as dependents:

[37] Matthews and Prothro, *New Southern Politics.*
[38] Alston, "Race Etiquette."
[39] This study included interviews with several hundred residents of Humphreys County, Mississippi.
[40] Dunbar, *Our Land Too,* p. 11.

Mechanization and the Disappearance of Paternalism

A point perhaps not yet overstated is that when people spend their lives depending upon others, the "others" do not feel like oppressors; they feel paternalistic. And, in fact, what made the plantation different from labor camps was that the planter tried to respond to the needs of his tenants as he saw them. . . . The kindness that might once have played a part in the relationship between planter and tenant is disappearing; it is being replaced by the callousness between management and labor.[41]

The benefits that paternalism provided to workers were withdrawn as mechanization removed the economic motivation for planters to provide paternalism. We have suggested that these benefits included Old-Age Assistance – giving a plot of land and some occasional work to tenants too old to toil in the fields. By the end of the 1960s, this aspect of paternalism was fast disappearing:

It is in the tradition of the plantation system that a tenant who had spent his life working on the place would be guaranteed a little bit of work here and there as long as he was able and a minimal sort of old-age security – a house to remain in until he died, occasional loans to see him through the winter, and help in paying medical expenses. . . . [Now] no tenants not working can believe the boss who says, 'You can live here as long as you need to.' They have seen too many families, believing the same promise, who were told one afternoon to leave by the next morning so that the house into which they were born could be burned and planted over in cotton.[42]

Even for the able-bodied, the system of paternalism was withering away by the late 1960s. Benefits like the provision of a small plot for growing vegetables, calling the doctor when the tenant is sick or injured, and making sure that enough work was provided even in bad seasons to tide tenants over until better times – benefits that were once part of the "plantation tradition," the unspoken protocol of paternalism – were now seldom offered:

The last years in the Delta have seen tenants go homeless, truck patches on plantations prohibited or restricted, people dying or being permanently disabled because the planter would not send for a doctor. . . . There is nothing predictable now about life on the plantation. No man knows if his home is secure, or if he will be given enough work to support his family.[43]

The author of this study concludes that these changes have occurred "not because the planters have decided to starve the black man out of the Delta, as some have said, but rather because planters no longer care, except as it affects their own operations, what happens to the tenants on their farms."[44]

[41] Ibid., p. 26.
[42] Ibid., p. 27.
[43] Ibid., pp. 28–9.
[44] Ibid., p. 28.

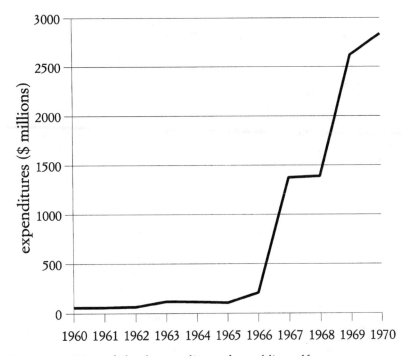

Figure 6.1. Direct federal expenditures for public welfare
    Excluding Social Security, Unemployment Compensation, and other in-
    surance trusts.
Source: U.S. Census Bureau, *Historical Statistics*, p. 1125

IV. Political Ability to Resist the 'Great Society'

Inspector Gregory: "Is there any point to which you would wish to draw my attention?"
Holmes: "To the curious incident of the dog in the night-time."
Inspector Gregory: "The dog did nothing in the night-time."
Holmes: "That was the curious incident."[45]

The point to which we wish to draw attention is the curious behavior of Southern Congressmen in the 1960s. They no longer blocked or limited the expansion of welfare activities as they had previously. The 1960s witnessed both the expansion of already existing programs such as Aid to Families with Dependent Children and the creation of programs such as the community action programs initiated by the Economic Opportunity Act. Direct expenditures by the Federal government for public wel-

[45] Doyle, *Complete Sherlock Holmes*, p. 320.

fare – excluding Social Security, Unemployment Insurance and other insurance trusts – increased dramatically during the 1960s (Figure 6.1). Transfers from the federal government to state and local agencies are a larger share of total federal expenditures for public welfare but we want to highlight the increase in the *direct* federal role in welfare.[46] The number of recipients under AFDC increased from 3 million in 1960 to 4.4 million in 1965 and to 9.7 million in 1970.[47]

Two explanations are possible. Either Southerners lost political power or they no longer had as much incentive to thwart the expansion of the welfare state. We argue that Southern politicians did not lose committee power in the 1960s, which suggests that paternalism did not die from an inability to sustain it, but rather from a declining economic incentive to employ it.

As we discussed at length in Chapter 2, political power in Congress from the 1920s through the 1960s was exercised through committees. Deering and Smith argue that the period from 1947 to the mid-sixties marked the zenith in power of committee chairmen. Before the reforms of committees in the early 1970s, chairmen could withhold legislation from the floor singlehandedly.[48] Knowing the power of the committee chairmen, other committee members shaped legislation to meet the approval of chairmen. In addition, in the House, committee chairmen catered to the chairman of the Rules Committee in order to get legislation to the floor.[49]

Because of the dominance of the Democratic party in the South, Southern Congressmen were more senior on average than Congressmen in other regions. Consequently, they disproportionately chaired and occupied the senior seats on committees in the postwar period, the era of strong committee chairs. In Chapter 2, we documented the strength of Southern Congressmen on committees from the 1930s to 1960. Here, we argue that their strength on committees did not decrease in the 1960s. In Tables 6.1 and 6.2, we present evidence on the continued dominance of Southern Democratic Congressmen on committees in the House and Senate. The committees examined were the same as earlier and were chosen because of either their importance in overseeing legislation in general or their jurisdiction over agriculture, welfare, labor, or civil rights. We consider three eras, all in the period of strong committee chairmanship: from 1947 through the election of President Kennedy in 1960; the New Frontier years and the first spate of welfare legislation

---

[46] U.S. Census Bureau, *Historical Statistics*, pp. 340–1, 1125.
[47] Ibid., p. 356.
[48] Steven S. Smith, *Call to Order*, pp. 8–9.
[49] Dierenfield, *Keeper of the Rules*, p. 231.

Table 6.1. *Seniority of Southern Democrats on House committees,*
1947–70

Committee	Years chaired by Southern Democrat			Average number of first five Democratic seats held by Southern Democrat		
	1947–60	1961–64	1965–70	1947–60	1961–64	1965–70
Rules	6	4	6	3.0	3.0	1.7
Appropriations	0	0	6	2.3	2.0	3.3
Ways and Means	10	4	6	3.4	2.0	2.7
Agriculture	10	4	6	4.7	5.0	5.0
Education/Labor	8	0	4	2.0	2.0	1.0
Judiciary	0	0	0	1.3	1.5	1.0

Notes: Democrats held a majority in the House from 1947 to 1970 in each Congress except 1947 to 1948 and 1953 to 1954. We employed the *Congressional Quarterly* definition of the South: the former Confederate states plus Kentucky and Oklahoma.
Source: Congressional Directory (various years)

from 1961 to 1964; and the years 1965 to 1970, which saw the arrival of more Great Society programs under President Lyndon Johnson and their continuation under President Richard Nixon, by which time cotton cultivation in the South was almost fully mechanized.

In the House, in the first period, a Southerner chaired the Ways and Means Committee and the Agriculture Committee every year Democrats enjoyed a majority. In addition, Southerners disproportionately occupied the other senior ranks. Southerners averaged 3.4 of the top five Democratic seats on the Ways and Means Committee and 4.7 on Agriculture. Their dominance did not significantly change on these committees in the second and third periods: Most importantly they chaired the committees from 1961 to 1970, while their senior representation increased slightly on Agriculture and fell on the Ways and Means Committee.[50] On the Education and Labor, and Rules Committees, Southern Democrats controlled the chairmanship from 1955 through the end of the first period. They also occupied more than their share of the senior ranks on Rules

[50] Though the number of Southern Congressmen in the top five Democratic seats on the Ways and Means Committee fell in the early 1960s, representation by the South was still considerable. In the period from 1961 to 1964 Southern Democrats held an average of 5.2 of the top 10 seats. Furthermore, in the same period, Republican Representative Baker (TN) was either the second- or third-ranking Republican on the committee.

Table 6.2. *Seniority of Southern Democrats on Senate committees,*
1947–70

Committee	Years chaired by Southern Democrat			Average number of first five Democratic seats held by Southern Democrat		
	1947–60	1961–64	1965–70	1947–60	1961–64	1965–70
Rules	0	2	6	1.0	1.0	1.3
Appropriations	4	0	2	2.7	3.5	4.0
Finance	10	4	6	3.5	3.5	3.3
Agriculture	10	4	6	4.0	5.0	5.0
Labor	6	4	6	1.4	2.0	1.7
Judiciary	4	4	6	2.3	4.7	3.2

Notes: Democrats held a majority in the Senate from 1931 to 1970 in each Congress except 1947 to 1948 (Republican majority), 1953 to 1954 (Republican majority), and 1955 to 1956 (tie). We employed the *Congressional Quarterly* definition of the South: the former Confederate states plus Kentucky and Oklahoma.
Source: Congressional Directory (various years)

and two of the five most senior positions on Education and Labor. From 1961 to 1964 Southerners continued to dominate the Rules Committee as they had since Representative Smith (VA) assumed the chairmanship in 1955. After 1953, Representative Colmer (MS) was the second-ranking Democrat on the Rules Committee, followed Smith to the chairmanship in 1967, and held it through our third period. In the Education and Labor Committee, though their senior representation stayed constant in the early sixties, Southerners lost the chairmanship in 1961.

Appropriations and Judiciary were the only committees in the first period on which Southerners were not well represented. Southerners lacked influence on the Appropriations Committee until 1965, when Representative Mahon (TX) ascended to the chairmanship. From 1965 on, Southern Democrats occupied more than three of the top five seats, and Representative Jones (NC) was the second-ranking Republican from 1965 through the remainder of the decade. On the Judiciary Committee, Southern Democratic representation was weak throughout all three periods and roughly constant. However, from 1959 through 1966, Southern Republican Representatives Poff (VA) and Cramer (FL) held two of the top five minority seats.

In the Senate, as in the House, Southerners had disproportionate power in committees. In the first period, Southerners held sway over the Agriculture and Finance committees, chairing them every year that the

Democrats held a majority. A Southerner chaired the Labor Committee after 1954 and the Judiciary Committee beginning in 1957. In the first period, Southerners were weakly represented as chairmen only on Rules and Appropriations. However, despite not having the chairmanship of Appropriations, Southerners were well represented in the senior ranks, averaging almost three of the first five senior Democratic positions. In the sixties, Southern Senators reigned virtually supreme over the committee hierarchy: they chaired the Agriculture, Labor, Finance, and Judiciary committees in every year; they chaired the Rules Committee from 1963 to 1970; and although Senator Russell (GA) chaired the Appropriations Committee only in 1969 and 1970, he was the second-ranking Democratic member of the committee after 1953, and because he had been on the committee since 1933, he had considerable influence.

Overall, there is no evidence that Southerners lost their control over committees in Congress in the sixties. Indeed, as judged by the number of chairmanships, by 1965 Southern agenda control had never been greater. Given the essentially static power position of Southerners in the House and their increased power in the Senate in the sixties, it is extremely unlikely that the welfare programs of the sixties could have emerged from Congress without the countenance of Southern Congressmen. Not only did Southerners have the agenda control which committee power and their importance within the Democratic party produced, but as we will see below, both Kennedy and Johnson needed the Southern vote in order to pass welfare legislation.[51] Schlesinger described the dependence of Kennedy on the South: "[Kennedy] could never escape the political arithmetic. The Democrats lost twenty seats [in the 1960 election] . . . , all from the North, nearly all liberal Democrats. . . . Many times in the next two years Kennedy desperately needed these twenty votes. Without them he was more than ever dependent on the South."[52] Donovan notes that Johnson faced the same situation as Kennedy.[53] Some scholars have suggested that the Great Society would never have come into being without the application of the particular political skills of Johnson. We do not dispute this view, but rather suggest that perhaps the presence of Johnson was a necessary though not sufficient condition for such legislation to have passed. In the presence of Southern opposition, even Franklin Roosevelt, a president as politically astute and as successful in pushing other aspects of his legislative agenda as any, was unable to pass a Social Security Act which encroached on the South's paternalistic labor relations.[54]

[51] Donovan, *Politics of Poverty*, p. 20.
[52] Quoted in ibid., p. 20.
[53] Ibid.
[54] See Chapter 3.

Mechanization and the Disappearance of Paternalism

Ornstein, Mann, and Malbin assembled data similar to ours and reached a similar conclusion:

In the 1950s and early 1960s, Democrats from the Deep South constituted a near majority of their party, but they held an even greater share of committee chairmanships. Their overall strength in numbers, however, discouraged any challenge to the system of selecting chairmen by nonsoutherners who opposed the system's unrepresentative results. By the late 1960s, the South's share of the Democratic party was on the wane, but its hold on chairmanships of committees, especially the most powerful committees, was more tenacious.[55]

Further evidence for the view that Southerners retained considerable power throughout the early 1960s through their control of key committees is provided by the various attempts to limit the power of committee chairmen in the late 1960s and 1970s. We are not interested so much in the effect of these measures as in the tenacity with which liberal Democrats pursued reform. The types of reforms passed only make sense if Southern Congressmen held considerable agenda power throughout the 1960s.[56]

Frustration over attempts to pass more liberal legislation led to the formation of the Democratic Study Group in 1959.[57] For a brief time (1964–6) House liberals believed that by sheer numbers they might be able to push through legislation, but conservative Southerners still had substantial gatekeeping power. Furthermore, after the 1966 election resulted in Republican gains, the liberals knew that their only hope in getting their agenda enacted was to diminish the power of committee chairmen.[58] They succeeded in doing this with reforms beginning in 1970.[59] Under the Legislative Reorganization Act of 1970, the almost absolute power of committee chairmen was diminished somewhat: (1) if

[55] Ornstein, Mann, and Malbin, "Committees."

[56] It is instructive to note that in 1974, the Democratic Caucus rejected three chairmen, all of whom were from the South: W. R. Poage (TX), chairman of the Agricultural Committee; F. Edward Hebert (LA), chairman of the Armed Services Committee; and Wright Patman (TX), chairman of the Banking and Currency Committee.

[57] The Democratic Study Group was a group of mostly Northern, liberal House Democrats whose purpose was organizing was the promotion of liberal policies; Rohde, *Parties and Leaders*, p. 17. The accounts by Sheppard, *Rethinking Congressional Reform*, pp. 11–17; and Stevens, Miller, and Mann, "Mobilization," pp. 668–71, also argue that the prime motivating force for the organization of the Democratic Study Group was the power of conservative Southerners. The discussion that follows draws most heavily on Rohde, *Parties and Leaders*, ch. 1-2.

[58] Rohde argues that after the 1966 election, liberals "believed that their preferred policies could still command majority support if given a fair chance, but now southern committee leaders were able to use the power generated to them through the seniority system to block that chance." Rohde, *Parties and Leaders*, p. 8.

[59] One ironic aspect of the reforms is that they may well not have been needed given the impact of the Voting Rights Act on the behavior of Southern politicians.

the chairman was absent, the most senior majority member could preside over the committee; (2) roll-call votes in committee were now publicly disclosed; (3) a majority of a committee could overrule a chairman and push legislation onto the floor, provided it had clearance from the Rules Committee; and (4) votes would now be recorded on amendments to bills in the Committee of the Whole making it easier for constituents to see how their legislator voted and more difficult for committee chairmen to influence the votes of committee members.

Within the Democrat Caucus, reforms to curb the power of committee chairmen began only in 1971: (1) Committee chairmen could now be subjected to a vote of approval if ten members requested; (2) Democrats could only hold one subcommittee chairmanship; and (3) all subcommittee chairman now had the right to hire at least one staff member. In 1973, the House Democratic Caucus adopted what came to be known as the "Subcommittee Bill of Rights," which substantially reduced the power of committee chairmen by reducing their ability to control subcommittees. The Democratic Caucus now guaranteed budgets for subcommittees, established bidding for subcommittee slots and ceded complete authority for staff hiring decisions to subcommittee chairmen. The House at large further diminished the power of chairmen and strengthened the hand of the majority party by passing legislation in 1974 that allowed the Speaker to refer a bill to more than one committee simultaneously.[60]

V. The South's Role in Shaping the War on Poverty

The Great Society "War on Poverty" was in practice a war aimed principally at urban ghettos. Piven and Cloward, as well as other scholars, argue that the reason for the urban bias was an effort by the administration to capture the Northern black urban vote, which if successful, would have enabled the Democrats to avoid a close call like the 1960 election.[61] We agree that there was a large constituency that demanded welfare legislation, but in light of Southerners' control over the Congressional agenda and control of the marginal votes needed for passage of Great Society welfare programs, a look is warranted at why Southerners allowed programs aimed at alleviating poverty in urban ghettos.

If paternalism was still valuable to the South, Southern legislators would have limited welfare programs aimed at alleviating poverty in the

[60] Rohde, *Parties and Leaders*, discusses other measures adopted by either the House or the Democratic Caucus that reduced the power of committee chairmen and strengthened the grip of the Democratic party over legislation.
[61] Piven and Cloward, *Regulating the Poor*, pp. 258–63.

urban North, because the option of welfare benefits in the urban North would have encouraged outmigration, which in turn would have raised labor costs. But instead of remaining valuable, paternalism became burdensome with the advance of mechanization because plantation owners may have felt a moral obligation to uphold their side of an implicit contract. Even if plantation owners felt no guilt over not caring for displaced workers, as long as the local community felt an obligation to provide some – albeit low – level of welfare assistance to displaced workers, the burden would have been felt most by the local elite in increased taxes. A way to avoid the obligations of paternalism or taxes was to encourage outmigration.[62]

Perhaps more importantly, civil rights were coming to the South whether white Southerners wanted them or not – and many white Southerners vehemently opposed them. But by the sixties, the threat of civil rights to the white South was no longer its impact on labor relations. Civil rights were actually beneficial to the business community and seen by many businessmen as such.[63] Rather, civil rights were a direct assault on white supremacy, a cornerstone of the institution of social control in the South. Given that federal welfare was no longer seen as a threat to labor relations and that civil rights were on the horizon, the white Southern rural elite chose to encourage black outmigration to limit the impact of civil rights.

Evidence from the birth and life of the Economic Opportunity Act is consistent with our view that mechanization destroyed the economic motive for supplying paternalism and that Southerners worked to limit the anticipated impact of civil rights in the South by promoting outmigration and assuring that control of new federal programs remained in their hands. The Economic Opportunity Act was conceived in the White House as the centerpiece of the Johnson administration's War on Poverty. The bill consisted of six parts, only the first three of which were controversial. Title I dealt with youth unemployment and was essentially a redraft of a bill that had previously stalled in the House Rules Committee, which was chaired by Democratic Representative Howard Smith (VA). The most radical part of the bill was Title II, which established urban and rural community action programs. What made the programs radical was that they gave no role to state and local governments. The goal was to involve the poor directly and make an end run around urban bureaucracies. Because poverty had previously been mostly a local issue, the biggest threat was to mayors of large cities. Title III, rural economic

[62] See the quotation from Quadagno, *Transformation of Old Age Security*, p. 94.
[63] Wright, *Old South, New South*, p. 268; Schulman, *Cotton Belt to Sunbelt*, pp. 209–10.

opportunity programs, included grants aimed at land reform, principally Southern land reform, the goal of which was to purchase tracts of land for resale to tenants and sharecroppers.

The important change made by Congress in Title I was that a new "emphasis [was] placed on large 'urban' training and remedial education centers rather than on conservation camps."[64] In Title II, Southerners ensured that governors were given the right to veto the placement of Job Corps Centers and Community Action Programs in their states.[65] Southerners were also concerned that community action grants would be disruptive to the Southern way of life. Their concern was that the grants might go to groups not under the control of the local power structure. To limit this threat, Southerners "modified the legislation to require grantee organizations either to be public agencies or, if private nonprofit agencies, to have an established record of concern with the problems of the poor, or else a link to such an established record by being created by an established agency."[66] It was not that Congressmen outside the South favored the administration's attempt at bypassing local control, but rather that Southern Congressmen were in a better position to do something about it. Grants for land reform in Title III were struck from the final bill as well.

Southerners continued to have disproportionate influence over the actions of the Office of Economic Opportunity (OEO). At the behest of Democratic Senator John Stennis (MS), the Senate Appropriations Committee began an investigation in the autumn of 1965 into a Head Start program grant in Mississippi. As a result of the investigation, the Senate tightened its controls over the OEO in November of 1965. In 1966, the House Education and Labor Committee placed additional constraints on the OEO.

The House passed the Economic Opportunity Bill by a roll-call vote of 226–185. Sixty Southern Democrats voted for the legislation. In the Senate, half of the Southern delegation voted in favor of the bill. It is important to remember that the votes were taken after the bills were altered in committee. The Economic Opportunity bill that emerged was aimed at fighting poverty in Northern ghettos by allowing local communities to bypass local urban bureaucracies. From the South's viewpoint, the bill as amended and passed posed little threat to the Southern way of life. In fact, it seems to have been part of an unsuccessful last ditch effort to maintain the Southern way of life by encouraging outmi-

---

[64] Sundquist, *On Fighting Poverty*, p. 26.
[65] Donovan, *Politics of Poverty*, pp. 36–7, argues that the veto was part of the price paid by the administration for Southern support.
[66] Yarmolinsky, "Beginnings of OEO," p. 46.

gration of blacks. Before mechanization and a shift toward less labor-intensive crops, outmigration would have threatened the Southern way of life because it would have increased labor costs. After mechanization and the demise of paternalism, encouraging outmigration was seen as a way of limiting the anticipated impact of civil rights. In fact, black workers displaced by mechanization "were frequently given a bus ticket, a token amount of cash, and the address of the welfare office in New York." Former New York mayor and Representative John Lindsay recalled that "his Southern colleagues would clap him on the back and say, 'John, we're sending 'em right up to you.' "[67] The final shape of the Economic Opportunity Act was one more piece of evidence demonstrating the death of paternalism in the South.

Schulman argues that Southerners were opposed to welfare programs in general.[68] Southerners, however, were not unanimous in their opposition, while they had been almost unanimous in the past: As we noted earlier, sixty Southern Democrats voted for this legislation in the House, and in the Senate half the Southern delegation voted in favor of the bill. Schulman's evidence on the opposition to welfare is consistent with our hypothesis that Southerners retained sufficient political power to shape welfare programs to encourage rural outmigration and thereby limit the impact of welfare in the rural South.

Additional evidence on the extent to which Southern votes changed as the economic interests of the rural Southern elite changed comes from an examination of the Food Stamp program. The overall level of Southern cohesiveness in voting on all legislation over this period is consistent with a clear change in Southern interests. Southerners in the House attained a 90 percent or higher degree of unity on 41 percent of all roll calls in the 1933–45 period; by the 1950s, they did so on only 19 percent of all roll calls, whereas in the 1960s, they achieved such high cohesion on only 6 percent of all roll-call votes.[69] The birth of the Food Stamp program is consistent with our hypothesis that with access to mechanization and with civil rights on the horizon, Southern Congressmen encouraged rural outmigration. Ferejohn documents the legislative history of the program. He shows that though the bill was clearly a piece of urban welfare legislation, it was actually sent to the floor by the House Agriculture Committee, a stronghold of the rural Southern Congressional delegation. In 1963, when the Agriculture Committee reported the Food Stamp bill, the committee was chaired by Democratic Representative Cooley (NC) and the seven senior Democrats on the committee were

[67] Adam Smith, "The City as the OK Corral," p. 64.
[68] Schulman, *Cotton Belt to Sunbelt*, pp. 180–1.
[69] Havard, *Changing Politics of the South*, pp. 644–5.

from the South. Though many Southern Representatives voted against the bill on the floor of the House, the votes of those Southerners who favored it were decisive – they provided the bill's margin of passage and continued to do so throughout the program's early life.[70]

VI. Conclusion

In the 1960s Congress passed legislation that increased the scope and scale of U.S. welfare activities. An important part of the story of this period was what went on behind the legislation – how changes in economic relationships led to the evaporation of opposition to much of that legislation. We have focused on what we believe was an important such change: the end of paternalistic relations in Southern agriculture.

For the first half of the twentieth century, the South represented a formidable obstacle to the expansion of the welfare state. In response to the constraints of technology, planters fostered the institution of social control, and adopted a paternalistic system of labor relations that reduced labor costs by reducing the cost of monitoring labor effort and discouraging labor turnover. The importance of Southerners within the Democratic party and the committee structure of Congress ensured that senior Southern Congressmen could block or significantly limit legislation that threatened that system.

Before mechanization, social control in the South and the rules of the game in Congress shaped not only the paternalistic relationship between Southern plantation landlords and their workers, but also the developmental pattern of the Federal welfare state. The complete mechanization of Southern agriculture reduced the economic incentive of Southern politicians to oppose uniformly Federal welfare programs and made possible the expansion of the welfare state in the 1960s.

[70] Ferejohn, "Logrolling in an Institutional Context," pp. 230–3.

Conclusion

We have used the methodology of the new institutional economics to understand paternalism and the forces that shaped it. Our work, then, is a case study in institutional analysis, an area in which the literature is still longer on theory than on empirical work. We believe that theoretical development in this area will come through the insights provided by the aggregation of case studies such as ours. We hope that our work will be a methodological aid to other scholars in the empirical analysis of institutions and institutional change. In conclusion, we offer a recapitulation of the main argument, a brief discussion of the lessons we learned that may be of use in the study of other cases, and an analysis of how our argument meshes with the existing literature on the growth of the welfare state in the twentieth-century United States.

In the Introduction, we provided a general framework for analyzing the interaction between institutions and contracting. In the remaining chapters, we used that framework to help us understand the economics and politics associated with paternalism in Southern agriculture. The framework highlights the importance of transaction costs in motivating the development of contractual relations. In our case study, we focus on the transactions costs associated with the use of labor in premechanized cotton production. We analyze the steps that landowners in the South took that reduced the supervision and turnover costs associated with premechanized cotton production after the abolition of slavery. They negotiated sharecrop and tenant contracts, provided paternalism to some workers, and maintained the value of paternalism by maintaining a discriminatory class and racial climate through their political agents. Though these actions were not solely undertaken to reduce the transaction costs of cotton production, our analysis indicates that this was the dominant motivation. After mechanization and other science-based technological changes reduced the transaction costs of cotton production, we find that sharecropping and paternalism virtually disappeared in the

South. As a result, the political position of many Southern Congressmen changed dramatically. Intransigent opposition to the welfare state was transformed into grudging acceptance, removing an important obstacle to the expansion of the American welfare state on the eve of the birth of the Great Society.

The preceding chapters contribute to our understanding of the use of paternalism in agricultural contracting in the American South for nearly one hundred years. The evolution of paternalism over time and its ultimate demise in the 1960s were shaped by economic and political factors within and outside of the South. The plantation elite valued paternalism because of the high labor turnover and monitoring costs in premechanized Southern agriculture. Agricultural workers in the South valued paternalism because it offered some protection from the prevailing discriminatory racial and class conditions in the South. Thus, we argue that paternalism offered benefits to both plantation owners and workers. This is not a normative judgment; rather, it is a recognition that *given the prevailing distribution of economic and political power and the resulting socioeconomic climate*, both parties would have been worse off without paternalism. But we emphasize that both parties did not have equal access to maintaining or changing the socioeconomic "rules of the game." Here only the rural elite were players.

In Chapters 3, 4 and 5, we chronicle the political actions undertaken by Southerners to maintain paternalism. The three legislative acts that we analyze are the Social Security Act of 1935 and its subsequent revisions, the Farm Tenancy Act of 1937, which established the Farm Security Administration, and Public Law 45 in 1943 and subsequent legislation and international agreements, which formalized the bracero program in 1951 and afterward. The actions of Southern politicians and their allies had profound effects outside the South. For example, all agricultural labor was excluded from the initial Social Security Act, not just Southern agricultural labor. Similarly, when the actions of the Farm Security Administration turned to reform, the appropriations were slashed for the entire nation, not just the South. Though the Southern region employed few Mexican workers under the bracero program, the South was the staunchest supporter of the program which enabled millions of Mexican workers to come legally to the United States.

Just as the literature in industrial organization illustrates that different outcomes will result from an unequal distribution of economic power, our analysis illustrates the importance of understanding the political institutions (e.g. committees or parties) that give rise to the distribution of political power in order to understand policy outcomes. Without an understanding of the levers of political power, it is difficult to understand why the more populous North could not "reform" the South or how the South could successfully limit the expansion of the welfare state until the 1960s. When landmark changes in welfare did come to the nation in the early 1960s, the underlying political institutions had not changed. Southern legislators still dominated the senior positions within the Democratic party and consequently held the most senior positions on the committees from which welfare legislation emerged, which gave the South agenda control. We argue, therefore, that much of the change in welfare legislation came about because economic conditions within the South had changed sufficiently to allow the expansion of the welfare state in ways that Southerners would have fought to limit in earlier years. Though the role of Northern politicians was crucial in that expansion, we contend that the South first had to change from within before it could be changed from the outside. The most important change within the South that undermined paternalism in Southern agriculture and led to an accommodation to welfare legislation was the mechanization of Southern agriculture.

Because our work has important implications for understanding the growth of the American welfare state in the twentieth century, it is worth considering briefly how our work fits in with existing theories of welfare state development. Though the implications of this study for that larger story are incidental to our main purpose – explaining how transaction costs, social control, and politics interacted to produce the South's system of paternalism in agriculture – these developments in the South played a role in how the welfare state developed in the wider American context.

Recent surveys of "theories of the welfare state" have suggested several broad though not mutually exclusive typologies of such theories.[1] Though most of these theories were developed to explain why the welfare state grows, in the American case, because the American welfare state's underdevelopment is often the thing that needs to be explained, the questions they address have often been formed in the negative rather than the positive. As Piven and Cloward note, the question becomes "Why was 'the great transformation' of nineteenth century market societies into welfare states which Polanyi thought had become literally essential to human survival impeded in the United States?"[2] Though our study is not a "theory" of welfare state development, it is nonetheless consistent with much of what other scholars conclude regarding the

---

[1] Surveys of welfare state theories include Skocpol and Amenta, "States and Social Policies"; Quadagno, "Theories of the Welfare State"; Skocpol, *Social Policy*, pp. 15–32; and Piven and Cloward, *Regulating the Poor*, pp. 407–56.
[2] Piven and Cloward, *Regulating the Poor*, p. 408.

forces that have shaped the U.S. welfare state. After briefly considering theories of the welfare state's growth, we will explore the similarities and differences between our work and these theories.

The earliest theories of the growth of the welfare system (apart from the often self-serving explanations of its expansion offered by early social welfare professionals who saw their own actions as the principal motive force in this epic) focused on the role of such systems in providing support for individuals suffering economic hardship in industrial societies that have cut them off from traditional sources of support like family, church, and community. In this view, the forces promoting the welfare state's growth are increasing urbanization and industrialization and the social dislocations they produce. In this approach – often termed "the logic-of-industrialism" view – the causes of welfare state growth are inferred from the structure and functions the welfare state has historically assumed. Unfortunately, this view is unable to account for the fact that many of the first welfare states were considerably less industrial than countries like the United States in which the welfare state developed only slowly and partially.[3]

The preceding chapters have offered another reason why this approach is less than complete: Even in the rural U.S. South (neither urban nor industrial), rudimentary social welfare benefits were offered by employers, outside the context of the family, church, or community. This suggests that the need for a "safety net" may exist even in nonmechanized agriculture but that the channels through which that need is met may bypass "the state" altogether. The "logic-of-industrialism" approach, at least for the United States, may tell us more about why the provision of benefits shifted from private employers to the state than about why such benefits were offered in the first instance. If the word "industrialism" is taken to include both the growth of large-scale, factory-oriented production in urban centers and a corresponding modernization in agriculture and labor migration from farms to cities, this approach captures the essence of the process we described in Chapter 6: mechanization reducing Southerners' demand for unskilled, dependent workers, industrial and urban growth creating a demand for welfare services in cities, and the burden of caring for the poor, aged, unemployed, and disabled shifting to the federal government, as Southern agricultural interests abandoned the system of paternalism and encouraged the outmigration of workers by allowing the growth of welfare programs in cities, which were mainly in the North.

The role of employers in offering early versions of what later became standard welfare state benefits (Unemployment Insurance, old-age pen-

---

[3] Ibid., pp. 417–19; Orloff and Skocpol, "Why Not Equal Protection?"

sions, health care) is emphasized in the "corporate liberal" approach to the welfare state's growth. Work in this tradition focuses on the role of businesses that offer benefits to workers and the competitive disadvantage they face from employers who do not offer benefits.[4] The assumption of the role of benefit provider by the federal government would put these "enlightened" businesses on an equal footing with less enlightened firms. Though there is ample anecdotal evidence for the crucial role played by some business interests in the formation of the early U.S. welfare state in the New Deal, this approach has been criticized for ignoring the roles of the state and more broadly based forces in the economy as actors influencing the welfare state.

The "corporate liberal" approach also does not fit the story we have told for the Southern United States. We have shown that the actions of the region's most powerful economic actors (the plantation oligarchy) reveal that absolutely the *last* thing they wanted was for the federal government to step in and assume the burden of providing social benefits to their workers, at least until the mechanization of the cotton harvest in the late 1950s and early 1960s. Before then, federal welfare benefits would have provided a substitute for the paternalistic services they offered to workers in exchange for "good and faithful" labor. Paternalistic services were provided to strengthen the ties between planters and their workers, ties that federal benefits would have loosened. The federalization of benefits would have put all planters on an equal footing, but it would have done so by removing a crucial device planters used to extract labor from their workers: the discretion to bestow nonvested, plantation-specific benefits on their "good" workers.

The "corporate liberal" view is a subset of a larger, neo-Marxist approach to the welfare state's growth in which the welfare state represents a response to the needs of both workers for basic protection (from sickness, old age, or unemployment) and employers for control over labor. Though this approach might seem the least closely related to the developments we have sketched in the preceding chapters – the term "advanced capitalism" is seldom associated with the system of production and social relations in agriculture in the Southern United States early in this century – this view's emphasis on the "labor control" functions of welfare benefits is nonetheless consistent with the behavior of Southern planter interests. Though that control occurs in the South through the provision of benefits by employers rather than by the state, the outcome it produces in the South is quite similar to that observed elsewhere. For example, Skocpol and Amenta note that "state-socialist

[4] Berkowitz and McQuaid, *Creating the Welfare State*; Quadagno, *Transformation of Old Age Security*.

authorities in centrally-planned economies closely tailor social insurance and housing policies to the exigencies of labor discipline and control of migration."[5] Substitute "Southern planters" for "state-socialist authorities" and "rural South" for "centrally-planned economies" and the resulting description is a succinct summary of the preceding six chapters.

A particularly well-known variant of the neo-Marxist approach is the work of Piven and Cloward, who suggest that the welfare state (the provision of relief in particular) serves a crucial function in the capitalist system.[6] The function is not primarily the support of the poor or the provision of services that had traditionally been provided through other channels; rather, relief is provided to prevent large-scale, urban unrest when economic conditions are unfavorable for workers, and it is withdrawn to enforce work norms when prosperity returns.[7] Like other neo-Marxists, they focus on the "labor control" function played by state-supplied welfare benefits, as opposed to the role played by privately supplied benefits like those provided by Southern planters.

Several scholars have recognized that, whatever the forces prompting the welfare state's growth, an important impediment to that growth in the United States was the attitude of rural elites in the South.[8] These studies recognize from the outset that the South had a unique system of social and labor relations (which Piven and Cloward refer to as its "caste" system), and that as a result Southern elites were particularly averse to the expansion of the welfare state.[9] The crucial role of the mechanization of Southern agriculture in the 1950s and 1960s in this process has been widely recognized.[10]

One result of mechanization was massive migration to Northern cities.[11] Piven and Cloward suggest that, combined with the weakening of traditional systems of social control that this migration produced and the lack of employment opportunities in cities already being deserted by

[5] Skocpol and Amenta, "States and Social Policies," p. 134.
[6] Piven and Cloward, *Regulating the Poor.*
[7] Ibid., pp. 1–41.
[8] Piven and Cloward, *Regulating the Poor*; Quadagno, *Transformation of Old Age Security.*
[9] Piven and Cloward, *Regulating the Poor*, pp. 131–4.
[10] Quadagno, *Transformation of Old Age Security*, pp. 142–9; Piven and Cloward, *Regulating the Poor*, pp. 200–20.
[11] For an alternative to the view that the mechanization of the cotton harvest was primarily responsible for migration from South to North in this period, see Heinicke, "Black Migration" and unpublished paper, who emphasizes other "push" factors (such as cotton acreage reductions in response to changing world cotton prices, the influence of government acreage restriction programs, and the introduction of tractors) as well as "pull" factors (such as wages in Northern cities).

industry, the migration created an explosive situation that culminated in riots throughout the 1960s.[12] The government's response was an expansion of relief spending. Again, our emphasis on the same event is somewhat different: We focus instead on the impact of mechanization *within* the South. We suggest that the need for paternalism was reduced when a large workforce of cheap, dependent labor was rendered obsolete by the mechanical cotton picker.

Piven and Cloward note the ways in which labor relations within the South were transformed by mechanization.[13] They do so, however, in the context of explaining how mechanization increased poverty in the South, why the South's relief system did not expand in response, and why there was no resulting social disorder in the South. They do not explore how this transformation in labor relations would have altered the willingness of the Southern rural elite to defend paternalism against competition from federal welfare programs. Quadagno also notes the transformation in the welfare system accompanying the mechanization of cotton cultivation, but focuses, as we do, on the change in Southern attitudes toward federal welfare programs brought about by mechanization.[14] Our research explains the economic basis of that change in attitudes toward federal welfare programs. The result was less frequent exercise of their veto power over federal welfare legislation by Southern representatives. Combined with the sort of pressures demanding welfare services in Northern cities and the willingness of entrepreneurial Northern politicians to offer them, this resulted in the expansion of the welfare state seen in the 1960s and early 1970s.

Quadagno sees Southern distinctiveness as one of three forces retarding the growth of the American welfare system, the other two being a weak organized labor movement and the heavy hand of corporate interests (described above in discussing the "corporate liberal" approach to the growth of the welfare state). Her description of how the Old-Age Assistance program was transformed in the 1960s and 1970s as a result of changes in the attitudes and political power of Southerners closely parallels our own. Our work differs from hers in two important respects: (1) in placing greater emphasis on Southern attitudes toward welfare programs than on changes in Southern political power as crucial in this process of transformation; and (2) in showing how the forces that prompted Southern opposition to the extension of the Social Security system from the 1930s through the late 1950s and early 1960s was but part of a persistent Southern strategy to prevent interference in the re-

---

[12] Piven and Cloward, *Regulating the Poor*, pp. 222–46.
[13] Ibid., pp. 201–12.
[14] Quadagno, *Transformation of Old Age Security*, pp. 187–8.

gion's paternalistic labor relations, a strategy that prevented tenure reform in agriculture, shaped an immigrant "guest worker" policy that had an impact far beyond the South, and oversaw an expansion of urban programs in the 1960s that went far beyond anything contemplated in the New Deal.

In addition, our work makes two important contributions regarding the role of Southern uniqueness in shaping the growth of the American welfare state. The first is to explain how the difficulty of monitoring and retaining labor in cotton cultivation and the South's system of social control combined to produce the peculiar system of labor relations we have called paternalism. Our second contribution is to show that the Southern elite's fear of the welfare state came not so much from the effect of relief spending on their ability to attract workers as from the effect of any intervention in their labor system on their ability to maintain a dependent labor force. For example, if the level and timing of relief spending through Aid to Dependent Children (later, Aid to Families with Dependent Children, or AFDC) had been the only issue in the South, the elite's fears would have been allayed by the retention of local control over the administration of the program (including benefit levels) and the imposition of "employable mother" rules like those used in Louisiana (1943) and Georgia (1952).[15]

Local control and the power to force recipients to work at times of peak labor demand (e.g., the cotton harvest) would have allowed local elites to enjoy the benefits of relief spending (subsidizing the maintenance of temporarily superfluous labor and preventing its unrest) and yet retain the ability to enforce work norms when labor was again in demand. To the extent that AFDC payments by states were supplemented by federal matching grants (within limits), such relief spending would have been an important subsidy to employers facing large seasonal variation in labor demand. That such spending was not welcomed in the South even though numerous restrictions could be placed on it by the Southern rural elite suggests that far more than federal money was the problem. We explain why not just relief spending but an entire range of federal programs would have been uniquely disruptive in the South. The mechanism through which federal programs would have interfered in Southern labor relations and disrupted the South's system of paternalism also explains Southern elite support for programs like the bracero program that enhanced the dependence of Southern farm workers on plantation owners.

Finally, more recent research has focused on political theories of the growth of the welfare state. This work is less concerned with the forces prompting the demand for welfare state services than with the political

[15] Bell, *Aid to Dependent Children*, pp. 46, 107.

Conclusion

mechanisms that intermediate between those demands (however they are formed) and the resources that can satisfy those demands.[16] These theories have examined the role of civic and worker-based organizations (e.g. labor unions and labor-based political parties) as vehicles through which demands for social welfare services can be articulated, given force, and eventually satisfied, and have similarly examined the roles of more narrowly defined interest groups and the effect of institutional arrangements (e.g. bureaucracies, bicameral legislatures, parties, and committees) in that process.[17] This approach recognizes that different outcomes (in terms of the shape or scale of welfare programs) can result where underlying economic conditions are identical simply because of differences in the degree of democratic participation, the extent of preexisting bureaucracies, or the arrangements in legislatures that allow some constituencies to wield disproportionate political power.

Of these views, the institutional perspective is the most satisfying: The role of working-class organizations has seldom been found to be crucial in empirical studies (and in any case, circumstances in the United States, which never developed a broad-based labor movement or a labor party, require that a prior question be addressed as well: Why has the labor movement been so weak historically in the United States?), while interest-group based theories fail to recognize that the distribution of political power may be quite unequal. The institutional view provides insight into these shortcomings of other perspectives, even as it helps explain other aspects of the system's development (e.g. how a system that is national in scope had to be made to conform with narrow sectional circumstances).

The institutional approach fits well with our explanation for how the South's regional interests were translated into national policy. It provides an explanation for how the distinctive economic features of a single region can have a disproportionate emphasis on national welfare policy. We have shown the enormous power Southern Congressmen wielded because of institutional realities in Congress, in particular the importance of the Senate, which gave influence to states regardless of their populations, and internal arrangements in the House, which gave senior members and committee chairs virtual veto power over legislation. When mechanization arrived in the 1950s and 1960s, because there were no institutional changes that would have weakened Southern veto power over welfare legislation, we infer that the desire of Southern representatives to block welfare legislation must have waned. Because institutional

[16] Skocpol, *Social Policy*, pp. 19–32.
[17] Skocpol, *Protecting Soldiers and Mothers*; Hibbs, *Political Economy of Industrial Democracies*; Korpi, *Democratic Class Struggle*; Janowitz, *Social Control*.

relationships in Congress had not changed, Southerners could have continued to prevent much of the expansion of the welfare state (both in
terms of overall spending on direct relief and later in terms of Great
Society programs). That they no longer did so with such tenacity suggests to us that mechanization had changed the economic environment
in the South and made the defense of paternalism against the appearance
of substitute benefits and benefactors less salient. Piven and Cloward
maintain, as we do, that Southern Congressmen were still powerful
throughout the 1960s. They were able to shape the Economic Opportunity Act so that its influence was felt mainly in the North: "[T]he powerful Southern congressional delegation was watchful and at least partly
successful in curbing implementation of these programs in its home-
land."[18]

The growth of the welfare system in this period forever altered the
economic and political landscape. Reform of the system has been a point
of contention for most of the last thirty years. In fact, the welfare state
in its current manifestations has now been with us so long that it is
difficult for anyone born since 1964 to imagine life in the United States
without it. What we have tried to show is how life in one area – the
rural American South – was considerably different before its expansion,
how the need to keep labor cheap and dependent led to the adoption of
an elaborate system of paternalism that provided some of what the welfare state later offered, and how mechanization in the South led to the
abandonment of paternalism and helped prompt the extension to the
entire nation of a welfare system that had been opposed by a Southern
rural elite defending the viability of a particularly Southern system of
economic and social relations.

[18] Piven and Cloward, *Regulating the Poor*, pp. 280–1.

References

CES RECORDS – Records of the Committee on Economic Security, National Archives, Record Group 47
CES REPORTS – *Reports of the Committee on Economic Security.* Vol. 6, pt. 2. Washington, D.C.: Unpublished, 1934
SSB RECORDS – Records of the Social Security Board, National Archives, Record Group 47

Abbott, Grace. *The Child and the State.* Chicago: University of Chicago Press, 1938.
"AFL Report Including Agricultural Workers." *New York Times,* 8 February 1937, 5.
Aiken, Charles S. "The Decline of Sharecropping in the Lower Mississippi River Valley." *Geoscience and Man* 19 (1978): 151–65.
Aiken, Charles S., and Merle Prunty. "The Demise of the Piedmont Cotton Region." *Association of American Geographers Annals* 62 (1972): 283–306.
Akerlof, George A. "Labor Contracts as a Partial Gift Exchange." *Quarterly Journal of Economics* 97 (November 1982): 543–69.
Alston, Lee J. *Costs of Contracting and the Decline of Tenancy in the South, 1930–60.* New York: Garland, 1985.
"Empirical Work in Institutional Economics." In *Empirical Studies in Institutional Change,* edited by Lee J. Alston, Thrainn Eggertsson, and Douglass C. North. New York: Cambridge University Press, 1996.
"Farm Foreclosures in the United States During the Interwar Period." *Journal of Economic History* 43 (1983): 885–903.
"Race Etiquette in the South: The Role of Tenancy." *Research in Economic History* 10 (1986): 199–211.
"Tenure Choice in Southern Agriculture." *Explorations in Economic History* 18 (April 1981): 211–32.
Alston, Lee J., and Joseph P. Ferrie. "A Model of In-Kind Compensation in Agriculture." University of California (Davis) Agricultural History Center Working Paper No. 34 (April 1986).
"Resisting the Welfare State: Southern Opposition to the Farm Security Administration." In *Emergence of the Modern Political Economy,* edited by Robert Higgs. Greenwich, CT: JAI Press, 1985.

153

References

"Social Control and Labor Relations in the American South Before the Mechanization of the Cotton Harvest in the 1950s." *Journal of Institutional and Theoretical Economics* 145 (March 1989): 133–57.

Alston, Lee J., Wayne A. Grove, and David C. Wheelock. "Why Do Banks Fail? Evidence from the 1920s." *Explorations in Economic History* 31 (October 1994): 409–23.

Alston, Lee J., and Kyle D. Kauffman. "Social Norms of Racial Discrimination and their Impact on Land Rentals in the U.S. South." Working Paper. University of Illinois. May 1998.

Alston, Lee J., Thrainn Eggertsson, and Douglass C. North, eds. *Empirical Studies in Institutional Change*. New York: Cambridge University Press, 1996.

"Alternative Plans for the Coverage of Agricultural Workers." 1940, SSB Records, Box 32, Agricultural Materials file, pp. 5–8.

Armstrong, Barbara N. "Provision for Old-Age Security." CES Records, Box 23.

Baldwin, Sidney. *Poverty and Politics: The Rise and Decline of the Farm Security Administration*. Chapel Hill: University of North Carolina Press, 1968.

Barraclough, S. L., and A. L. Domike. "Agrarian Structure in Seven Latin American Countries." *Land Economics* 42 (November 1966): 391–424.

Barry, John M. *Rising Tide: The Great Mississippi Flood of 1927*. New York: Simon and Schuster, 1997.

Bean, Louis H. "The Economic Security Program in Relation to Farm Operators and Employees." CES Reports.

Bell, Winifred. *Aid to Dependent Children*. New York: Columbia University Press, 1965.

Benedict, Murray R. *Farm Policies of the United States, 1790–1950*. New York: Twentieth Century Fund, 1953.

Bensel, Richard F. *Sectionalism and American Political Development, 1880–1980*. Madison: University of Wisconsin Press, 1984.

Berkowitz, Edward, and Kim McQuaid. *Creating the Welfare State*. New York: Praeger, 1980.

Bloch, Marc. *Feudal Society*. Chicago: University of Chicago Press, 1961.

Slavery and Serfdom in the Middle Ages: Selected Essays. Berkeley and Los Angeles: University of California Press, 1975.

Bowles, Samuel. "The Production Process in a Competitive Economy: Walrasian, Neo-Hobbesian, and Marxian Models." *American Economic Review* 75 (1985): 16–36.

Brannen, Claude O. "Relation of Land Tenure to Plantation Organization." *U.S. Department of Agriculture, Bulletin* 1269 (1924).

Brinkley, Alan. "The New Deal and Southern Politics." In *The New Deal and the South*, edited by James C. Cobb and Michael V. Namorato. Jackson: University Press of Mississippi, 1984.

Bruce, Phillip A. *The Plantation Negro as a Freeman*. New York: G.P. Putnam's Sons, 1889.

Bureau of Research and Statistics, Division of Old-Age Benefits Research, "Expansion of Coverage." 27 September 1938, SSB Records, Box 4, pp. 4–15.

Carmichael, H. Lorne. "Efficiency Wage Models of Unemployment – One View." *Economic Inquiry* 28 (April 1990): 269–95.

"Self-Enforcing Contracts, Shirking, and Life-Cycle Incentives." *Journal of Economic Perspectives* 3 (Fall 1989): 65–83.

"CIO Urges Inclusion of Agricultural Workers." *New York Times*, 14 October 1937, 9.

References

Cloud, N. B. "Cotton Culture in 1866." In U.S. Department of Agriculture, *Report of the Commissioner of Agriculture for the Year 1866*. Washington, D.C.: Government Printing Office, 1867.

Committee on Economic Security. *Reports of the Committee on Economic Security*. Vol. 6, pt. 2. Washington, D.C.: Unpublished, 1934.

Social Security in America – the Factual Background to the Social Security Act as Summarized from Staff Reports to the Committee on Economic Security. Washington, D.C.: Government Printing Office, 1937.

Congressional Directory. Washington, D.C.: Government Printing Office, various years.

Congressional Quarterly Almanac. Washington, D.C.: Congressional Quarterly, 1953–63.

Corson, John J., to O. M. Powell. "Conference with Farm Labor Committee of the Department of Agriculture." 25 November 1940, SSB Records, Box 32, Agricultural Labor file, p. 1.

Cox, Gary W., and Matthew D. McCubbins. *Legislative Leviathan: Party Government in the House*. Berkeley and Los Angeles: University of California Press, 1993.

Craig, Richard B. *The Bracero Program: Interest Groups and Foreign Policy*. Austin: University of Texas Press, 1970.

Crain, W. M., D. R. Leavens, and R. D. Tollison. "Final Voting in Legislatures." *American Economic Review* 76 (1986): 833–41.

Daniel, Pete. *Breaking the Land: The Transformation of Cotton, Tobacco, and Rice Culture Since 1880*. Urbana: University of Illinois Press, 1985.

Davis, Allison, Burleigh B. Gardner, and Mary R. Gardner. *Deep South: A Social and Anthropological Study of Caste and Class*. Chicago: University of Chicago Press, 1969.

Davis, Ronald L. F. *Good and Faithful Labor: From Slavery to Sharecropping in the Natchez District*. Westport, CT: Greenwood Press, 1982.

Day, Richard H. "Technological Change and the Sharecropper." *American Economic Review* 57 (June 1967): 427–49.

Deering, Christopher J., and Steven S. Smith. *Committees in Congress*. Washington, D.C.: Congressional Quarterly Press, 1984.

Denzau, Arthur T., and Michael Munger. "Legislators and Interest Groups: How Unorganized Interests Get Represented." *American Political Science Review* 80 (March 1986): 84–106.

Dierenfield, Bruce J. *Keeper of the Rules: Congressman Howard V. Smith of Virginia*. Charlottesville: University of Virginia Press, 1987.

Donovan, John C. *The Politics of Poverty*. New York: Pegasus, 1967.

Doyle, Arthur Conan. *The Complete Sherlock Holmes*. Garden City, NY: Doubleday, 1930.

DuBois, W. E. B. "The Negro Farmer." In *Twelfth Census of the United States: 1900, Special Reports, Supplementary Analysis and Derivative Tables*. Washington, D.C.: Government Printing Office, 1906.

Three Negro Classics: Up from Slavery. The Souls of Black Folks. The Autobiography of an Ex-Colored Man. New York: Avon Books, 1965.

Dunbar, Anthony. *Our Land Too*, New York: Pantheon, 1971.

Fenoaltea, Stefano. "Authority, Efficiency, and Agricultural Organization in Medieval England and Beyond: A Hypothesis." *Journal of Economic History* 35 (December 1975): 693–718.

Ferejohn, John A. "Logrolling in an Institutional Context: A Case Study of Food

References

Stamp Legislation." In *Congress and Policy Change*, edited by Gerald C. Wright, Jr., Leroy N. Rieselbach, and Lawrence C. Dodd. New York: Agathon Press, 1986.

Ferleger, Louis. "Sharecropping Contracts in the Late Nineteenth Century South." *Agricultural History* 67 (1993): 31–46.

Fite, Gilbert C. *Cotton Fields No More: Southern Agriculture, 1865–1980*. Lexington: University Press of Kentucky, 1984.

Richard B. Russell, Jr., Senator from Georgia. Chapel Hill: University of North Carolina Press, 1991.

Fogel, Robert W. "Circumstantial Evidence in 'Scientific' and Traditional History." In *Philosophy of History and Contemporary Historiography*, edited by David Carr. Ottawa: Editions de l'Universite d'Ottawa, 1982.

Without Consent or Contract: The Rise and Fall of American Slavery. New York: Norton, 1989.

Folsom, Josiah C. "Economic Security of Farmers and Agricultural Workers." CES Reports.

"Perquisites and Wages of Hired Farm Laborers." *U.S. Department of Agriculture Technical Bulletin* 213 (1931).

Foner, Eric. *A Short History of Reconstruction*. New York: Harper & Row, 1990.

[Freedmen's Bureau] U.S. Congress. Senate. *Report of Freedmen's Bureau*. 39th Cong., 1st sess., 1866. S. Doc. 27.

Galarza, Ernesto. *Strangers in Our Fields*. U.S. Section, Joint United States–Mexico Trade Union Committee. Washington, D.C.: Government Printing Office, 1956.

Genovese, Eugene. *Roll, Jordan, Roll: The World the Slaves Made*. New York: Pantheon, 1974.

[Godwin, J. R.] U.S. Industrial Commission. "Testimony of J. R. Godwin." *Report*. Vol. 10. Washington, D.C.: Government Printing Office, 1900–2.

Grove, Wayne A. "Cotton Economy in Transition, 1950 to 1964: Mechanization, Southern Out-Migration, and Foreign Labor." Ph.D. diss., University of Illinois, forthcoming.

Ham, William T. "The Bearing of the Program of the Committee on Economic Security Upon Farmers and Farm Laborers." CES, *Reports*.

Hammer, Philip G., and Robert K. Buck. "Idle Man Power." *Land Policy Review* 5 (1942): 9–18.

Hancock, Richard H. *The Role of the Bracero in the Economic and Cultural Dynamics of Mexico: A Case Study of Chihuahua*. Stanford, CA: Stanford University Press, 1959.

Havard, William C., ed. *The Changing Politics of the South*. Baton Rouge: Louisiana State University Press, 1972.

Hawley, Ellis W. "The Politics of the Mexican Labor Issue, 1950–1965." *Agricultural History* 40 (1966): 157–76.

Hayami, Yujiro, and Masao Kikuchi. *Asian Village Economy at the Crossroads: An Economic Approach to Institutional Change*. Baltimore: Johns Hopkins University Press, 1982.

Heinicke, Craig W. "Black Migration from the Rural American South and Mechanization in Agriculture, 1940–1960." Ph.D. diss., University of Toronto, 1991.

Unpublished paper, 1993.

References

Hibbs, Douglas A. *The Political Economy of Industrial Democracies*. Cambridge: Harvard University Press, 1987.

Higgs, Robert. *Competition and Coercion: Blacks in the American Economy 1865–1914*. New York: Cambridge University Press, 1977.

Crisis and Leviathan: Critical Episodes in the Growth of American Government. New York: Oxford University Press, 1987.

Higgs, Robert, and Lee J. Alston. "An Economist's Perspective on Southern Paternalism." Unpublished paper, 1981.

"Contractual Mix in Southern Agriculture Since the Civil War: Facts, Hypotheses, and Tests." *Journal of Economic History* 42 (June 1982): 327–53.

Hoffsommer, Harold, ed. *The Social and Economic Significance of Land Tenure in the Southwestern States: A Report on the Regional Land Tenure Research Project*. Chapel Hill: University of North Carolina Press, 1950.

Holmes, William F. "Whitecapping: Agrarian Violence in Mississippi, 1902–1906." *Journal of Southern History* 35 (May 1969): 165–85.

Hughes, Jonathan R. T. *The Governmental Habit Redux: Economic Controls from Colonial Times to the Present*. Princeton, NJ: Princeton University Press, 1991.

Hutchinson, T. W. *Village and Plantation Life in Northeastern Brazil*. Seattle: University of Washington Press, 1957.

Janowitz, Morris. *Social Control of the Welfare State*. New York: Elsevier, 1976.

Jaros, Natalie. "Agricultural Workers in Foreign Unemployment Insurance Schemes." November 1934. CES Records.

Jaynes, Gerald D. *Branches Without Roots: Genesis of the Black Working Class in the American South, 1862–1882*. New York: Oxford University Press, 1986.

Johnson, Allen W. *Sharecroppers of the Sertaõ*. Stanford, CA: Stanford University Press, 1971.

Johnson, Charles S. *Shadow of the Plantation*. Chicago: University of Chicago Press, 1966.

Statistical Atlas of Southern Counties. Chapel Hill: University of North Carolina Press, 1941.

Kaufman, Jacob J. "Farm Labor During World War II." *Journal of Farm Economics* 31 (1949): 131–42.

Key, V. O. *Southern Politics in State and Nation*. New York: Knopf, 1949.

Kiehel, Constance A. "Agricultural Workers and Farmers in Foreign Social Insurance Systems." 25 October 1934, CES Records.

Kiewat, D. Roderick, and Matthew D. McCubbins. *The Logic of Delegation: Congressional Parties and the Appropriations Process*. Chicago: University of Chicago Press, 1991.

Kirby, Jack Temple. *Rural Worlds Lost: The American South, 1920–1960*. Baton Rouge: Louisiana State University Press, 1987.

Korpi, Walter. *The Democratic Class Struggle*. Boston: Routledge and Kegan Paul, 1983.

Kousser, J. Morgan. *The Shaping of Southern Politics: Suffrage Restriction and the Establishment of the One-Party South, 1880–1910*. New Haven, CT: Yale University Press, 1974.

Larson, Olaf F., ed. "Ten Years of Rural Rehabilitation in the United States." Washington, D.C.: Unpublished, U.S. Department of Agriculture, Bureau of Agricultural Economics and Farm Security Administration, 1947.

References

Lebergott, Stanley. *Manpower in Economic Growth.* New York: McGraw-Hill, 1964.

LeRay, N. L., G. L. Wilbur, and G. B. Crowe. "Plantation Organization and the Resident Labor Force, Delta Area." *Mississippi State University Agricultural Experiment Station Bulletin* 606 (1960).

Leuchtenburg, William E. *Franklin D. Roosevelt and the New Deal, 1932–1940.* New York: Harper & Row, 1963.

Levy, Brian, and Pablo T. Spiller. "The Institutional Foundations of Regulatory Commitment: A Comparative Analysis of Telecommunications Regulation." *Journal of Law, Economics and Organization* 10 (October 1994): 201–46.

Lieberman, Robert C. "Race and the Development of the American Welfare State from the New Deal to the Great Society." Ph.D. diss., Harvard University, 1994.

Litwack, Leon F. *Been in the Storm So Long: The Aftermath of Slavery.* New York: Knopf, 1979.

Lyon, Richard M. "The Legal Status of American and Mexican Migratory Farm Labor: An Analysis of U.S. Farm Labor Legislation, Policy, and Administration." Ph.D. diss., Cornell University, 1954.

Maddox, James G. "The Farm Security Administration." Ph.D. diss., Harvard University, 1950.

Maier, Frank. "An Economic Analysis of the Adoption of the Mechanical Cotton Picker." Ph.D. diss., University of Chicago, 1969.

Mandle, Jay R. "The Re-establishment of the Plantation Economy in the South, 1865–1910." *Review of Black Political Economy* 3 (Winter 1973): 68–88.

Not Slave, Not Free: The African American Economic Experience Since the Civil War. Durham, NC: Duke University Press, 1992.

Matthews, Donald R., and James W. Prothro. *Negroes and the New Southern Politics.* New York: Harcourt, Brace & World, 1966.

McConnell, Grant. *The Decline of Agrarian Democracy.* Berkeley and Los Angeles: University of California Press, 1953.

McMillen, Neil R. *Dark Journey: Black Mississippians in the Age of Jim Crow.* Urbana: University of Illinois Press, 1989.

Mokyr, Joel. *The Lever of Riches: Technological Creativity and Economic Progress.* New York: Oxford University Press, 1990.

Mowry, George E. *Another Look at the Twentieth Century South.* Baton Rouge: Louisiana State University Press, 1973.

Musoke, Moses S., and Alan Olmstead. "The Rise of the Cotton Industry in California: A Comparative Perspective." *Journal of Economic History* 42 (1982): 385–412.

Myrdal, Gunnar. *An American Dilemma.* New York: Harper & Row, 1944.

"National Urban League Asks Inclusion of Domestic and Agricultural Workers." *New York Times,* 15 January 1937, 7.

Newby, Howard. *The Deferential Worker: A Study of Farm Workers in East Anglia.* London: Allen Lane, 1977.

North, Douglass C. *Institutions, Institutional Change, and Economic Performance.* New York: Cambridge University Press, 1990.

Structure and Change in Economic History. New York: Norton, 1981.

Nourse, Edwin G., Joseph S. Davis, and John D. Black. *Three Years of the Agricultural Adjustment Administration.* Washington, D.C.: Brookings, 1937.

158

References

"Old-Age Insurance for Agricultural Workers." 22 April 1940, SSB Records, Box 32, p. 4.

Orloff, Ann, and Theda Skocpol. "Why Not Equal Protection? Explaining the Politics of Public School Spending in Britain, 1900–1911, and the United States, 1800s–1920." *American Sociological Review* 49 (1984): 726–50.

Ornstein, Norman J., Thomas E. Mann, and Michael J. Malbin. "Committees." In *New Perspectives on the House of Representatives*, edited by Robert L. Peabody and Nelson W. Polsby. Baltimore: The Johns Hopkins Press, 1992.

Otken, Charles H. *The Ills of the South, or Related Causes Hostile to the General Prosperity of the Southern People*. New York: G. P. Putnam's Sons, 1894.

Patterson, James T. *America's Struggle Against Poverty, 1900–1985*. Cambridge: Harvard University Press, 1986.

Percy, William Alexander. *Lanterns on the Levee*. New York: Knopf, 1941.

Pitts, Phillip H. Papers. Southern Historical Collection, University of North Carolina: Chapel Hill, NC.

Piven, Francis Fox, and Richard Cloward. *Regulating the Poor*. New York: Pantheon Books, 1993.

Powdermaker, Hortense. *After Freedom: A Cultural Study in the Deep South*. New York: Athenaeum, 1978.

Quadagno, Jill. "Theories of the Welfare State." *Annual Review of Sociology* 13 (1987): 109–28.

The Transformation of Old Age Security. Chicago: University of Chicago Press, 1988.

Ransom, Roger L., and Richard Sutch. *One Kind of Freedom: The Economic Consequences of Emancipation*. New York: Cambridge University Press, 1978.

Raper, Arthur F. *Preface to Peasantry*. New York: Athenaeum, 1968.

Rasmussen, Wayne D. "A History of the Emergency Farm Labor Supply Program, 1943–47." U.S. Department of Agriculture, *Agricultural Research Monograph 13*. Washington, D.C.: Government Printing Office, 1951.

"Returning Relief to the States." CES Records.

Rich, Spencer A. *U.S. Agricultural Policy in the Postwar Years, 1945–1963*. Washington, D.C.: Congressional Quarterly Research Service, 1963.

Roback, Jennifer. "Southern Labor Law in the Jim Crow Era: Exploitative or Competitive." *University of Chicago Law Review* 61 (1984): 1161–92.

Robertson, Paul L., and Lee J. Alston. "Technological Change and the Organization of Work in Capitalist Firms." *Economic History Review* 45 (May 1992): 330–50.

Rockoff, Hugh. *Drastic Measures: A History of Wage and Price Controls in the United States*. New York: Cambridge University Press, 1984.

Rohde, David W. *Parties and Leaders in the Postreform House*. Chicago: University of Chicago Press, 1991.

Rosengarten, Theodore. *All God's Dangers: The Life of Nate Shaw*. New York: Knopf, 1974.

Rubin, Morton. *Plantation County*. Chapel Hill: University of North Carolina Press, 1951.

Schlesinger, Arthur, Jr. *The Coming of the New Deal*. Boston: Houghton Mifflin, 1965.

The Politics of Upheaval. Boston: Houghton Mifflin, 1970.

Schuler, Edgar A. "Social Status and Farm Tenure – Attitudes and Social Con-

References

ditions of Corn Belt and Cotton Belt Farmers." U.S. Department of Agriculture, Bureau of Agricultural Economics and Farm Security Administration, *Social Research Report IV*. Washington, D.C.: 1938.

Schulman, Bruce J. *From Cotton Belt to Sunbelt: Federal Policy, Economic Development, and the Transformation of the South, 1938–1980*. New York: Oxford University Press, 1991.

Schumpeter, Joseph. *Capitalism, Socialism, and Democracy*. New York: Harper, 1950.

[Schurz, Carl.] U.S. Congress. Senate. *Report of Carl Schurz*. 39th Cong., 1st sess., 1866. S. Doc. 2.

Scruggs, Otey M. "Evolution of the Mexican Farm Labor Agreement of 1942." *Agricultural History* 34 (1960): 140–9.

Seltzer, Andrew. "The Political Economy of the Fair Labor Standards Act of 1938." *Journal of Political Economy* 103 (1994): 1302–41.

Shapiro, Carl, and Joseph E. Stiglitz. "Equilibrium Unemployment as a Worker Discipline Device." *American Economic Review* 74 (1984): 433–44.

Sheppard, Burton D. *Rethinking Congressional Reform: The Reform Roots of the Special Interest Congress*. Cambridge: Schenkman Books Inc., 1985.

Shepsle, Kenneth. *The Giant Jigsaw Puzzle: Democratic Committee Assignments in the Modern House*. Chicago: University of Chicago Press, 1978.

Shepsle, Kenneth A., and Barry R. Weingast. "Legislative Politics and Budget Outcomes." In *Federal Budget Policy in the 1980s*, edited by Gregory B. Mills and John L. Palmer. Washington, D.C.: Urban Institute Press, 1984.

"The Institutional Foundations of Committee Power." *Brooking Papers on Economic Activity*. 1994

Shlomowitz, Ralph. "The Freedmen's Bureau." Ph.D. diss., University of Chicago, 1978.

Skocpol, Theda. *Protecting Soldiers and Mothers: The Political Origins of Social Policy in the United States*. Cambridge: Harvard University Press, 1992.

Social Policy in the United States: Future Possibilities in Historical Perspective. Princeton, NJ: Princeton University Press, 1995.

Skocpol, Theda, and Edwin Amenta. "States and Social Policies." *Annual Review of Sociology*, 12 (1986): 131–57.

Smith, Adam [pseud.]. "The City as the OK Corral." *Esquire*, July 1985, 64–7.

Smith, Steven S. *Call to Order: Floor Politics in the House and Senate*. Washington, D.C.: Brookings Institution, 1989.

Southerner [pseud.]. "Agricultural Labor at the South." *Galaxy*, September 1871, 328–40.

"Staff Report on Unemployment Insurance." 24 December 1934, CES Records.

"Statement of Arthur J. Altmeyer, Chairman of the Social Security Board, Before the Senate Finance Committee on Amendments to the Social Security Act." SSB Records, Box 4, Amendments 1939 file, p. 10.

"Statement of the Secretary of the Treasury to the Ways and Means Committee on the Economic Security Act." CES Records.

Stearns, Charles. *The Black Man of the South, and the Rebels; or, The Characteristics of the Former, and the Recent Outrages of the Latter*. New York: Negro Universities Press, 1969 [1872].

Steckel, Richard. "The Economic Foundations of East–West Migration During the Nineteenth Century." *Explorations in Economic History* 20 (January 1983).

References

Stevens, Arthur G., Jr., Arthur H. Miller, and Thomas E. Mann. "Mobilization of Liberal Strength in the House, 1955–1970: The Democratic Study Group." *American Political Science Review* 68 (1974): 667–81.

Stone, Alfred Holt. "The Negro in the Yazoo-Mississippi Delta." *American Economic Association Publications*, 3rd Series, 3 (February 1902): 243–94.

Street, James H. *The New Revolution in the Cotton Economy*. Chapel Hill: University of North Carolina Press, 1957.

Sundquist, James, ed. *On Fighting Poverty: Perspectives from Experience*. New York: Basic Books, 1969.

Taylor, H. C. *Outlines of Agricultural Economics*. New York: Macmillan, 1925.

Taylor, Paul. "Relation of Tenancy and Labor in Agriculture." 1940, SSB Records, Box 32, Agricultural Labor to 1939 file, p. 1.

Tebeau, C. W. "Some Aspects of Planter–Freedman Relations, 1865–1880." *Journal of Negro History* 21 (April 1966): 130–50.

Tindall, George B. *Emergence of the New South*. Baton Rouge: Louisiana State University Press, 1965.

[Truman, Benjamin C.] U.S. Congress. Senate. *Report of Benjamin C. Truman.* 39th Cong., 1st sess., 1866. S. Doc. 43.

U.S. Census Bureau. *Historical Statistics of the U.S.: Colonial Times to 1970.* Washington, D.C.: Government Printing Office, 1975.

Sixteenth Census of the United States – 1940. Vol. 3, pt. 1. Washington, D.C.: Government Printing Office, 1942.

U.S. Congress. House. *Report of the Select Committee to Investigate Interstate Migration of Destitute Citizens.* 77th Cong., 1st sess., 1941. H. Rept. 369.

Committee on Agriculture. *Hearings on the Department of Agriculture Appropriation Bill.* 1942–4.

Committee on the Judiciary. *Hearings on Admission of Aliens into the United States for Temporary Employment and Commuter Workers.* 1963.

Committee on Ways and Means. *Hearings on the Economic Security Act.* 74th Cong., 1st sess., 1935.

Joint Committee on Reconstruction. *Report of the Joint Committee on Reconstruction.* 39th Cong., 1st sess., 1866. H. Rept. 30. Serial 1273.

U.S. Congress. Senate. Committee on Agriculture. *Hearings on the Department of Agriculture Appropriation Bill.* 1942–4.

Committee on Education and Labor. *Report on Relations Between Labor and Capital.* 1885.

Committee on Military Affairs. *Report on Deferment from Military Service of Persons Engaged in Agricultural Occupations.* 78th Cong., 1st sess., 1943.

U.S. Department of Agriculture. *Report of the Commissioner of Agriculture for the Year 1866.* Washington, D.C.: Government Printing Office, 1867.

U.S. Department of Agriculture. Economic Research Service. "Statistics on Cotton and Related Data 1920–1973." *Statistical Bulletin 535.* Washington, D.C.: Government Printing Office, 1974.

"Termination of the Bracero Program: Some Effects on Farm Labor and Migrant Housing Needs." Washington, D.C.: Government Printing Office, 1964.

U.S. Department of Labor. Bureau of Employment Security. *Farm Labor Market Development and Farm Labor Developments.* Washington, D.C.: Government Printing Office, 1954–69.

U.S. Industrial Commission. *Report.* Vols. 10 and 11. Washington, D.C.: Government Printing Office, 1900–2.

References

U.S. Selective Service System. *Selective Service as the Tide of War Turns: Third Report of the Director of Selective Service, 1943–44.* Washington, D.C.: Government Printing Office, 1945.

Valelly, Richard M. "Party, Coercion, and Inclusion: The Two Reconstructions of the South's Electoral Politics." *Politics and Society* 21 (March 1993): 37–67.

Van Onselen, Charles. *The Seed is Mine: The Life of Kas Maine, a South African Sharecropper, 1894–1985.* New York: Hill and Wang, 1996.

Wallis, John J. "The Political Economy of New Deal and Fiscal Federalism." *Economic Inquiry* 29 (July 1991): 510–24.

Wayne, Michael. *The Reshaping of Plantation Society: The Natchez District, 1860–1880.* Baton Rouge: Louisiana State University Press, 1983.

Weingast, Barry R., and William Marshall. "The Industrial Organization of Congress: Or Why Legislatures Like Firms Are Not Organized as Markets." *Journal of Political Economy* 96 (1988): 132–63.

Weisskopf, Thomas E., Samuel Bowles, and David M. Gordon. "Hearts and Minds: A Social Model of U.S. Productivity Growth." *Brookings Papers on Economic Activity* (1983).

Whatley, Warren C. "Labor for the Picking: The New Deal in the South." *Journal of Economic History* 43 (December 1983): 905–30.

"Southern Agrarian Labor Contracts as Impediments to Cotton Mechanization." *Journal of Economic History* 47 (March 1987): 45–70.

Wiener, Jonathan M. *Social Origins of the New South: Alabama, 1860–1865.* Baton Rouge: Louisiana State University Press, 1978.

Wilcox, E. V. "Lease Contracts Used in Renting on Shares." *U.S. Department of Agriculture Bulletin 650.* Washington, D.C.: Government Printing Office, 1918.

Wilcox, Walter W. *The Farmer in the Second World War.* Ames: Iowa State College Press, 1947.

Williams, Edward A. *Federal Aid for Relief.* New York: Columbia University Press, 1939.

Williamson, Oliver. *The Economic Institutions of Capitalism.* New York: Free Press, 1985.

Witte, Edwin E. "Major Issues in Unemployment Compensation." December 1934, CES Records.

"Major Issues in Unemployment Compensation." February 1935, CES Records.

The Development of the Social Security Act. Madison: University of Wisconsin Press, 1963.

Woodman, Harold D. *New South – New Law.* Baton Rouge: Louisiana State University Press, 1995.

"Post-Civil War Southern Agriculture and the Law." *Agricultural History* 53 (January 1979): 319–37.

Woodward, C. Vann. *Origins of the New South.* Baton Rouge: Louisiana State University Press, 1951.

Woofter, T. J. *Negro Migration: Changes in Rural Organization and Population of the Cotton Belt.* New York: Negro Universities Press, 1969 [1920].

"The Plantation Economy." Works Progress Administration and Farm Security Administration, *Social Research Report IV.* Washington, D.C.: Farm Security Administration, 1936.

References

Wright, Gavin. *Old South, New South: Revolutions in the Southern Economy Since the Civil War.* New York: Basic Books, 1986.

———. "The Economic Revolution in the American South." *Journal of Economic Perspectives* 1 (Summer 1987): 161–78.

Yarmolinsky, Adam. "The Beginnings of OEO." In *On Fighting Poverty: Perspectives from Experience,* edited by James Sundquist. New York: Basic Books, 1969.

Young, Richard P., Jerome Burstein, and Robert Higgs. "Federalism and the Demise of Prescriptive Racism in the United States." Paper presented at the annual meeting of the American Political Science Association, 1992.

Index

Abbott, Grace, 71
agenda control, 9, 41–2, 44, 136, 145
Agricultural Adjustment Administration
  (AAA), 45, 54, 56, 69, 77, 89, 125
agricultural labor
  deferment from military service in
    World War II, 101, 104, 105
  exclusion from Social Security, 9, 61–3,
    65–71, 73–5
  monitoring costs of, 1, 5, 7, 10–11, 39,
    142, 144
agriculture
  and paternalism 13–14, 20, 23, 31, 126,
    142–3, 145, 150
Agriculture Committee, 11, 41–2, 46, 80–
  1, 94, 109, 115, 120, 134–6, 141
Aid to Dependent Children (ADC), 9, 58–
  61, 67, 70–2, 150
Aid to Families with Dependent Children
  (AFDC), 59, 70, 132–3, 150
Aiken, Charles S., 121, 122
Akerlof, George A., 24
Alston, Lee J., 4, 6, 7, 13, 14, 16, 17, 23,
  24, 25, 26, 30, 31, 57, 76, 77, 121,
  122, 123, 125, 126, 127, 128, 130
Amenta, Edwin, 145, 147, 148
antienticement laws, 35
Appropriations Committee, 40, 44, 46–7,
  81, 94–5, 97, 135–6, 140, 144
Armstrong, Barbara N., 66

Baldwin, Sidney, 76, 77, 78, 80, 83, 88,
  90, 91, 93, 94, 96, 97
Bankhead, John, 81, 104
Bankhead-Jones Farm Tenancy Act, 75,
  80, 91, 97
Barraclough, S. L., 14
Barry, John M., 22
Bean, Louis H., 63, 65

Bell, Winifred, 150
Benedict, Murray R., 104, 105
benefit levels
  Aid to Dependent Children (ADC), 70,
    150
  Mothers Aid, 62
  Old Age Assistance, 70–3
  Southern states, 55
Bensel, Richard F., 43, 44, 47
Berkowitz, Edward, 147
Bloch, Marc, 14
Bowles, Samuel, 59, 126
bracero program
  bribery, 114
  impact of cotton mechanization, 117–18
  impact on cotton mechanization, 122
  impact on migration, 113
  origins, 107–9
  political support, 109, 111, 144
  reasons for termination, 115–18
  Southern motivation for support, 99,
    105–6, 109, 113, 150
  work effort of braceros, 112
bracero wages, 112
Brannen, Claude O., 122
Brinkley, Alan, 44, 45
Bruce, Phillip A., 17
Buck, Robert K., 102
Byrd, Harry, 69, 95

Carmichael, H. Lorne, 126
cash income and declining tenancy rates,
  129
civil rights
  impact of mechanization, 126–7, 130
  impact on Economic Opportunity Act,
    11, 139–41
  lack of, and impact on paternalism, 7–8,
    21, 39

165

Index

Index

mechanization of cotton cultivation (*cont.*)
  and monitoring costs, 10–11, 23, 119,
    121–2, 126–7
  and labor turnover, 11, 121
  impact on paternalism, 11, 119, 121,
    124, 127, 130–1, 139, 141–2, 149,
    152
  impact on race relations, 121
  impact on tenancy, 121–2, 126–7, 143
Mexican labor, 10, 106–9, 112, 117–18
migration
  capital from North to South, 33
  in centrally planned economies and wel-
    fare programs, 148
  tenants within the South, 23
  workers from Mexico, 107; *see also* bra-
    cero program
  workers from Southern farms
    after World War II, 40
    and emigrant agents, 105
    and interests of Southern Congress-
      men, 11
    and Great Society programs, 11, 121,
      139, 141, 149
    and hostility toward blacks, 22
    and mechanization of cotton cultiva-
      tion, 119, 123, 128–30, 141, 146, 148–
      9
    and paternalism, 33–4, 119, 124, 139,
      141
    and Unemployment Insurance, 65
    during World War II, 102–3, 106, 126
    factors preventing, 33
    impact of bracero program, 10, 74,
      99, 107
    push factors, 123
    pull factors, 124
Miller, Arthur H., 137
Mokyr, Joel, 3
Morgenthau, Henry, Jr., 67–9
Mothers' Aid, 57, 59
Mowry, George E., 9, 28
Munger, Michael, 6
Musoke, Moses S., 113
Myrdal, Gunnar, 30

New Deal
  and committee power, 41, 43
  and Resettlement Administration, 76–7;
    see also Resettlement Administration
  and Southern labor relations, 2, 8–9, 30,
    37, 40
  corporate liberal view, 147
  relief programs, 50, 61; *see also* Federal
    Emergency Relief Administration
  shift from relief to reform, 76–7, 88

Southern political support, 45, 56, 60
welfare programs, 50, 59; *see also* Social
  Security
New Frontier, 12, 133
Newby, Howard, 14
Nixon, Richard M., 74, 134
norms
  and Farm Security Administration, 54,
    87
  and transaction costs, 5
  and violence, 21
  and welfare programs, 148, 150
  as constraints on behavior, 1, 3
  in Congressional committees, 42
  in the South, 2, 7
North, Douglass C., 3, 7
Nourse, Edwin G., 56, 89

Old-Age Assistance
  inclusion of farm workers, 63
  expansion of federal funding and over-
    sight, 74, 149
  local control, 9, 60–1, 67, 69, 70–2
  provided by planters, 13, 131
  Southern opposition to federal program,
    39, 58
Old-Age Insurance
  and racism, 58
  benefit to the South from participation,
    57–8
  exclusion of farm workers, 62–3, 65–70
  inclusion of farm workers, 73–4
  provided by planters, 59
Olmstead, Alan, 113
Orloff, Ann, 146
Ornstein, Norman J., 137
Otken, Charles H., 18

Pace amendments, 10, 105
Pace, Stephen, 81, 105
paternalism
  and actions by Southerners in Congress,
    2, 8, 128, 133, 138–9
  and bracero program, 10, 99, 150
  and economic and political transforma-
    tion, 1, 12, 144
  and Farm Security Administration, 75–6,
    81, 83–94
  and migration from the South, 11, 124,
    141, 146
  and plantations, 28, 31
  and relief, 50
  and social control, 2, 7, 130
  and worker mobility within the South,
    27
  causes, 1–2, 7

Index

disappearance after mechanization of cotton cultivation, 1, 10–11, 119, 121, 125, 131, 145, 149, 152
evidence from non-U.S. contexts, 14, 24
evidence from the South, 20–3, 30–1, 82, 128, 131
functions, 1, 8, 19, 23
origins, 2, 8, 14, 17–18
preventing substitutes, 34, 36–8, 43, 48–51, 63, 70, 72–3, 92, 98, 144
patron, 8, 19, 24–5, 27, 50
Patterson, James T., 52, 53, 72
pensions, 57, 62, 69, 70–1
Percy, William, 22, 30
Perkins, Frances, 71
Pitts, Phillip H., 19
Piven, Francis Fox, 73, 128, 138, 145, 148, 149, 152
plantation elite, 8, 35–6, 124, 144
Poage, W. R., 109, 137
policy outcomes, 144
political parties, 7, 151
Poor Laws, 51
poor relief, 49–51
Powdermaker, Hortense, 21, 24, 30, 31, 128, 129
Powell, O. M., 73
property rights, 4–5, 7–8
Prothro, James W., 130
Public Law 45, 105, 108, 144
Public Law 78, 109, 115–17

Quadagno, Jill, 57, 71, 73, 74, 139, 145, 147, 148, 149

racism
and Southern pension and Mothers' Aid levels, 56, 58
and Southern politics, 39
in post-Reconstruction era, 15
Ransom, Roger L., 16
Raper, Arthur F., 24, 30, 31, 85, 128, 129
Rasmussen, Wayne D., 105, 107
Reconstruction
and origins of social control, 2
and turnover in plantation elite, 15
appearance of paternalism following, 15
planter political power following, 28, 34–7
rise of racism following, 15, 18
Redeemers, 34
reform
in Congressional committee system, 133, 137–8
in Second New Deal, 9, 40, 56, 76–7

in Southern agriculture, 40, 48, 74–5, 89, 92, 140, 144–5, 150
Resettlement Administration (RA)
activities, 77–8, 83
impact, 9, 16, 78, 80–1, 125
origins, 76–7
Reconstruction Finance Corporation (RFC), 52
Rich, Spencer A., 104
Roback, Jennifer, 106
Robertson, Paul L., 4
Rockoff, Hugh, 99, 101
Rohde, David W., 137, 138
Roosevelt, Franklin D., 44–5, 47, 52, 56, 60, 72, 76, 81, 108, 136
Rosengarten, Theodore, 128
Rubin, Morton, 23, 24, 30, 31, 87, 128
Rules Committee, 40, 42, 44, 46–7, 133, 135–6, 138–9
rural rehabilitation, 78, 83, 87, 90–1, 93, 95, 97
Russell, Richard B., 47, 81, 84–5, 93, 96, 104–5, 136

Schlesinger, Arthur, Jr., 44, 45, 76, 136
Schuler, Edgar A., 20, 31, 82, 83, 86
Schulman, Bruce J., 139, 141
Schumpeter, Joseph, 6
Schurz, Carl, 16, 18
Scruggs, Otey M., 107
Secretary of Labor
role in bracero program, 116–18
Seltzer, Andrew, 10
seniority on committees, 9, 43–7, 60, 120, 137
Shapiro, Carl, 126
sharecroppers, see croppers
Sheppard, Burtin D., 137
Shepsle, Kenneth A., 7, 41, 120
Shlomowitz, Ralph, 16
Skocpol, Theda, 145, 146, 147, 148, 151
Smith, Adam, 141
Smith, Ellison, 95
Smith, Howard, 135, 139
Smith, Steven S., 42, 43, 44, 133
social control
as an institution, 2, 7–8, 139, 145
deference, 128
impact of mechanization on, 121, 130, 142, 148
impact on paternalism, 7–8, 19, 121, 130, 142, 145, 150
impact on poor whites, 39
measure of, 121, 130
origins, 8, 19
Southern defense, 9–11, 50–1, 53, 99

169

ARTHUR LUPIA AND MATHEW D. MCCUBBINS, *The Democratic Dilemma: Can Citizens Learn What They Really Need to Know?*

MATHEW D. MCCUBBINS AND TERRY SULLIVAN, eds., *Congress: Structure and Policy*

GARY J. MILLER, *Managerial Dilemmas: The Political Economy of Heirarchy*

DOUGLASS C. NORTH, *Institutions, Institutional Change, and Economic Performance*

ELINOR OSTROM, *Governing the Commons: The Evolution of Institutions for Collective Action*

J. MARK RAMSEYER, *Odd Markets in Japanese History*

J. MARK RAMSEYER AND FRANCES ROSENBLUTH, *The Politics of Oligarchy: Institutional Choice in Imperial Japan*

JEAN-LAURENT ROSENTHAL, *The Fruits of Revolution: Property Rights, Litigation, and French Agriculture*

CHARLES STEWART III, *Budget Reform Politics: The Design of the Appropriations Process in the House of Representatives, 1865–1921*

GEORGE TSEBELIS AND JEANNETTE MONEY, *Bicameralism*

JOHN WATERBURY, *Exposed to Innumerable Delusions: Public Enterprise and State Power in Egypt, India, Mexico, and Turkey*

DAVID L. WEIMER, ed., *The Political Economy of Property Rights*